An
AMERICAN CADDIE
in
St. Andrews

An AMERICAN CADDIE in ST. ANDREWS

Growing Up, Girls, and Looping on the Old Course

OLIVER HOROVITZ

GOTHAM BOOKS

GOTHAM BOOKS
Published by the Penguin Group
Penguin Group (USA) Inc., 375 Hudson Street,
New York, New York 10014, USA

USA / Canada / UK / Ireland / Australia / New Zealand / India / South Africa / China
Penguin Books Ltd, Registered Offices: 80 Strand, London WC2R 0RL, England
For more information about the Penguin Group visit penguin.com.

Insert photograph on page 1 (middle) copyright © Rory Jackson; bottom photograph on page 1
copyright © Lindsay Allen; top two photographs on page 2 copyright © Matt Fouchek; bottom
photograph on page 2 copyright © Gillian Horovitz; second photograph on page 3 courtesy of St.
Andrews Link Trust; top photograph on page 4 copyright © Getty Images, Richard Heathcote;
middle photograph on page 4 copyright © Israel Horovitz; bottom photograph on page 4 copyright © Greg Savidge; top photograph on page 5 copyright © Kenny Goosen; all other photographs are courtesy of the author.

LIBRARY OF CONGRESS CATALOGING-IN-PUBLICATION DATA
Horovitz, Oliver.
An American caddie in St. Andrews : growing up, girls, and looping on the old course / Oliver
Horovitz.
pages cm
ISBN 978-1-59240-729-3 (hardback)
1. Horovitz, Oliver. 2. Caddies—United States—Biography. 3. Royal and Ancient Golf Club of
St. Andrews. 4. Saint Andrews Links (St. Andrews, Scotland) I. Title.
GV964.H67A3 2012
796.352092—dc23
[B]
                                    2012029331

Printed in the United States of America
10 9 8 7 6 5 4 3 2 1

Set in Janson Text
Designed by Spring Hoteling

Penguin is committed to publishing works of quality and integrity.
In that spirit, we are proud to offer this book to our readers;
however, the story, the experiences, and the words
are the author's alone..

To Uncle Ken.

"I don't blame you, I don't blame you!
I blame me for choosing you!"

—What Seve Ballesteros once yelled
to his caddie after a bad clubbing

PROLOGUE

"Please welcome your 2003 graduates!"

The raspy voice of our principal, Stanley Teitel, booms into the loudspeaker. Jack Welch, our class day speaker, takes a seat, having just finished his speech. I'm pretty sure he's the CEO of General Electric. I know he just talked about GE washing machines, a lot. It's 10:12 A.M., June 25. I'm onstage at Avery Fisher Hall in New York City, trumpet on my lap, facing three thousand fellow Stuyvesant High School students, parents, and teachers, all assembled for our graduation ceremony. It's ridiculously hot. My cell phone vibrates, signaling a call that could define my life. I'm waiting to hear from Harvard College's admission office. I've been on their waiting list for the past three months, and they're supposed to let me know today if I've been admitted. As the orchestra strikes up a rousing march, I exit stage left, semi-discreetly, and take the call. It's Sally Champagne, Harvard's admissions officer. The news is good. I've been moved off their wait list: I'm in. But Sally Champagne keeps talking. There's a small catch: All class of 2007 spots have been filled. I've been accepted for the following year. I need to take a gap year, which is a euphemism for killing 365 consecutive days. But how?

I stumble back to my third-trumpet seat. Dr. Raymond Wheeler taps his baton and scowls at me to pay attention. Trumpet touches lips. We play "Pomp and Circumstance March No. 4" and there is no doubt whatsoever that high school is ending.

I strain, unsuccessfully, to hit my high E-flat and catch Dr. Wheeler wincing as if his firstborn child has just been hit by a truck. It's no good. I can't concentrate; my immediate future's playing out alongside Edward Elgar's overture. Measure thirty-two arrives, giving me a nine-bar rest. While resting, I tear through coming-year options. After I rule out 1) waiting tables, 2) chopping wood, 3) chopping tables, an idea hits me: a year at the University of St. Andrews, in Scotland, where I'd also applied. I've been going to St. Andrews since I was a little kid, to play golf with my family and to visit my mother's uncle Ken Hayward, who lives four hundred yards from the Old Course's first tee.

As soon as I get home from graduation, I call the University of St. Andrews. I discover that they have a special freshman-year-abroad program. I call Harvard to see if I can do it. Harvard says it's okay, if I don't matriculate for transfer credit. I also discover that the University of St. Andrews has a 70/30 girl-to-boy ratio. I'm also a 1.8-handicap golf junkie. This is all sounding good.

. . .

"First place goes to Duncan Montgomery!"

Everyone around me applauds. Several bang on tables. Others scream, "Montayyyyyyy!" at inappropriate volumes. Duncan Montgomery, a third-year student from Edinburgh, waves cheerfully from his seat.

It's a warm Wednesday night in mid-May, and I'm near the end of my gap year in St. Andrews, Scotland. I'm at the weekly meeting for the University of St. Andrews golf team. True to British university form, the team is entirely student run (no adults, no coaches) and meets once a week, at a pub called the Gin House. It also contains, this year, twenty-five students with handicaps of 2 or better. Results are being announced now from the weekly club medal on the Old Course, from which team standings are determined. The winning student this week ("Montayyyyyy!"), currently necking a pint of Tennent's lager, has casually shot a 5-under 67. Last weekend, facing a match against Clark University (visiting from the States), the club captain, a party animal from Northern England, showed up on the first tee at nine A.M., sleepless, disheveled, and still in a tuxedo from the night before. He rubbed his eyes, hit his opening drive 280 down the middle, and won his match 6 and 5.

I'm sitting at the crowded team table in the back of the Gin House, beside Michael Choong, a posh Chinese-English third-year student from Wimbledon, and Richard Hooper, a six-foot-three Welsh fourth-year student who last week broke his putter in anger against a tree on the third hole of a match against the University of Stirling and had to subsequently putt with his 4-iron (he shot 68). I lean back in my chair, think about my own relatively puny score of 75, and roll up my sleeves for the ensuing drinking games. It's going to be a messy night.

Thus far, my gap year in St. Andrews has been unthinkably wonderful. With my £105 student links ticket, I've been allowed unlimited play on St. Andrews's six golf courses. I play a round virtually every day on the Old Course and have dinner at least once a week with my dapper, plaid-tie-wearing uncle Ken. My classes are superb. I read English with Robert Crawford, the good great poet, who has us imitating Wordsworth and Keats. I also study modern history and international relations, taught by brilliantly eccentric old Scottish guys with big ears and impenetrable brogues. I have my first serious girlfriend. I try haggis. I meet kids from all over the world, and together we discover St. Andrews's thirty-one pubs (the highest per capita pub population in the UK).

Maybe because of its age (nearly six hundred years old), or maybe just because it's in Scotland, ancient arcane traditions abound at the University of St. Andrews. And I've tried to take part in them all. There's the bimonthly Pier Walk, for which hundreds of students don ceremonial red academic robes and walk down the harbor pier in pitch-darkness, every third student holding a candle for (totally inadequate) illumination. There's the May Dip, held on May 1, when all seven thousand students stay up through the night attending various parties, then charge into the North Sea at five A.M., totally naked (while a choir sings hymns and bagpipers play from the rocks). And there's Raisin Weekend, an Animal House–esque weekend in November "supervised" by every first-year student's "academic parents" (all third- or fourth-year students), involving obscene levels of drinking and culminating in a nine A.M. sixteen-hundred-person shaving foam fight in St. Salvator's Quad. There's also the student charity fashion shows, at which ultracool European students dressed to the nines sit at tables stocked with champagne. And the notorious May Ball, held in a gigantic converted farmhouse outside St. Andrews. Here, the VIP "Gold Ticket" gets you a limo ride . . . to the *helicopter*, which sweeps you along the coast and touches down on the farm, where bumper cars, a Ferris wheel, and chocolate fountains await.

There's another quirk to the University of St. Andrews. For the last three years, Prince William has been a student here—bringing fame, fortune, and gloriously high numbers of girl applicants to the university. Protecting its prized possession, the university has a special agreement with the royal family: Any student attempting to sell photographs of William to the British tabloids will find him or herself promptly expelled from school. Uncle Ken lives across the street from William's flat, exchanges pleasantries with him daily, doesn't ask for autographs or photo ops.

But my most important discovery—by *far*—is that everyone at the University of St. Andrews seems to play golf. Including very cute girls. For the first time in my life, my golf playing is an *asset*, as cool (perhaps) as being a quarterback on an American college football team. In St. Andrews, golf runs alongside life. This is not a small deal.

By this point in May, it has become clear to me: I do not want this gap year to end. As glasses clink and club captain Benny Kelly announces upcoming matches, I ask kids at my table what students do for paid work during vacation. Amazingly, I learn that many of my golf team friends stay on in St. Andrews over the summer to caddie on the Old Course. I'm told that caddies earn fifty pounds a round or more, and can, on a good day, loop two rounds a day. The exchange rate for the dollar is terrible, so fifty pounds translates to nearly $100—a hell of a lot more than the $35 a round I'd been earning caddying at Bass Rocks Golf Club in Gloucester, Massachusetts, where my family lives during the summer months. Over pints of Belhaven Best, my friends also tell me hilarious stories of tourist golfers and famously gruff old Old Course caddies. It all sounds good.

I fill out the forms, buy official Old Course caddie rain gear, sign up for the official Old Course caddie training program, change the date of my flight home to America, and find cheap student digs for the summer.

I'm good to go—which is to say, I'm ready to stay.

PART
ONE

ONE

"Horovitz, you're with Kenny."

Rick Mackenzie thrusts a pin sheet into my outstretched hand. Twenty old Scottish caddies mill about the window of the caddie shack. It seems like a slow day. I nod to Rick, thank him, offer up a sunny smile. I want to make a good first impression, to charm him, and the smile usually works with most people.

Rick does not return my smile. "Get going," he barks instead.

I get going.

I'm about to do a "shadow round"—the final stage of my official Old Course caddie training program before I can begin earning money. I'll be following a professional caddie around the Old Course, observing how he operates. Secretly, I'm pretty sure I don't need this shadow training. I've played the Old Course close to 150 times this year. I had the best round of my life (2 under, the only time I've ever broken par) on these very eighteen holes back in December. I've also caddied summers at Bass Rocks Golf Club since I was twelve. The way I see it, I'm already qualified. Still, a shadow round is what Rick's requiring, and I tell myself it'll be good to hang with one of the professional caddies, to pick up some tricks. In fact, going in, I have a romanticized view of this relationship; I see us as Caddie and Shadow, teacher and student, father and son even.

I find Kenny by the first tee. He is a Scot with an accent so thick, even other Scottish caddies have difficulty understanding him. He has three friendly American women in his group, all, like me, from New York City, and I happily chat with them while we await our tee time. My caddie mentor, observing this friendly chat, is all smiles, and I feel my caddie career is off to a great start. As we walk onto the first tee, Kenny yanks me aside, motions to his mouth, and whispers fiercely, "Yuh see what ahm pointin' to, Jimmah? Shut it!"

The high point of this shadow round, beyond my raking traps and searching cacti-sharp gorse bushes for lost balls, comes on the fifteenth hole, when I'm told (not asked . . . told) to run to the Eden Clubhouse to grab a bottle of water. Upon my breathless return, the professional caddie takes the bottle, turns to his player (who has, of course, witnessed none of my excursion), and charmingly announces, "Here, Judy. I got you some water." This is not the opening day of my dreams.

. . .

By nine P.M. I'm back in my rented St. Andrews flat, and the memory of the day's caddie humiliation is mercifully fading in the recesses of my mind. From my closet, I pull out a crimson-colored packet that's arrived in St. Andrews. There's a boldfaced message on the front cover: *Welcome (in 3 months!) to the Harvard Class of 2008.*

I open up the packet, revealing twelve pages of advance orientation info. Move-in dates, freshman-year academic requirements, a picture of a dorky kid smiling in pastel green shorts. I really don't need to look at this packet yet—there are still months before freshman registration—but tonight, I pore over everything. I'll be living in Weld Hall, the welcome sheet says. That sounds nice. It looks like it's in the middle of Harvard Yard. There's also a laundry room in Weld. Sweet.

I count the days till I start. Eighty-three. A part of me wishes it were less. I notice my pin sheet from today lying on the bed and tuck it away in my drawer. I realize I'm actually scared to go back to the shack tomorrow.

My great-grandfather was a junk man. My grandfather was a truck driver until age fifty. My father did all kinds of odd jobs until he was able to earn an adequate living as a playwright. By comparison, I had it pretty easy growing up. I spent my childhood summers in Gloucester, Massachusetts, and from age nine, these summers were mostly spent on a golf course. If I wasn't playing golf, or hitting balls until my glove wore out at the pads, I was probably somewhere sulking and wishing that I were playing. I also watched golf on TV religiously; I could tell you everything about Viagra and Lipitor by age twelve. Occasionally, I had a job teaching golf to little kids in the city of Gloucester golf program (frequently forgetting our age difference and dropping F-bombs in front of seven-year-olds). I also caddied at Bass Rocks. But more than anything else, my summers meant golf.

I guess for me, spending thousands of hours hitting golf balls felt sort of like a job in itself. Because in the way that all twelve-year-old boys are pretty sure they are going to be professional athletes, I was always pretty sure I was going to be a professional golfer. And in the same way that every twelve-year-old boy keeps a running narrative of his personal details for future TV interviews, I secretly stored away my golf eccentricities, secretly waited for when I would tell Bob Costas about how I always used a women's putter (I won it when I was eleven, not noticing the green and purple color scheme). I never told anybody at Bass Rocks how I was secretly filing our private conversations away for future Golf Channel specials—how when I played with Pat O'Donnell and shot 2 under on the front nine, that that was the first time I *knew* I'd be a pro. I never told anyone these things. But each day I went to work. And each week I had to buy a new golf glove.

Obsessions are funny things. When you're in the midst of them, they don't seem in any way strange. Or perhaps it's when you're young that they don't seem strange. In elementary school, while some kids drew Spider-Man comics in their notebooks, I drew golf holes. In fourth grade, I conducted a putting demo in my class for show-and-tell day. I also dressed up as a golfer for Halloween. Two years in a row. Yeah, I was that cool.

I felt like I had another job, too, aside from golf: school. I was, by light-years, never the smartest kid in class, but I worked hard. At Stuyvesant High School, a public school with an entrance exam taken by twenty-four thousand New York City kids for eight hundred spots, I made the cut by one question. All stereotypes of high school were thrown out the window at Stuyvesant. Stuy's football team had perfect SAT scores. Cheerleaders took eight AP courses. My classmates were seriously interesting, funny, but also shamelessly dorky. Everyone knew everyone else's running grade point average, to the decimal place. The more exciting days of the year were report card days. Our robotics team was nationally ranked. While at Stuyvesant, I would sometimes study five hours a night; there weren't a lot of chances to relax. But I felt like it was my job to get good grades. I felt like in my family, it was a way to distinguish myself, to carve out some kind of niche. Getting into Harvard, a school that my dad and his buddies in Wakefield, Massachusetts, had only seen and heard of from the outside—this made me feel, I dunno, good.

A St. Andrews seagull squawks outside my window, snapping me back to Scottish reality.

I stare outside at Market Street, past the seagulls and down toward the Central, a pub where my friends and I would grab post-round pints during the school year. The sun is sinking lazily behind chimney tops and church steeples, bringing dusk down onto the cobblestone street. I think more about my gap year in St. Andrews, how great it's been. How it's given me a (forced) chance to finally breathe. To have fun. To live. I'd been hoping that this summer of caddying would be all that, and maybe more. Because at the moment, I see myself not as a St. Andrews caddie, but as an American kid about to start at Harvard. Sure, I know the course, but I feel a lot more like the American golfers teeing it up here than the guys carrying their bags. I'm here because it'll be a cool summer job. A thing I can brag about to my friends. And maybe I'm pathetically leafing through my Harvard information packet in my room right now because I'm sure I don't belong in the caddie world. Because I'm trying to convince myself that there are more important things in my life than the humiliation of this afternoon's shadow round. Because I'm trying to pretend that I don't care. I look down at the dimpled blue folder.

Ninety-six percent of Harvard seniors find immediate job placement in their field.

• • •

The old caddie doesn't respond.

I repeat my question. "Is that what he paid you in?"

Again, no response. I'm outside the caddie shack, on the damp concrete path, waiting for another round. The caddie I'm addressing—Neil Gibson, it says on his badge—has been showing another caddie a traveler's check, seemingly made out to him by his golfer. I've walked over to the two Scots, interested and wanting to join in on the conversation. But I'm getting the silent treatment. Both caddies are acting as if I'm literally not there. Other caddies are staring now. This is humiliating. Stunned, I walk back to my bench and sit down. I guess I was somehow out of line.

My first few days here have been a quick introduction to the caddie social structure—which is extremely complex and as firmly in place as the hierarchy of any Mafia "family," the only discernible differences being that Old Course caddies 1) don't tend to speak Italian, and 2) drink a lot more Guinness. At the top of the pecking order you've got your old-timers—the wrinkly, complaining guys, who've spent years earning their stripes. Just below them are the full-time adult caddies. Currently in their caddying prime, these guys pound out thirty-six holes daily, and many have caddied in British Opens, or on the European or LPGA tours. They know their stuff. Below these guys are the university (or university-aged) kids, who've been caddying for a couple of summers and have achieved a decent level of cockiness. And at the very bottom of the pack, generally regarded as the scum of the caddie yard, are me and my kind: the trainee caddies.

I'm quickly realizing that the St. Andrews caddie world is not a safe place for newcomers. Less so for young newcomers. Even less so for *student* newcomers. And infinitely less so for young *American* student newcomers. Down here, the world is fiercely local, startlingly insular, strongly resistant to additions. There's no hand-holding, no shortcuts. If you don't know the run-out to Shell Bunker on 7, the caddies in your group will not come to your rescue. If you misclub your golfer over 11 green, word will get back to the shack. Mistakes are not taken lightly; the attitude is "If you don't know your stuff, you shouldn't be out here."

Different laws govern the grounds of the caddie shack, invisible laws that extend out onto the courses, undetectable to your visiting golfers. If you answer the questions of another caddie's golfer, you're dead. If you mistakenly walk left down the first fairway, blocking golfers driving on 18, their caddies will scream *"FORRRRRE!!!!"* at you furiously. At every step, there's a sense of danger for newcomers. And truthfully, I feel scared here. I'm far away from the university dorms and the friends I've made in St. Andrews, far from my family and the people who know I'm a good guy. I'm in a new, gruff world. I feel lost.

. . .

A few days pass. I'm promoted to the "official trainee caddie" rank and begin my first paid round on the Old Course, replete with blue

caddie bib and an embarrassingly huge badge reading TRAINEE CAD-
DIE (it resembles the STUDENT DRIVER signs you see on American
cars or the big red L on British cars). My golfer is an exceedingly
large Swiss journalist who resembles Michael Moore on a very bad
day. As the round progresses, so do his drives, from straight, to gentle draw, to mild hook, and (from hole 10 onward) to frightening
duck hooks, diving ninety degrees left, before entangling themselves
in whatever rough, gorse, or other groups of golfers await. All advice
I offer does little to remedy the situation. By hole 16, he is on pace to
not break 130, with mulligans. On hole 17, the world-famous Road
Hole, he simply stops playing. After we finish, he scribbles all 3's on
my trainee caddie report card (a perfect score) and hands me a crum-
pled fifty-pound note, telling me not to mention this round to anybody. My mood lifts. My career is off and running.

I practically gallop back to the shack to hand in my card to Rick.
I'm eager for a compliment about my perfect report card. I'm feeling
more secure right now; I've just taken a test, and I've passed. This
world, I know. Like a dog eager to be petted, I wait impatiently as
Rick glances at the card. The caddie master puts down the card and
leans out the window threateningly. "I want you to tone it down out
there. Caddies are already starting to talk about you." Before I can
respond, Rick closes the window on me. I have no idea what he's
talking about.

If caddie masters came in cooked-beef choices, Rick Mackenzie
would not be tender. Originally from western Scotland, Rick has
been the caddie master at St. Andrews for twelve years. He's a rough-
looking man in his late forties, with hair that might have once been
blond and a stern, stormy face. When he scowls—which is often—he
doesn't seem far away from violence. This is all to say that I am pro-
foundly terrified of Rick. He's notorious for firing even experienced
caddies who have looped for years, for offenses as minor as not shaving before a caddie round. Legend has it that the bruises and scars on
Rick's weathered face are from beatings by previously fired caddies.

It's apparent that when Rick is around, caddies become worried. Anything you say that Rick takes the wrong way—which is 82 percent of what you say—results in your being pulled into his office. Caddies always feel like they are one step away from being fired. Compounding this is the fact that Rick is deeply suspicious. Witness: Yesterday in the shack, five caddies were watching Alistair Taylor falling asleep and laughing as his head kept slipping from his hands. Hearing the laughter, Rick came charging in and roared, "Does something I said seem fuckin' funny to you?" Laughter ceased. Everyone had to now desperately convince Rick that this was a misunderstanding.

· · ·

As caddies in 2004, we're available for work on all six existing St. Andrews courses.

Course #1, where the majority of our rounds take place, is the famous Old Course (of course). Taking a caddie here is absolutely essential, since without one, a golfer would have zero clue where he or she was heading (almost every tee shot appears as if one is hitting into wilderness). Course #2 is the tighter, tougher New Course ("new" being a relative term here, since it opened in 1895). Course #3 is the Jubilee Course, the toughest golf course in St. Andrews. Course #4 is the calendar-pretty Eden Course, which is not often worked for caddie rounds. Course #5 is the short, straightforward Strathtyrum Course. It's primarily for high-handicap golfers, and although it does happen occasionally, taking a caddie on the Strath would be a bit like hiring Pete Sampras to restring your tennis racket. Lastly, course #6 is the wee nine-hole Balgove Course. The Balgove is basically a beginner's pitch-and-putt course, and I have never heard of a single caddie round taking place there (although veteran caddies will frequently joke that upon retiring, they will someday return to the shack, request a trainee for the Balgove, and treat him like shit). All told, that's ninety-nine holes within walking distance of the town, with rumors of another eighteen in the works. That's a lot of golf. And a lot of chances for caddie rounds. Which is what I need.

"Man, that's something, huh, Rog?"

My golfer stands with his hands on hips, looking straight ahead and talking to his friend. I'm on the Old Course, at the par-3 eleventh, a hole that runs toward the stunningly beautiful Eden Estuary and is described by Old Course caddies as the "most difficult par-3 in the world." (This is absolutely not true. I've seen 30-handicap golfers make birdie here.) It's my fourth round so far as a trainee. There's a sixty-year-old caddie in the group with me who's been caddying on the Old Course for the last fifteen years. He lights a freshly hand-rolled cigarette on every tee box. On this occasion, after the initial puff, he announces to the group that we've got 160 yards to the front edge. I look down at my official Old Course yardage book and notice that the old caddie's calculation is dead wrong.

"Um, are you sure?" I ask. "I think it's actually only one fifty-four to the *pin*."

The old caddie shoots me an iceberg stare. "I've been caddying here for fifteen years, you think I'm gonna let a bloody *trainee* tell me about yardage?" he screams, in plain view of the other players. Clearly, I've crossed a line here. As we leave the tee box, I try to apologize, but he's having none of it. He strides out to two caddie friends in the opposite fairway and starts speaking privately (and furiously) with them. I curse under my breath, noting that my absolutely correct advice was, in my new caddie world, a mistake.

After the round, Rick again wants to see me. This time I'm less eager to get to the window. After a fifteen-second "chat," I gather that Rick is not pleased about what happened on 11. I begin an eloquent excuse, but Rick cuts me off. "You're on thin ice, mate," he says, and slams the window shut.

Quietly, I leave the window. I don't know what to do. As I'm replaying today's events in my mind, a gentle-looking older caddie passes me. He looks me up and down. I want to meet as many new caddies as possible. I'm also in need of a friend right now. I nod, say hello to him. He does not respond. He glares and walks by.

I shuffle away from the shack and over to the Old Course putting green, to watch four wind-shirt-clad American golfers putting. They look so happy, so friendly. They joke with each other. I suddenly realize that I'm extremely jealous. They'll be heading back to the States soon. I could be as well. I remember that today was my original flight date. A sudden pang seizes me. It's homesickness, mixed with a longing to fit in, and above all, loneliness. I want to just rip off my bib, hop the fence, and run over to the Americans. I want to join them, talk to them, play golf with them. Anything but stay here. All at once, I feel trapped—pinned to my caddie identity. *I don't need this shit*, I think. *Why do I have to put up with this?* I could just go home. Enjoy my summer. I wish I hadn't changed my flight. I wish I hadn't done any of this. I bite my lip, hold back tears. I feel like Harvey in *Captains Courageous*, and I've just fallen off the ship.

Two

The doorbell ring dances around the house.

I can hear the sound of a creaking chair, then movement toward the door. Above me at number 4 Howard Place, St. Andrews seagulls dart and dive, landing on the chimneys of surrounding flats. Ten seconds pass; then I hear the door being carefully unlocked, along with an unmistakable cheery giggle. It's Uncle Ken.

I'm here for my twice-weekly dinner with my great-uncle Ken Hayward. Throughout the school year, I've been supping with him on Friday evenings, and I'm praying that these meals continue during my caddie summer. Uncle Ken first came to St. Andrews during World War II. A Royal Air Force pilot squadron leader, he was stationed at RAF Leuchars, directly across the Eden Estuary from the Old Course. Uncle Ken fell in love with St. Andrews, and with a St. Andrean lass named Betty. They married in 1944, and after living for twenty years in England, Ken and Betty retired to St. Andrews in 1964. Uncle Ken's been here ever since. Betty died in the 1970s, and Isobel, Ken's second wife, died suddenly in 1991.

Now eighty-three, Uncle Ken lives alone in a huge, elegant Georgian town house at Howard Place that he inherited from Isobel. Uncle Ken was a town councilor for more than twenty years. He was a reasonable golfer (7 handicap) and a member of both the St. Andrews Golf Club and the New Golf Club (whose clubhouses overlook the eighteenth fairway of the Old Course). For the past twenty years, Uncle Ken has been president of the St. Andrews and District Horticultural Society. He knows every shop, every street sign, every house, every tree, and every St. Andrean over the age of seventy-five. You could say, with accuracy, that Uncle Ken's got the town under wraps. Ever dapper, he always wears a dress shirt and tie, even at home, even in the garden. When on the streets, he sports a tweed jacket and tartan cap. He has a cheery, youthful (and high-pitched) giggle, and a deadly putting stroke. He also has an adorable Jack Russell terrier named Bonnie, who has the look and energy of a wind-up toy. Uncle Ken and I go to a different restaurant every week—which provides a welcome change from my caddie diet of morning cereal, midday chicken sandwich, and nightly pasta. At these dinners Uncle Ken is all business as he enthusiastically fills me in on the town gossip, the state of his garden, and his motor caravan (RV) club trips with "the gang," plus seriously interesting stories of his time in the RAF and subsequent travels around the world. Uncle Ken has endless plans, a full agenda (which he calls his "gen"). I always fire back with detailed reports of my own golf scores, often hole by hole, shot by shot. I love my time with Uncle Ken. I never want the nights to end.

This evening, over poached salmon at the Grill House, I explain to Uncle Ken what's been happening so far in my caddie world. I tell him that I'm having a rough go of it. I confess that I'm having second thoughts about this summer job choice. Uncle Ken takes this all in; then he takes in a bite of Tay salmon. A few seconds later, he speaks. "Give it time, Ollie. This will be good for you." I nod. I want to believe him. But I'm not sure he speaks the truth.

• • •

"Alistair Taylor," the caddie shack loudseaker bellows.

Alistair, an older caddie with aviator sunglasses and legs so skinny and pasty that they've been described as "two out-of-bounds stakes," is just getting his coffee from the shack's instant machine. He hears the announcement milliseconds before coffee hits lips and does a huge double take. He's on the course in five minutes and now can't enjoy his coffee. "Typical," he mutters as the others in the shack laugh loudly, "fookin' typical!"

The epicenter of caddie life is the caddie pavilion (aka the caddie shack). About twenty feet long and twenty feet wide, it is barred from the public's reach by a stern sign reading REGISTERED CADDIES ONLY (although UNASSUMING tourists often stumble in through any door left ajar, in search of toilets). The room is furnished with wooden benches, a table, a TV, old magazines, decks of playing cards, random golf clubs, and a KLIX machine that dispenses, among other things, vegetable soup with the inexplicable texture and flavor of minced carrots floating in paint thinner. Caddies assemble in the shack early mornings before their rounds (a tinny intercom intermittently blares out the name of the next caddie up), where they play cards and read tabloid newspapers (*The Scottish Sun*, featuring a different nude girl on page 3 every day, is a highly popular read). On the inside doorway of the room hangs a NO SMOKING sign—shrouded in a constant fog of cigarette smoke.

A caddie's day begins at different times, depending on how ambitious (and outrageously sleep deprived) one chooses to be. The first thirty rounds are reserved for the Top 30 Group: caddies with the highest number of rounds the previous year. The rest of the bags are awarded on a first-come, first-served basis, unless a paying player books a specific caddie in advance. The caddie manager arrives at six A.M. to start taking down names, but caddies begin to line up outside the shack well before that, sometimes as early as four A.M. Legend has it that Old Course caddies used to arrive when the pubs

shut and sleep on the benches by the shack till morning lineup. Ultimately, R & A members complained of the noise, sight, and smell
of these unshaven men, and bench rest was banished.

Once caddies sign in and get a number, they are free to do as
they please, provided they are at the caddie shack when their name is
called. I've already learned the art of correlating number and time to
wait. Each morning I arrive at five thirty A.M. for sign-in, pajamas
under my waterproofs; collect my number; and return to my bed for
one to three hours of blissful sleep.

"You're fookin' ridiculous! Right is *miles* easier in!"

Three caddies near me are now debating the ideal line off the
twelfth tee (to avoid four hidden bunkers in the middle of the fairway). Alistair has left for his round, coffeeless, bequeathing the untouched cup to another caddie with the accompanying description
"White coffee, nae sugar, to'ally *virginal*." I'm sitting at the far end
of the shack bench, over by the cubbyholes—by myself. I feel as cool
as the fifth grader sitting with his teacher on the school bus during
a class trip.

Beyond the twelfth-hole-debating group, another pack of caddies is fervently discussing Lee Westwood ("Nice swing, like, but
he's a poncey bastard"). Near them, a balding forty-year-old caddie
is telling a joke crescendo-ing exponentially in dirtiness about a
golfer and a farm animal. Caddies all around are laughing. They're
hanging out with their friends. They're having a perfect Tuesday
morning. And I'm in no way a part of it.

I adjust my bib self-consciously, pretend to look at my pin sheet.
I'm confused about why I'm so excluded. What the hell is going
wrong down here? What have I done to deserve this? I don't get it,
and I don't like it. I resent these guys for their unfriendliness. *You
know what? Fuck 'em.* I start reading a newspaper. More laughter
from around me. I try to concentrate on the paper. More banter. No
use. I put the paper down, take a deep, quivering breath. I realize
something: I desperately want to be accepted by these guys.

THREE

"Now, careful, Henry, it'll be very hot!"

Uncle Ken places three steaming mugs of Nambarrie tea on the table. Henry, sitting across from me, looks very pleased. He takes a sip, emits a satisfied eighty-three-year-old sigh.

"Aye, this is what I like."

"Oliver, I've got a rock bun from Fisher & Donaldson for you as well," Uncle Ken calls from the pantry, very seriously. "Would you like it now?"

Hell yes.

Whenever I have long gaps between loops, I've been biking up to Howard Place to have tea with Uncle Ken and various gardeners' club cronies (all elderly men wearing tweed jackets and tweed caps). Here I am treated to heated discussions on horticultural society event planning ("gen"), golf stories, tourist stories, reports of fallen trees, medical reports with more deaths than births, and the center of any local conversation: the weather in St. Andrews. My tea sessions with Uncle Ken and his cronies are extremely cool. They are full of good cheer. They make growing old seem, in a word, hopeful.

Today it's Uncle Ken and his closest friend, Henry Anquetil. An Englishman himself, Henry was also in the RAF, and married a "WAAF" (Women's Auxiliary Air Force), as he still labels his wife, Grace. Henry was the head gardener for forty years at the University of St. Andrews. Henry knows every single tree, flower, and bush growing on the university's massive grounds. He knows them because he planted them.

"How you gettin' on down there, laddie?"

Henry is interested. Together, both he and Uncle Ken are ardent trackers of my caddie and golf life. They're the first to applaud me (very Englishly) on good rounds. When, as a St. Andrews student, I broke par for the first time, shooting a 2-under 70 on the Old, Henry's response was a murmured ". . . By golly, well, I'm blowed!" I tell Henry that I'm trying my best down there. Henry nods. "I'm sure you young lads are doing well." I nod back in agreement, stiff upper lip firmly in place.

Henry, like Uncle Ken, is tracking steadily toward ninety. Henry, like Uncle Ken, is impeccably dressed every day in shirt, tie, and tweed jacket. Henry, like Uncle Ken, likes to stay on top of all town "gen." Such information is gathered by Henry daily during his waits at the Market Street bus stop, alongside the other "ancients" (as Henry and Uncle Ken call themselves). All gen is then disseminated at the kitchen table daily. As they hold forth over the town, Henry and Uncle Ken bring to mind Statler and Waldorf, the balcony-seated old men in *The Muppet Show*.

Henry turns his attention to another important matter.

"Did you see the leeks at the Kingsbarns flower show, Ken?"

Henry is now holding some pictures (of leeks) that he took from the vegetables competition. Scouting photos.

"I did, Henry, yes." Uncle Ken is all ears.

"Were as big as my cup!" Henry shows me an approximation of

their size. "I went like this . . . one, two, three. I said, 'By *golly*, they're good leeks.'"

Henry and Uncle Ken are alternating presidents of the St. Andrews Gardeners' Club and travel frequently to flower shows around the surrounding towns. Together, they spy on other vegetables that have won top prizes—six-foot-long leeks, immaculate carrots—to see how their St. Andrews show in September will compare. Fierce competition simmers on these flower-show circuits. The first-prize cucumber will be talked about in surrounding towns; eighty-year-old women with poor flower showings will sulk for weeks.

Dong dong dong.

The grandfather clock chimes three o'clock. It's time for me to head back down to the Old so Rick doesn't kill me. Uncle Ken sees me off at the front door, wishes me a good second round. Henry joins him out front, towering over my uncle (Henry, unlike Uncle Ken, is pushing six feet tall). "I hope they tip you well, lad," Henry says, a twinkle in his eye. It's obvious that both men are proud to know a young caddie on the Old. I tell Henry I hope they tip well too, and unchain my bike from the fence. As I pedal away, I glance back up at the stoop, where Uncle Ken and Henry stand, tweed coated and walking stick steady. They both tip their caps at me. I smile. I can't help thinking that they're the last remnants of a time past.

FOUR

"We've got Yanks."

Willie Stewart, a mustachioed Scottish caddie who looks permanently annoyed, motions to his two friends. I'm in the group too, although I'm not motioned at. The three Scots start walking to the first tee. Before I follow, I have to first pay my five-pound "admin fee" at the shack window. Every caddie pays Rick five pounds at the start of each day, as a kind of sign-on payment. Since caddies are technically self-employed, this money connects the caddie department to wages earned from golfers. The "admin fees" go toward the upkeep of the shack, as well as various caddie supplies like bibs, hats, and caddie waterproofing subsidization.

Rick's at the window as I approach, and he sticks his hand out immediately for my fiver. I scrounge around in my pockets (underneath my waterproof pants) and finally pull out four pound coins. Nothing else. I remember that I brought down only five pound coins this morning. I also remember that I bought a bottle of water ten minutes ago from Rick, for a pound, because my throat was dry. I probably should not have done this.

"Rick, I guess I'll have to pay you the final pound after my round," I say.

I *definitely* should not have said this.

Rick turns a volcanic shade of maroon and leans out the window toward me. "Well, you won't be caddying today then, that's for sure!" he bellows. This is not good. I'm considering trying to trade back my half-empty water bottle when someone taps me on the shoulder. It's an older caddie who's witnessed this scene. He hands me a pound coin. I take it and thank him.

"You owe me two back," he growls.

This is round number six for me in my quest for thirty. That's the golden number for trainees. It is the number of rounds, supposedly, after which Rick Mackenzie reviews our progress and (hopefully) promotes us to the rank of full caddie. Nothing is guaranteed, though. First you need to pass a difficult written exam, in which you must name many of the 112 bunkers and provide accurate sketches of the breaks in several Old Course greens. Plus, Rick seems under no particular pressure to take on new caddies. He'll promote to the rank of official caddie only those trainees who are near flawless.

All paid up now, I jog to catch up with the other three caddies, headed toward the first tee. At the tee box, Willy distributes pin sheets to the other caddies in the group. I ask if he has an extra one.

"You'll hafta get one for yourself, kid," Willy grunts. "I just got 'em for me boys!"

I walk back to the starter's hut to pick up my own pin sheet, aware that 1) I'm still at the insect end of the food chain, and 2) I'm probably not one of Willie's "boys."

The Old Course gets roughly twenty-five thousand visitors every year. The overwhelming majority of these twenty-five thousand are Americans. English, Japanese, and Canadians come next in frequency. Then it's Spanish, followed by French, followed by Germans. As Willie predicted, we've got Americans today, and from hole 1, I go to work. I've been picking up some crucial unwritten rules of caddying, either observed from my older counterparts on the course or overheard as I eavesdrop on conversations in the shack.

There are a few key rules: First, a young caddie who's out in a group of veterans *has* to tend/pull most of the pins on the greens. If he doesn't do his share, he will incur the wrath of the other caddies. The pin rule actually applies to most caddies—so anyone not pulling enough pins will quickly become known as lazy. Caddies who discover at the window that they're out with such-labeled guys will mutter, "Well, *I'll* be getting every fucking pin this round then . . ."

Second commandment: Before rounds, it's considered bad form for a young caddie to go up early to the tee before the other caddies (shit, I *always* do this!) to introduce himself to the group. Holding court in front of the whole group treads on the other caddies' toes. They've been here longer, the thinking goes, so let them play to the group.

Unwritten rule number three applies to bag selection. As a trainee caddie, you should always pick up the heaviest bag. If there's a cart bag, you need to take it. This isn't *required*, but it's a way to gain respect.

Rule number four: If you're asked questions during the round about history, course changes, and things of that nature, it's considered respectful to defer to the older caddies. ("Hey, Fergus, John was just asking when the Swilcan Bridge was built. You'd say it was in the fourteen hundreds, right?")

And finally, number five, and the most important rule of caddying ever: You must never, ever, question another caddie on the course in front of his golfer. If putt reads are wrong, if lines off tees are suspect, do *not* throw your fellow caddie under the bus. There is nothing to gain from correcting an older caddie. You make him look foolish, and you will quickly incur the wrath of the other caddies. These rules all have something in common: Don't be a big shot. I wonder if they think I am.

FIVE

"Do you want anything else?"

The English girl in Luvians Bottle Shop is staring at me. She's tall, blond, and outrageously good-looking.

"Uh . . ."

I glance over the counter. I've already bought two bottles of whiskey (which I don't particularly need) and a packet of pork chips (which I definitely don't eat). But I'm desperate for an excuse to keep talking to her. For the last few days, I've been passing this store and this girl and gradually falling in love. Now I'm inside, and I'm finally in front of her, and . . .

"Um . . ."

I keep scanning the counter. Over the past fifty-one seconds, several facts have made themselves abundantly clear to me. 1) I'm physically shaking, 2) I'm way too nervous to say anything remotely cool to this girl right now, and 3) my only hope of getting her number is to stall for a further, unspecified amount of time, until I can calm down. I have to find something else to buy . . . *anything.*

"Oh, uh, I'll take those sweets."

The girl nods, scoops up a packet of lemon drops. "These?"

"Yup!" I say brightly, and then for some unclear reason add, "For my niece." The girl rings up the final item, pretty sure that I don't have a niece, and looks at me.

"That's forty-nine pounds."

Shit. This was more than I was expecting. I pull out a grubby fifty-pound note that I received less than fifteen minutes ago and realize that I've just blown all my caddie earnings from today. Somehow I'm emboldened by this depressing detail, and leap into action.

"So . . . are you a student here?"

There's a long pause.

"Yes," the girl finally answers.

Another pause.

"Oh . . . cool. What do you study?"

The girl makes a face that seems to ask, "Is this actually happening?"

"English."

I'm about to begin the next bar of my conversational concerto when she adds with finality, "Well-have-a-*great-day.*"

I leave the store, tossing my pork chips into a bin on the way out.

I've been single since the last week of May, when Claire and I broke up. And I'm remembering that my skills with girls are, strictly speaking, not award winning.

Claire was my first serious girlfriend. A hilarious, cute brunette from Charlestown, South Carolina, she was, like me, a first-year student at St. Andrews. We dated for the second half of the school year, including a Valentine's Day weekend (yep, I finally had a girlfriend on Valentine's Day) spent exploring the Scottish Highlands together— forty-eight hours that, for me, approached dream status. Then summer arrived, and several facts became unavoidable. Claire would be back here next year; I wouldn't. Claire was heading back to America for the summer; I was staying here to caddie. The decision that followed made sense. The scene that followed this decision was less orderly—with my leaving Claire's dorm room, then running head-first into her four roommates, who collectively looked ready to administer my life's second, and possibly more violent, circumcision.

Several weeks later, I've still got that afternoon on regular repeat. I'm pretty sure that splitting up was the sensible thing to do. But I'm also realizing that sensible, when applied to romantic relationships, rarely makes a great deal of sense.

* * *

"Hurry up! It's starting!" Everyone's already in the living room.

"Yeah, I'll be there in ten seconds!" I yell back from the kitchen. The microwave's cycle is almost done, and the cheese is starting to bubble. I grab my creation and dash into the main living room as fast as my throbbing legs will turn over. Five other kids are already there, glued to the UK's smash-hit reality show *Big Brother*. They all turn as I enter. Eva looks at me.

"*What* is that?"

"Pasta with butter and cheese."

Sarah looks inside the bowl and remarks hesitantly in a Northern English accent, "That's a lot of cheese . . ."

"Yeah."

"And a lot of butter."

I nod. "Yeah."

Dave elaborates on this point. "It looks like shit."

"Yeah, well . . ." I search for a clever retort. "You're shit." And then I sit down. Clever retorts are harder after double caddie rounds.

I'm growing to love my digs, a rented garret room in a flat that occupies the top three floors of a stunning Victorian house overlooking Market Street, St. Andrews's half-mile-long main artery. From my door, I have no more than a three-minute bike ride to the

Old Course. As important, my building is flanked by a pub called the Red Reiver and a wine seller called Luvians Bottle Shop. Five other university kids are also living in furnished rooms in the same flat this summer: 1) a nice English kid named John, whose parents own the flat, 2) his girlfriend Sarah A, 3) John's older brother Dave, 4) Sarah B, a University of St. Andrews third-year, and 5) Eva, a Russian girl who spends summers working in Scotland. I quickly discover that all of my flatmates are very European, and very cool. And everyone, like me, has a busy summer job. John and his brother Dave caddie at Kingsbarns Golf Links; John's girlfriend, Sarah A, waitresses at a coffee shop on South Street; and Sarah B and Eva bartend at the Pilmour Hotel, a pub frequented by Old Course caddies (and known to insiders as "TP's").

"Any good tips today?" Dave is asking Sarah B.

"Yeah, two American golfers were chatting me up all afternoon."

"Minted?"

"Big-time."

"Oh, wonderful. I'll just pass that along to your boyfriend then . . ."

"Get stuffed, Dave!" Sarah B replies with a sharp kick to Dave's shin.

Early this morning, our flat bustled with action as six roommates prepared for their day jobs. Now, ten sunlit hours later, the flat is transformed into a haven of immobility. We are collectively so exhausted that the mere notion of being horizontal is enough excitement for any of us.

"I had a legend on Kingsbarns today," John announces, nursing his Stella.

"Yeah?"

"It was a corporate outing, so the shack has to pay us fifty quid before we even start, right? My guy's a Vegas hotel owner. He gives me a hundred-dollar bill at the end, and I tell him, 'That's really generous of you, sir, but you only have to pay the tip today—we're already getting fifty quid from the shack.' And the guy says, 'Oh,' looks in his wallet, clearly *only* has hundred-dollar bills, and goes, 'Ah fuck it, just keep it.'"

The others laugh. Sarah A turns to me.

"What time are you down tomorrow, Ollie?"

"Eh, not too bad. Five."

Dave whistles. "Good effort!"

"Yeah, well, you know . . . I'm trying. Long as I don't have that Polish guy again."

I set my bowl down on our coffee table and sink back happily into my couch cushion. Most nights of ours seem to follow this same routine: preparing and eating dinner together, usually pasta, and trading highlights, lowlights, and no-lights of our particular work-days. It's my first time living in a flat away from home, and I like it. A lot.

Six

I'm heading to the first tee to meet my golfers for my second round of the day. It's four P.M., and dark clouds have begun to roll off the North Sea, toward the Old Course. I'm exhausted. My golfer introduces himself. He's a tall, clean-cut forty-five-year-old from Spain. In his halting English, he lets me know that his bag is waiting, just by the fence. I follow his pointing finger to a cow-sized cart bag, obviously stuffed to the brim with an assortment of useless golfing items. (Witness: He packs a twenty-five-foot extendable golf-ball scooper. There is a total of one water hazard on the Old Course, and there are at least three ball scoops lying right alongside said hazard.) I suck in my breath, lift his cow, force a smile, and follow him to the tee. As we walk down the first fairway, I look over at the other caddie in our group, a strong-backed six-foot-three fellow trainee, cantering along. He is smiling. He is also pulling a cart, rented for him by his player, who uses no more than a ferret-sized Sunday bag.

At the end of the round, I limp up the concrete steps to the front of the R & A building, where golfers always pay their caddies. I dump the bag on the ground for the last time, just as my fellow caddie perkily glides his ferret-on-a-cart to a halt beside me. My golfer reaches into his pocket and takes out a crisp fifty-pound note. "That's what I'm talking about," I say to myself. My jolly mood crashes to earth as my golfer says, "Split this between you two." I've had about as much as I can take.

"Excuse me, you know the trainee rate is twenty-five pounds *plus tip*, right?"

"Ohhhh! I apologize," my golfer says, and looks genuinely sorry. He reaches into his pocket and produces a fifty-pence coin, which he places in my hand. "There we are. Sorry about that."

. . .

I've been trying to pump out the rounds lately, in my quest for trainee-scrub promotion. I'm desperate to shed my trainee identity and be moved up to the promised land of full caddie-dom. So this week, I've decided to go into caddie overdrive, doing doubles (two rounds in a day) whenever possible. And already, I'm starting to understand some key elements to caddie life.

Like tips.

Along with pace of play and golfer ineptitude, tips rank as the biggest subject of caddie shack discussion. Officially, the full-caddie rate in 2004 is thirty-five pounds, plus tip. The trainee rate is twenty-five pounds, plus tip. This tip, or "caddie gratuity," is left unspecified, and it creates a vast gray area, which will often (*always*) determine what caddies think of their golfers. A wonderful round with a pleasant golfer who then tips badly leaves a sour taste in caddies' mouths and will assuredly induce post-round complaining in the shack. Caddies even have slang for certain tips. A fifty-quid total payment (fifteen-pound tip) is known as the "Hawaii Five-0," after the popular TV show. It is considered a low tip, worthy of complaint. So a caddie might say to another, "I think we're gonna see the Hawaii

Five-0 today," or use an even looser spin-off of the idea, such as "Fook me, we're definitely goin' to Hawaii today." It is inner-shack lingo, and Hawaii, or the need to "get your surfboards out," will be frequently mentioned out loud right beside golfers, who have no idea what their caddies are talking about.

A well-liked story in the shack involves the caddie last summer who asked his elderly golfer, on the first tee, what he did for a living. "Oh, I'm an actor," the man replied. "I was on this show for years that used to be with CBS. You might have heard of it, *Hawaii Five-0*?" The caddie's face fell. He knew what was coming. And as if confirming the presence of divine caddie law, he received fifty pounds at the end of the round.

Above the Hawaii Five-0, a payment of fifty-five pounds (the "Britvic 55," after a UK soft drink) is still bad. Sixty pounds is considered good. Nothing special at all, but fine. A caddie would be slightly disappointed if certain things throughout the round *had* pointed toward a higher tip—a miraculous green-read on 18 for birdie, or leading the golfer to the round of his life—but sixty is normally considered good. In no way, however, would sixty be considered a "reward" for great caddying. Seventy is a nice reward, and anything higher will be talked about in the shack appreciatively. Triple-digit tips are not that uncommon. Everyone gets a "ton" (one hundred pounds) at some point each summer. And any payment below fifty is deemed equivalent to stabbing a caddie's child.

What tip each golfer will likely dispense is frequently discussed among caddies throughout the round. The predictions take into account a stunning variety of factors, including the golfer's perceived talent, personality, gender, hired tour company, and nationality. Nationality is big. Americans are not only the most frequent visitors to the Old Course, but also tip the best. Just north of the U.S. border live the people considered the worst tippers in the world—Canadians. Scottish caddies will frequently grumble, "He was a nice guy, like, but the fucking Canadians can't tip." (There's also a regularly repeated saying in the shack: "What's the difference between a Canadian and a canoe? A canoe tips.") The English are bad too. So are the Germans. So are the Japanese, but that's more complicated. The Japanese aren't particularly stingy (golf drivers sometimes go for eight hundred dollars in Tokyo), but their golfers are usually on highly regimented tours with greedy Scottish operators who want extra tips for themselves and will often direct their Japanese golfers toward low caddie gratuities.

As a trainee, all rules governing my own pay are out the window. My trainee caddie badge is an embarrassing reminder to golfers of my lowly class, my supposed blithering ineptitude. The caddie report cards that I have to distribute to my players above the eighteenth green seem to scream, "I'm just learning! Pay me less!" And if that's not enough, there's the humiliation of standing there while Rick Mackenzie notes to my golfer—directly in front of me—that I am a *trainee caddie* (implying that if I suck, it's not really his fault), and that my rate is thus "only twenty-five pounds plus tip." So for me and my kind, fifty pounds is a *great* payday, and the money is usually lower than that.

It's disheartening—I have to work much harder to prove myself to golfers, to overcome my trainee status and show them that I know my stuff. And that's another reason I'm doing doubles whenever possible. I need to show Rick that I'm a hard worker and show the other caddies that I'm serious about this. Respect isn't given freely out here. It has to be *earned*. And that's what I intend to do.

. . .

St. Andrews is different in summertime. The town has changed form. The students are gone, their popped pink collars replaced by roving packs of American golfers (always in foursomes) and sunburned Scottish "holidaymakers" on pub terraces sipping Magners cider. The days are longer, the seagulls more restless as they swoop over the Scores (a scenic street near the North Sea). Golf is in full bloom, at peak season. The ballot is crammed full each day, hopeful walk-on golfers begin lining up at four A.M., and the caddie shack is heaving to keep up with the demand. In spite of my lower trainee rate, the money is good, and for the first time in my life, I'm making a bunch of it. I'm paying my own rent, buying my own food, depositing grubby twenty-pound notes into Lloyds bank. I feel like an adult, and it's exciting. I'm still not respected in the shack (by a long stretch), but I think I'm moving in the right direction.

At day's end, I'm handed fifty-five quid for my eighth round as a trainee. I hop on my bike and cruise back into town. The streets are still filled with people, and I still wear my caddie bib proudly, fully conscious of the awed looks American tourists give me as I ride by: an Old Course caddie. I'm loving the attention.

Suddenly, a car screeches noisily to a halt ten yards from my bike. A voice screams out, "Take that goddamn bib off, you know you can't wear that in toon!" It's another Old Course caddie. I remove my bib.

Caddies' nights out are defined by job prospects for the following morning. During the early part of the week (the packed days), when most caddies will be getting down to the course between five A.M. and six A.M. for sign-up, the thought of a late night out—of arriving at sign-up groggy eyed and hung over—is, in a word, unappealing. However, when the next day's ballot displays a slow workday, caddies sportingly make up for lost time. Enter St. Andrews's pub scene.

A common view among Americans is that Old Course caddies predominantly congregate in the Jigger Inn—the famous pub located right alongside the seventeenth fairway, adjoining the Old Course Hotel. This is as accurate as the belief that a haggis is actually a ferocious animal (of which, interestingly, many caddies have been known to convince ignorant unsuspecting tourists). Caddies avoid the Jigger for a number of reasons: 1) It's too far from town, 2) it's too expensive, 3) it's filled with tourist golfers who think Old Course caddies hang out there.

Older Old Course caddies opt for more centrally located pubs like the Dunvegan and TP's. There is, however, a locally known game called the Jigger Challenge. In this game, whoever comes down 17 on the Old Course stops in the Jigger and helps themselves to a certain number of pints. The amount is up to the contestant, but that person then must play the eighteenth hole in fewer strokes than downed pints. To my knowledge, there have been very few winners of this game.

. . .

I'm pedaling up to Howard Place.

I've got an especially important midevening job here—green bean planting with Uncle Ken. The baby-blue gardening gloves are waiting for me when I pull up, as is Uncle Ken. He's on the stoop, intently staring down Hope Street, and waves at me with relief. I'm six minutes late, but in eighty-three-year-old Uncle Ken's world, this is enough to necessitate active stoop-watch duty. As we begin planting out in the garden, the frustrations of my day melt like snow. The work is wonderfully simple, relaxing. Inside this little garden, it's just me and Uncle Ken. I pat down another bed of green beans, with Uncle Ken instructing me on proper planting procedure. Then I hear a bark and feel a warm lick on my cheek. Bonnie has joined us.

For the past sixteen years, Bonnie has been Uncle Ken's constant companion. They share thrice-daily long walks by the Old Course, where Bonnie hunts and finds unlucky golf balls, sometimes two dozen in a single outing. They travel together on weekend motor caravan trips. (Uncle Ken is a stalwart member of the Scottish Motor Caravanners' Club.) The two are inseparable. Whenever he eats a meal in a restaurant, Uncle Ken brings a small brown bag with him and discreetly slips a portion of his beef into the bag for Bonnie. (Uncle Ken confesses, with the sigh of a longtime spouse accustomed to his wife's picky habits, that Bonnie will only eat the very finest Scottish beef.)

I quickly realize that as much as Bonnie needs Uncle Ken, he in return, living alone in such a large, lonely house, equally needs the company of his now-elderly terrier. It is charming to watch the two of them, sharing sprightly old age together, the firmest of friends.

• • •

The rounds keep coming. I'm assigned to a group from America—the Deep South. My player, after learning that I'm a John Kerry supporter, announces that by round's end he'll convert me to Republicanism. He doesn't. What the other players in the group *do* manage to accomplish, however, is to deeply upset another caddie in the group—one of my friends. They trade anti-French Freedom Fries jokes throughout the entire front nine, which they share frequently with him. On 10, he reveals that his mother is French, and gives them dead-wrong green reads the rest of the way in.

I'm walking back to the shack to sign on for my next round. Rick is at the window. He takes down my name for a second round. "You're not doing the motormouth thing still, are you?" he asks. Rick is implying that I'm somehow talking too much on the golf course. It's something he heard regarding my very first trainee round, and he hasn't let the matter die since. I think he picks on certain caddies that he considers to be "weaker," and my eighteen-year-old-American-student status must qualify me for this category.

"Well, I'm doing the caddie chat if that's what you call it, and I'm averaging threes on my assessment cards so I must be doing something right!" is what I want to say, Paul Newman–style.

"Oh no, I'm not, Rick," is what I actually say, sounding meeker than a church mouse. And then I degrade myself even further. "I'm going to run into town quickly, can I get you a candy bar from Tesco?"

Rick beams. "Oooh nooo, Ollie, that won't be necessary." I leave the window to a smiling Rick and walk past a dorky trainee caddie with thick glasses, who has heard the exchange.

"Way to stand up to Mackenzie," he taunts, his eyes squinting gleefully behind the bifocals.

"Well, we can't all be the Fonz like you!" I snap, then leave to go buy a yogurt.

I'm learning more caddie "tricks" out here. If my golfer putts out first, I often head to the next tee, carrying the other bags with me. This speeds up play but also gives the older guys a rest. While not required, it earns you serious suck-up points with the other caddies. It also provides opportunities for your golfers to see you carrying four bags at once, which is always funny (the secret: put one bag over each shoulder, and carry the others by their side handles). Another trick is forecaddying. On certain holes, like number 6 with its blind tee shot over seemingly unending gorse, I always volunteer to go forecaddie. You have to be careful, though, as some older caddies like to do this themselves. One tall caddie joined me on top of the hill above the sixth tee, after I'd already gone to forecaddie. Looking down at our annoying New Jersey golfers, I said, "Least we're outta range for a bit." The caddie looked out to sea and sighed. "Best forty-five seconds of my day."

There's another important lesson to learn. In the caddie shack, like anywhere else, knowledge is power. The more a trainee knows about the Old Course, the more respected he will be by his fellow caddies. I begin studying my caddie yardage books whenever I can. I memorize the names of as many bunkers as possible. The cluster to the right of the fifth fairway is the Seven Sisters. The two between 6 and 13 are the Coffins. The bunker eighty-five yards short of 14 green is called Hell. The bunkers just left of 14 green are the Graves. There are a lot of death references out here.

. . .

It's the next day, and I'm assigned a group of Japanese golfers, just in from Tokyo this morning. They're dazed, jet-lagged, and absolutely euphoric to be on the Old Course. (Their excitement reminds me of myself as a five-year-old, on my first trip to Water Country, a theme park in New Hampshire, when I began to hyperventilate and had to breathe into a paper bag.) The Japanese group speaks no English. None. I walk up to my golfer, eager to impress, and utter the one scrap of Japanese I know, "*Ohayo-gozaimasu*," which means (I think) "Good morning." My golfer's eyes light up, and a torrent of babbling Japanese answers my greeting. I nod my head and smile back inanely. It's going to be a long day.

My copious double-round days are having a good effect. Ken Henderson, the kindly assistant caddie master, tells me in the caddie shack that Rick is impressed with my "vitality." He says that they can barely keep up with me and all my trainee-caddie report cards. In contrast to Rick, Ken is Mother Teresa. He's a cheery sixty-year-old Scottish chap with bushy eyebrows and spectacles with string attached behind his ears. Ken is a keen golfer, and belongs to Crail Golfing Society, a course twenty-five minutes from St. Andrews and set on headlands overlooking the sea. Ken has a pleased, grandfatherly smile whenever I sign on for late double rounds, and an easy laugh. I get the feeling that he's rooting for us youngsters. I receive Ken's report about Rick with a nod, then immediately sign on for a second round. I want to keep up my "vitality."

I'm back out on the course now for round two, caddying for a loud American guy from Los Angeles. He quickly establishes himself as a total jerk, making comments about a variety of things, including the slow pace of play (it isn't) and the faults in his playing partners' swings. After one particularly harsh put-down of his friend's chipping stroke on 6, the criticized friend, a nice old guy with Coke-bottle-thick glasses, who could have understudied Uncle Junior on *The Sopranos*, shoots back with, "When God gave out the assholes, did you say yes twice?" Today is not my golfer's day. It is not his day, in the same way that the arrival of a Plague of Locusts would not be a barley field's day. As the round progresses, my golfer's golf grows worse and worse, as does his temper. By 18, he is out of control. As the other players slow down in front of the Swilcan Bridge to take a group photo, my player keeps going. When told to wait for the picture, my guy, sentimental to the end, screams, "I don't wanna take any more fuckin' pictures!" and charges over the bridge. He slips, falls, skins both knees. His opponents laugh and applaud.

Days later, I am told the following story by an elderly caddie: He was looping for a middle-aged golfer who obviously used to be a below-scratch player. The golfer started to cross Swilcan Bridge, stopped, began to cry. The caddie gently asked him, "What's the matter?" The man answered softly, "I used to have dreams about walking over this bridge and thousands of fans screaming my name." I think about all the times, while caddying, I've walked over that same bridge with the same thought in my head.

SEVEN

"Tom Greaves. Ollie Horovitz."

The shack intercom booms its caddie call to duty.

Greaves and I laugh and exchange a fist-pound. This'll be a fun one.

Greaves is my age and has just finished his first year at the University of St. Andrews. We were in the same English section together, spending two hours each week tackling *Frankenstein*, *Wuthering Heights*, and *Beowulf*. Greaves is Scottish but sounds absolutely English, as do most Scottish kids who went to private school. He's also in his first year of caddying, also still a trainee. Days before beginning his summer caddie career, he inexplicably dyed his hair bleach-blond to "get ready for caddying." A few sun-drenched rounds, and it's begun to turn green. Greaves and I head outside, passing another young trainee, Kevin Fogarty (*Foggy!*), at the door. We all smile as we pass. It's nice knowing you're not the only wretch out on the mountain.

A month has passed since I started at the shack, and I've begun making friends with many of the other caddies my age. Most of these kids attend or have just graduated from the University of St. Andrews, although quite a few others come from all over the world, just staying for the summer to earn some spending money (or attempting to do so). As we are all climbing the figurative "caddie ladder" together, I grow to know all fellow trainee scrubs well. There are some definite characters, including Patrick, a cheery Irish kid who's been staying in the youth hostel in St. Andrews for the last five months (he's the only full-time boarder), uses the terms "Mighty!" and "Grand!" frequently, and keeps a comb in his back pocket for midround touch-ups; a Swedish kid named Olle, whose occupation before being a caddie was soldier in the Swedish army; and Melissa, a stunningly attractive blond English girl who is unceremoniously hit on by every male golfer for whom she caddies (and on whom I develop an instant crush, before receiving the tragic news that she has a boyfriend—one of Prince William's flatmates).

Altogether, there are about fifteen of us in our caddie circle. I'm the lone American. Although we've come to St. Andrews from totally different parts of the world, we have a ton in common. At night, our group heads to the livelier pubs in St. Andrews, like Ma Bells, the Lizard, the Raisin, or the West Port (where Prince William often hung out during the school year). After the pubs shut at one A.M., my friends and I head to various flat parties that run into the wee hours of the morning. After working so hard during the week, one comes to feel like Saturday night/Sunday morning out has been, in a word, earned.

As luck would have it, most of my caddie mates, like me, are also obsessive golfers. Most, like me, have schlepped their clubs to Scotland with them. All, like me, soon happily realize that it stays light in St. Andrews, during the summer, until eleven P.M. As most loops end for the day at around seven or eight P.M., there is still ample time for the especially devoted (or mildly insane) of the lot to head home, grab their clubs, and return to the course for a quick nine holes of their own. Counting ourselves among those of the latter category, my group does this frequently. It's worth the effort. There is nothing quite like playing golf in St. Andrews in the evening. All wind dies down. Stillness settles over the landscape. Hares dart out from the gorse. Birds hunker down for the night. As the sun dips lower in the Scottish sky, greens and fairways are brilliantly lit at a striking angle. It all resembles a movie set. And it's ours. A secret world of no wind and beautiful oak-red light, a private privilege for the ones who work the course. Against this backdrop, my caddie friends and I stage brutally competitive nine-hole matches, some extending until the very last rays of the sun sink below the North Sea and darkness ends our match. At this point, we usually head straight from the course into town, to meet other caddies at the pubs. It's not a bad life.

Greaves and I are out this afternoon with two cool guys from South Africa. It is freezing cold, and they look miserable. "Is it always this cold?" my golfer asks me as we walk up the third hole. Apparently, it's fifty degrees warmer in Johannesburg at the very same moment—and it's winter there.

My golfer tells me that he owns a bank in Johannesburg, and his friend owns an insurance company. They are both decked out in top-of-the-line DryJoy waterproofs, play high-end Callaway clubs, and hit nothing but Pro V1s. They're rich but also incredibly stingy. My player spends two to three minutes looking for his tee on every tee box, even if it's broken. On 7, we discover that I've lost his putter cover. He looks as if he might cry. Or strangle me. At the end of the round, I receive all 3's on my assessment card, except for the category "equipment service," where a 2 is filled in. I figure "2" is a euphemism for "He lost my goddamn putter cover."

I'm starting to carve out a place for myself in the shack. I'm still not accepted by the top caddies, but I also don't feel like I'm on my own anymore. The caddie world is a slightly friendlier place now. I'm starting to feel like I can handle it. In fact, I'm starting to have fun down here. Maybe, just maybe, this summer won't break my heart.

EIGHT

"You know, this will be absolutely super for the garden."

Uncle Ken is driving and looking very pleased. He and I are heading to Cupar. Specifically, he and I are heading to Cupar to buy garden pebbles.

I have the afternoon off from caddying (Rick informed me of this after my morning round, in typical Rick fashion, by simply screaming out "*No!*" at me from fifty feet as I walked back toward the shack). Instead, I'm along for the ride as Uncle Ken grips the steering wheel tightly, navigating us as if in one of the Lancaster bombers he flew during World War II. The red '82 Vauxhall we're in has no power steering (or power anything for that matter), and I can't imagine how an eighty-three-year-old can handle this thing. But handle it Uncle Ken does, gunning us along at speeds that make me incredibly uneasy.

"Now we'll have to pull up here a minute," Uncle Ken remarks, turning us (sharply) left onto Tom Morris Drive. Soon I see a familiar figure walking toward our car. Henry climbs in.

"Golly, I just *had* to get out of the house," Henry breathes, stretching out dramatically in the front passenger seat. "Grace and our daughter Louise are having the carpets redone. Made me stay in with them all morning!" Henry, it's safe to say, doesn't do well indoors.

After a few minutes, the Old Course passes by on our right-hand side. Henry quickly relaxes, now that he's out on the road with the boys. He removes three sweets from his right-hand pocket, offers two to us. Henry always has sweets in his right-hand pocket.

"A lad down at the shops, he told me that they're gonna be renovating the bus station soon. Said it'll take foive weeks."

The gen has begun.

"Oh yes, I'd heard that too," Uncle Ken replies.

"He said to me, 'Harry, mark my words, things are changing around 'ere!' "

The St. Andrews skyline slowly sinks away in the background. We drive along the edges of the more distant links courses—the Eden (ironically nicknamed "the Garden of Eden" by caddies, since it's annoyingly far from the shack) and the Strathtyrum—then it's just farmland.

"The Leuchars flower show is coming up, you know," Henry says, turning around to me.

"Yes, Oliver might be coming with us, *if* he can get a caddie round in before!" Uncle Ken replies.

"Oh aye."

Uncle Ken looks at me in the mirror. "You know, I think it would be a *good* idea for you to see it!" Uncle Ken loves the idea of educating me in Scottish life. Apparently, the Leuchars flower show is a part of it.

"I'd love to go," I reply, and both men in the front seat nod. We continue toward Cupar, passing through Guardbridge and Dairsie. These towns are still as foreign to me as the pebble-centric lives of my carmates. But I'm learning.

NINE

Caddies like having good golfers. With a good golfer, rounds are easier. Balls do not have to be scrounged for in the rough, swing and chipping lessons do not have to be constantly administered. In fact, most St. Andrews caddies who have looped on tour will tell you that tour rounds are much easier. "You just basically have to give yardages and babysit," one tour caddie tells me, on the benches outside the shack. Out on the Old, a good straight driver of the ball does make rounds much more pleasant. "Steady ball makes all the difference," old Jimmy Bowman adds, sitting next to us.

As might be expected by applying the same logic, caddies do not like having bad golfers. Rounds are harder, more frustrating, more demanding. You cannot exercise the "top tier" of your talents—picking dangerous but rewarding lines off the thirteenth tee, being tested on controversial club choices and putt reads—because your golfer simply won't give you this opportunity. Plus you have to walk more. When caddies find out their golfers are bad, they become angry. One extreme example of this involves a minuscule caddie known as Switchy. Switchy will ask his golfers what their handicaps are on the first tee. If their handicap is over 4, he will promptly "switch off" for the round. Tempting fate, Switchy even has the phrase SWITCH OFF emblazoned on his caddie golf cap, subtly alerting his golfers to this practice. Incidentally, Switchy (whose moniker is also inscribed on his own cart bag) used to caddie for Samuel L. Jackson each year in the Dunhill Links Championship—a pro-am event similar to the AT&T Pebble Beach pro-am. While appearing on *The Late Show with David Letterman* one night promoting a new film, Jackson told Letterman, "The only thing I'm afraid of in life is my caddie at St. Andrews." Somehow this comment got back to the shack three thousand miles away, and Switchy was pulled into the office and screamed at by Rick. Samuel L. Jackson had tattled on Switchy.

I'm thinking about this story as I walk along Market Street after my round. I love to see the veteran caddies impersonate Rick in the shack. Almost every caddie can bust out a hilarious rendition on the spot. Most involve some version of the long low "mmmmm," which expresses Rick's displeasure at something, followed by a low-pitched declaration of "What's going on here?" or "You're not doing enough rounds for me," or "Have a shave." I've been developing my own Rick impersonation, spending time to get the "mmmmm" at the exact pitch.

I do a little "mmmmmm" practice to myself now ("Mmmmm . . . I'll need your fiver now") as I pass the Student Union, then the Electoral Roll office. On the opposite side of the street, near Jim Farmer's golf shop, I look over at the bus stop. It's packed with "ancients," all waiting for their three P.M. bus. There are old men with baby-blue coats and argyle sweaters, older women with light bonnets and heavy shopping. And in the middle of this hubbub, I spot Henry. He's sitting on the bench and (of course) chatting with five fellow ancients. I can only hear a murmur of thick Scottish accents, but I know that everyone is trading gen. I stare at this group, all between the ages of eighty-one and ninety-four, and keep walking. I'm proud to know their ringleader.

. . .

"Can you fookin' believe it?"

Nathan Gardner is taking off his waterproofs, still in disbelief. It's the next day, and Nathan is sharing his latest misery story with the rest of the shack. I'm eagerly listening in. Apparently, Nathan's just had an American 13-handicapper who questioned everything that Nathan told him.

"Lines off tees . . . reads . . . everything. But here's the kicker." Nathan is getting excited now. "We're on fifteen, right? I hand him a five-iron for his second shot. He tells me he doesn't think it's the right club. And I tell him, 'Just hit it.' The guy hits, holes it out for an eagle."

Both of Nathan's hands are now raised in the air.

"And *then* this arsehole turns to me and says, 'I still don't think that was the right club!'"

The rest of the shack howls with laughter. Nathan continues. "I take the guy aside, and I say to him, 'Look, what's the problem here? You've just holed out, you can't get better than that. What the fuck's the problem?' The guy gives me no more lip after that."

Nathan's story makes it clear: Questioning your caddie is the worst thing a golfer can do. Not buying him a snack at the turn, having a heavy bag, forgetting his name—they all pale in comparison to questioning his advice. Because for all the expertise of the caddies, for all the high stakes that are attached to a round at St. Andrews, the ultimate responsibility for the shot is with the golfer.

Many people seem to forget this. Alec Howie, a veteran caddie who's looped for Arnold Palmer, and whom I have never once seen misclub a golfer, was caddying for a guy from Detroit last year. After hitting a shot on 7, the man turned to Alec, pointed his finger at him, and said, "That was the wrong yardage!" Instantly, Alec grabbed the man's finger, pulled him in violently. "Don't you *ever* point your finger at me again," Alec breathed murderously. I've heard this story repeated by caddies a hundred times, and with biblical respect.

As Nathan continues his rant, it strikes me how much pride caddies take in their work, and how insulted they are by disrespectful golfers. For caddies, forging routes for golfers around the Old Course's 112 bunkers isn't just a lark—it's their art. It's their expertise. It's why, for four hours, the president of Xerox, or Amazon.com, or the United States of America, absolutely depends on them—

"Ollie Horovitz."

The shack intercom snaps me out of my daydream. I go to wet my caddie towel in the shack's bathroom, and have a wee pee. This'll be my fifth double since Monday. It's kind of shocking when I think about it—I'll have done ten rounds in five days. But the doubles are starting to come easier now. My calves and hamstrings are less sore after loops; I'm acting less like a zombie in front of my roommates at night. Even the five thirty A.M. wakeups are starting to seem almost pleasant. My body's getting into the flow, getting used to the new normal. I guess this is a good thing.

TEN

I'm out with a sixty-year-old nerdy American lawyer, who is playing with three other nerdy American lawyers, who I assume are his friends. On 3, however, after waiting twenty-five minutes for the other three players to hole out, my golfer takes me aside, just past the green, and tells me, "I fuckin' hate these guys." The lawyer has mood swings that vary from the highest of highs, with childish giggles, to kicking his clubs into pot bunkers. These fluctuations can occur at any second, caused by a missed putt or a (frequently) skulled chip. He is quite possibly the most annoying golfer I've met to date. He tells embarrassingly corny jokes and uses several catchphrases, like "You're gonna give me the teach here." Nonetheless, I suck up like crazy, laugh at his jokes, and make fifty pounds for the round.

And then it happens.

I'm back at the shack window and about to hand in my forty-first assessment card to Rick Mackenzie. It's been seven weeks since I began the caddie training program. Suddenly Rick grabs me by the bib and wordlessly pulls me toward the window. I have zero clue what's happening. It occurs to me that Rick is either going to kiss me, or kill me. Instead, in one deft act, Rick removes my trainee caddie badge from my caddie bib and slips in a blank badge. He nods. In the background, I can see Ken beaming. I realize what's happened. Rick shakes my hand.

"Mmmmmm, you've done well," he says, almost reluctantly. "Now don't fook everything up."

The other trainees crowd around the window. They all start clapping me on the back, congratulating me. More than a few look envious. Greaves gives me a high five. I can't think of what to say, and I can't wipe the gigantic grin from my face. It's a new and wonderful feeling. No more assessment cards. No more stupid trainee badge that I have to work to overcome. I've done this totally by myself, off my own back and legs and putt reads. I'm an official Old Course caddie. I've started at the bottom, gotten no shortcuts from anyone—I've earned this. I'm three thousand miles from home, and it's starting to rain, and a little piece of plastic has just been removed from my caddie bib—and this might be the proudest moment of my eighteen-year-old life.

I have to complete one final task before it's official. Rick's told me to bring him two passport-sized photos for my new caddie badge. He wants me to bring him the photos right away. I'm now sitting in the instant-photo machine in the back of Woolworths, having used all the change in my pockets to cover the exorbitant three-pounds-fifty-pence charge. I'm getting myself ready for a winning photo, gloriously happy, when suddenly the curtain is pulled back. I jump a foot out of my seat and look left. A cute three-year-old girl stares up at me. As I'm wondering what the hell she's doing in here, the first of four flashes goes off. The machine's rolling. I instantly pull the curtain back while forcing the fakest, most strained, dorky smile for—*pop!*—the second flash. *Can't use that one*, I tell myself, *I look like Davis Love III!* Suddenly, the curtain is pulled back again, and the same pair of innocent eyes looks up at me. I try to push her out of the booth, when—*pop!*—the third flash goes off, catching the right side of my ear. I manage to shove the kid out of the booth, slam the curtain closed, and turn to the camera for the last time. The flash captures a hideous scowl on my face as I realize I've just wasted three pounds fifty. I rush back to the caddie shack. Photo number two, with the strained, dorky smile, is pasted onto my badge. I cover up the picture when among other caddies.

•   •   •

Our taxi driver is speeding.

The Renault Transport is easily doing eighty, barreling down the motorway toward Dundee. St. Andrews cabdrivers love these trips, because they can charge thirty quid (sixty dollars) each way—more if the kids piling in seem particularly drunk. But to get back quickly for more work, they drive furiously. Our cab's interior is strangely quiet, considering the speed we're doing and the corners we're taking with screeching tires. The roads are tightrope narrow, and every so often, other cars come hurtling past us with only inches between. I'm not loving this.

Soon we're onto the Tay Bridge, tearing over water that shimmers in the night sky. Across the Tay River, Dundee emerges into view, a city that has seen better days but still provides thrilling nights for surrounding Fife. Its nickname is "Scumdee," and it features, among other late-night attractions, the Gala Casino, which comps late-night five-course meals to new members, and where my friend Helen almost got beat up last month by a drunk prostitute. Capping off Dundee's "oeuvre" is a strip club and a disco called Mardi Gras ("the Mardi"). But my friends and I are bound for a different destination: Fat Sams—a nightclub with a reputation for being meaner than Rick Mackenzie. Tonight we're celebrating.

"This is gonna be fookin' epic," Craig firmly announces inside the taxi, mainly to himself. Craig Morris is a tall, stringy twenty-four-year-old Scottish caddie from Dunfermline ("Funfermline") blessed with good looks and a quiet Scottish swagger to go with it. Craig, it can be said, lives for the weekends. And in particular for Fat Sams, or as he calls it, "Fatty's."

"It's one A.M.," Patrick McGinley, the Irish caddie, reports, looking at his watch.

"Perrrrrfect," Craig replies. Greaves and Iain Begg, another caddie mate of mine, are trading slurred caddie stories in the backseat. I'm just trying to not look out the window. We've been out since nine o'clock at the Vic, a pub on Market Street that served one-pound drinks all night for some reason. And the night is becoming more and more slippery. I shudder privately as our taxi takes a sharp corner extra sharply and continues thrashing along. Outside, Dundee's lights pierce their darkened surroundings, exposing a city that was once the shipping capital of Fife and now boasts one of the highest teen-pregnancy and drug rates in Scotland (as well as Europe). Dundee during daytime is a nice place. Dundee at night is a wilderness. A Scottish wilderness.

"We're here," our driver barks, and we spill out onto the main drag, outside the club. This is unfiltered Scotland. Not quaint St. Andrews. There are fights outside these clubs, occasional stabbings. The Scottish accents come thick and fast and loud, and the police are out in force tonight. This is a Scotland the tourists don't see. There's almost a sense, as I watch our steel-doored taxi disappearing into the night, that we might never make it back to St. Andrews, limbs intact.

Tonight South Ward Road is packed, and the scene is raucous. Hordes of Scottish boys and girls stand in large crowds in the middle of the street. Copious members of hen (bachelorette) parties and Dundee girls' eighteenth-birthday parties queue up outside the club. The reverberations of techno music spill out past the bouncer-guarded club doors. A boy in a tiger costume is throwing up against a fence.

"Loving it," Craig announces. "Absolutely loving it." We head for the entrance.

Inside, Fat Sams is a netherworld. Three levels of garish dance floors rise high above, obscured by smoke billowing out of smoke machines. Pounding techno pulses through the rooms, and hundreds of Scottish youth grind on the dance floors. I am, without a doubt, the only American here. Our group moves through the ground-floor mosh pit, heading for the bar. When I meet anyone and they find out I'm American, they are shocked. Girls whisper into their friends' ears that I'm from New York, as if I've taken part in the last moon landing. It's all a little surreal. More girls move past us now, dressed in outfits totally different from anything I've seen in America. Leopard pants. Short pink skirts. Petticoats. Metallic silver hair. I feel a little like I've stepped onto the set of *Blade Runner*.

Craig grabs my shoulder. "Get on it, son!" he shouts before diving into the mass of people on the dance floor. Greaves follows, emitting a loud whoop. I vaguely recall that I have to caddie tomorrow. In fact I think we all do. Early.

A Britney Spears techno remix blares thunderously, thumping upstairs into the second-level corridor, where Patrick and I are heading. Two girls catch our eyes, start giggling. They're cute, dimpled, and both their shirts read "Happy 18th Burf-day Jen!!" We introduce ourselves.

"I like your accent!" one of the girls says to Irish Patrick.

"I like you," Patrick says back, not missing a beat. Both girls giggle again.

This is heading in the right direction.

. . .

We're in a taxi again.

Now the speedometer says ninety.

It is four fifteen A.M., and we're heading, supposedly, to a pool party—in a town called Auchtermuchty (*Uk-ter-muk-tee*). I don't know where that is, but it doesn't sound very close to St. Andrews. The girls are giggling in the backseat. I look at Patrick.

"What time are we booked again?"

Patrick reaches into the inner workings of his brain. Signs of struggle pass over his face. Then he lights up.

"Six thirty!"

This number sinks in. There's a troubled silence—which I break.

"Shit."

Patrick looks out the window. He's always optimistic.

"It's grand! It's grand! At least it'll be nice weather."

I show up for work at six thirty A.M.—sleepless and hung over. It is not nice weather. It is pouring. Trees blow sideways with the wind. Lakes begin to form on the fairways. Although wearing a large sweater and two rain suits, I'm shivering and soaked to the skin after two holes. My player, a middle-aged Swedish doctor named Fritz, insists that I keep his umbrella open, even though the forty-mile-per-hour gusts make such a feat a near impossibility. I remember once playing golf in Ipswich, Massachusetts, with my dad during a hurricane. This seems worse.

You're an official caddie now, I remind myself as I walk up the blustery sixth fairway, sideways—sort of how a crab might walk if he was cold and deeply unhappy. "You can deal with anything," I add, aloud this time (my golfer hears and wonders what the hell I'm talking about). The pep talk doesn't make me feel any drier. My head resumes its spinning. I decide that celebrations from now on should take place only during weekends.

ELEVEN

I've got a voice mail waiting. It's from my dad, and he sounds excited.

"Ollie. Call me right away."

My parents are here visiting for a week. They're staying with Uncle Ken and playing golf every day. I've just come off the course from a caddie round (loud Austrian banker with the social graces of a mollusk). From behind the eighteenth green, I dial the house. The news is a shock. A good shock. Dr. Jake Davidson, Uncle Ken's next-door neighbor, has invited Dad and me to be two-day guest members of the R & A. Jake is a famously hard-of-hearing eighty-two-year-old radiologist from Glasgow who has had us round for tea several times over the years. I also cut his hedge a few months ago and badly scratched my arms and legs in the process. This may have helped make Jake feel generous. I run behind the shack to grab my bike, already thinking of whom I can ask for black dress shoes. The two-day membership starts tomorrow.

* * *

The Royal and Ancient Golf Club is one of many semiaffiliated clubs with ties to the Old Course. It's divided into two parts: the organization that serves as the governing golf body for a vast part of the world—the "equivalent" of the United States Golf Association—and the social golf club, with twenty-five hundred members, preferential times on the Old, and a lot of pink trousers.

The R & A represents, in St. Andrews, the effective pillar of the social pyramid. The crème de la crème. It's for the wealthy and the powerful. Although there are exceptions—not everyone is a duke or a lord—the R & A undeniably represents privilege. Uncle Ken is not a member; he was never invited. His place is the New Golf Club, located about a hundred yards from the R & A but a planet apart; a club for golfers neither royal nor ancient.

I've never been inside the R & A, but I did wait tables at their special 250th anniversary celebrations earlier this summer—serving blackberry compote to the white bow-tied. (On my first night, I tripped up a chef. On my second night, I got moved to toilet duty. On my third night, I saw Arnold Palmer. He didn't see me.) Now I'm fascinated. For two days, I'll be able to peek inside. And try the compote myself.

The next day our R & A membership begins. At six A.M. caddie sign-in, however, I discover that I am booked to loop two rounds for an English guy who hits short and right. He plays with the speed of an injured snail, and each round takes four-plus hours. I completely miss R & A day one. My father goes alone, brings his laptop, and spends the day working in the R & A's library. He confesses to me that, during the day, he snuck upstairs and peeked into the R & A's most private rooms.

"What was it like?" I ask.

He smiles and answers quietly, "I've been to church."

The next day is possibly my last chance ever to be an R & A member. My game plan: I will caddie a morning round and have lunch with Jake and my dad. At six A.M. I get my number but discover

54

I've been rebooked by the guy who hits short and right for an eleven A.M. tee time on Jubilee. If I don't get him through his round by two thirty P.M., I won't get to the R & A (in a jacket and tie) by three P.M., and I will miss lunch. I give this guy reads the likes of which he's never dreamed about. He holes his (fourth) putt on 18 at two forty-five P.M. I Lance Armstrong it to my flat and get to the R & A at 3:03. On my way in the door, I'm spotted by three caddies who know me well, giving me the blankest of stares. The table captain knows I'm coming. He also knows I've looped seven rounds in four days. He personally serves my meal, loading my plate with enough food for a foursome. We who live to serve grow to understand each other's pain.

The R & A is like a time capsule. Any member of over forty years gets his locker in the main coffee room—the room with the huge bay windows looking out over the first tee. The ceilings are miles high, and the walls are covered with elegant paintings of past R & A captains, most of them with multiple honors following their names. Any member of over sixty years (as well as many professional golfers) gets their locker in the lobby. Thus, there are lockers practically everywhere within the R & A. Coat and tie are required, as are dress shoes, which I've had to borrow from a friend. They are two and a half sizes too small, which I think will be fine, since I don't anticipate much walking around. However, Jake gives us a grand tour. There's the collection of ancient golf clubs on the walls. There's the reading room. There's the bathroom with fully functioning scales. There's the 1920s barometer, still working perfectly, which traces out the Old Course's air pressure for the past week. The tour concludes, and Jake decides we're having coffee. My toes are now bleeding.

R & A members spend lots of time in the main room, either staring out the window at the first tee and making fun of Japanese golfers' swings or having tea while reading the papers. Many peruse the large books called *Who's Who in Scotland*, pointing out their biographical sketches to one another. Many also look at "The Red Book," on the cover of which is written, "For R & A Members' eyes only." This contains, I've heard, the list of all potential R & A members around the world currently under consideration. Actual nominations have to be unanimous, and if any one R & A member doesn't want a nominee, that nominee is blackballed. According to club policy, if "The Red Book" is ever left open on a table, staff members have to shut it. Floating around the room, waiters in starched white jackets serve drinks from "the tankards"—big expensive serving pitchers that keep drinks extra cold, because their insides are literally gold. I kind of feel like I'm on board the *Titanic*.

There is an overwhelming sense of *satisfaction* within this clubhouse, as members smilingly look out over other members in equally posh jackets and ties. A feeling that—simply by being inside these walls—they've made it. And maybe, in a way, they have. The rich and the richer gather in this clubhouse. Members we meet are eager to provide the pedigrees of all their hallowed members. It's a different kind of gen.

Jake is hilarious within this setting. He holds court in the middle of the big room expertly. Being nearly deaf, he screams. When he moves, he kind of just leans to one side and takes off, moving slowly and steadily like a ship. There's no stopping him. There's also no stopping him when he decides that we'll be joining a rather shy and standoffish member, David, for coffee—despite the man's many vigorous protestations. We all take our seats for coffee (David looks like he's been captured in battle), and after calling the waiter, Jake points out a large painting on the right side of the room. It depicts a scene from the 1800s of an R & A captain taking office by striking a ceremonial first tee shot. All of the R & A members from that era are pictured near the captain, their faces realistically captured for posterity.

"There's a modern version of this painting hanging across the street, Izzy!" Jake announces loudly. He's been shortening Dad's name from Israel to Izzy, for some reason. "I think it's rather good. In fact, it's got all the current R & A members depicted." There's a pause in which Jake suddenly remembers something. "Well, in fact, not everyone. I didn't hear that I had to pay to be in the painting, so I never sent in my check." Our host suddenly looks very unhappy. The waiter arrives, perking Jake up just enough to order our coffee. He gives one last wistful glance at the R & A painting, then looks over to me. "Maybe someday, Ollie," Jake says, "you'll be a member as well."

After lunch, Jake heads home for an important game of bridge with his wife, Edith, leaving us free rein of the clubhouse for our final hour of membership. My dad and I play three rounds of snooker, a game with seemingly as many rules as golf. My dad calls his brown-ball shot but accidentally pots the pink and the yellow. He steps next door to the library and asks a gaggle of Yahs (twenty-first-century British yuppies) for a ruling. I hear a voice tell my father to give me points for the brown and the yellow. I hear my father's voice say, "Thank you." I hear another voice tell my father, "You should be disqualified and lose the game." I hear my father say, "I didn't ask *you*, I asked *him*!" Then I hear dead silence. My father reappears in the snooker room with a worried look. He whispers, "I just made a joke, but nobody laughed."

Twelve

I spot her as I'm walking down to the shack.

Brunette. Petite. Probably nineteen. Definitely European. She wears a stylish white golf sweater and mega-tight royal-blue corduroys. She is, immediately and unmistakably, drop-dead beautiful.

"Morning, guys."

I plop down on the caddie bench, next to Jim Napier, Bill Bucelli, and Grant Fisher. It's nine in the morning, and most of the guys are already out on the course.

"You all right?" Grant grunts, in the typical Scottish equivalent of "How's it going?"

"Yeah, fine," I say back. I place my caddie bib beside me. A few moments pass. I look around. I realize that everyone on the bench is staring at this girl.

"You see the ass on her?" Bill asks, practically licking his lips.

"Should be illegal," Napier replies.

"Think she's French?"

"Spanish."

"Ach no, she looks Dutch."

"What the fook does Dutch look like?!"

"She looks fookin' *hot*, whatever she is!"

There's something about the caddie bench that encourages otherwise rational men to act out like construction workers whenever cute girls play on the Old. For one thing, it doesn't happen that often. We usually see fifty-year-old men. But I think there's another issue at play. Girls like Little Miss Corduroy, in this setting, seem so totally unattainable. Too rich. Too young. Too well-traveled. They're here with husbands, and fiancées, and boyfriends with bottomless pockets. The fact that, as caddies, we'd never be able to get close to these girls is probably the greatest motivator of our animal behavior.

"Hey, look, there's no young guy in the group," I observe.

"She's gotta be here with her parents," Jim replies.

"Those two?"

"Yeah, I bet."

"I bet she's totally bored here."

"Aye! She wants ta be shown a good time!"

Our bench snickers. We're like sixth graders sneaking into a XXX video store.

The girl and her parents move to the practice green with their Scotty Cameron putters and start stroking putts. The girl's stroke looks silky-smooth. So does her body. Totally unaware that she has an audience, the girl turns away from us and extends her perfect rear end outward—which shoots another shock wave of excitement down our bench.

"I can't believe none of them are taking a fucking caddie!" Jim says.

"Cheap bastards," Bill adds.

I disagree with Jim. I think it's almost better this way. I've seen similar situations play out, in which other caddies get put in groups like this and make everyone else feel totally jealous all round the Old

Course. For the outsiders, it's almost too much to bear. The girl turns to leave, and I nod my head. Yeah, it's probably better this way.

"Ollie Horovitz."

Ken is calling to me from the shack. I look up.

"Nine ten. On the tee right now."

Everyone freezes in silence as the full meaning of this news hits our bench. Then Bill suddenly explodes with . . .

"*Fook me* . . . You're in her group!"

All at once, there's an upheaval around me.

"*Yes!*" I scream, doing an uncontrolled fist pump. Then, even louder, "*YES!*"

I dash toward the window, rummaging around awkwardly in my inner trouser pockets for my fiver, while the other caddies' voices trail me.

"You lucky bastard!" Jim yells after me.

"I don't believe it . . . how did *Horovitz* get in there!" Grant shouts, holding his head in his hands.

I dash to the tee now, frantically throwing on my bib. Midway there, I realize I've left my caddie cap on the bench and do a rapid about-face, sprinting back to retrieve it, while the other caddies explode with laughter.

"Nine ten game?"

I stride out onto the tee box. The girl is there (!), doing some practice swings. So are her parents. So is another guy, a short, kind of runty-looking sixty-year-old with a Pine Valley golf cap on, who now turns to me.

"Yeah, uh, hi. You're with me. Name's Bob."

"Oliver. Nice to meet you."

We shake hands, my eyes not leaving the girl the entire time.

"This is Fritz and, uh, I think Helen," Bob says in an American accent, motioning to the parents.

"Nice to meet you guys," I say to the couple, heart kabooming inside. The mother smiles and speaks to me in a thick German accent.

"And dis is awr dott-ah, Barbara."

Barbara turns her bright blue eyes up to me for the first time. And does . . . I don't believe it . . . a small double take . . . *Did that just happen?? Did she just do that?? I think she did! Oh my God!*

"Hello," Barbara says shyly, and meets my eyes in a smile. She has "the smile," the one that I'm pretty sure exists only in a total of seven girls in the world . . . the one that convinces you that at this moment, only *you* matter to her . . . that suddenly makes you quite certain that the only thing you want in this entire world is for this girl to just keep smiling at you like this, forever . . .

"Hi," I say back.

Not my wittiest reply. But it'll have to do.

Our group exchanges pleasantries, and I point out our opening tee shot to Bob.

"Let's start this on that yellow house down there . . . we're only looking for two thirty or so with this wind."

I'm kind of playing it cool at the moment, only talking to Bob, basking in the delicious knowledge that I have the *entire* round with this girl. Then the Old Course starter cuts into our chatter from his starter's-hut loudspeaker.

"Nine ten game, play away, please."

We're off.

"One twenty-eight front, one thirty-six pin. I like our nine-iron here."

I hand Bob his Callaway X-series 9-iron. We're on the third hole. And by now I've gathered a few facts about our group.

First, Bob doesn't actually know this family; he was randomly assigned to their group as a single.

Second, Bob is not a very good golfer. We've lost four balls in the first two holes.

Third, and most evident, everywhere we go, *every single person* is staring at Barbara. Caddies, rangers, greenskeepers, middle-aged golfers. Everyone. On each double green, in each double fairway, all conversations cease, and eight pairs of eyes lock squarely in disbelief on those royal-blue corduroys. So completely does Barbara cut into this world that entire games come to a standstill. And then the men see me trotting alongside Barbara, and their mouths drop open. It is Cleopatra's bedroom. And I'm fluffing the pillows.

"Ah. Shit."

Bob has completely knifed his 9-iron approach. The ball skids mercilessly over the green and plugs into deep rough, behind. The lob shot reached, at its absolute apex, a total of three inches in height. This is one of the best shots Bob has hit today.

"Yeah, that'll be all right, we'll get it," I say, and give Bob a pitching wedge.

"These fairways are so damn tight!"

"I know, they're very difficult." I pat Bob on the back, feigning support.

Bob is turning sixty next week. He's a lawyer, divorced, with a girlfriend who's flying over next week for his birthday. He's also got a daughter, who's a junior at the University of St. Andrews.

Bob is a nice guy, but . . . how do I put this delicately . . . I *literally* do not care about him. The only thing I want to do in this round—in this world—is to be near Barbara. Because Barbara is not just stunningly beautiful. She is not just in possession of a jaw-dropping smile and breasts to die for. She is also, perhaps, the best golfer I have ever seen.

"Gude shot."

Barbara has just crushed another perfect drive, 265 yards down the middle. Her swing is effortless, flawless, thrillingly perfect.

"Thank you." Barbara smiles modestly. The family is used to these drives.

"Nice shot!" I chirp, running loudly with Bob's golf clubs clanging on my back to catch up to Barbara. I should be helping Bob look for his ball embedded in the gorse jungle off 6 tee, but I'm going AWOL.

"There is gorse every-vere!" Barbara is amazed.

"Uh, yeah. There's a lot of it."

"I vas so nervous off tee one." She giggles.

"Really? I totally couldn't tell!" I giggle back excitedly. I'm her mobile cheering section.

Barbara, I've coaxed out of her mom, is studying law in Zurich. The family is Swiss, and Barbara and her mom have bought this trip as a surprise for her father, who, like Bob, turns sixty next week. He seems very happy. Although not as happy as me—because right now, Barbara and I are on the cart path that winds through the gorse, and for the moment we're alone.

"You play in tournaments, right?"

"Yah, I used to. On the Swiss girls' tour."

"Oh wow!"

"Noooooo. It doesn't mean much. You know."

So modest. So perfect. I could marry this girl at the ninth hole.

"Actually, back in America, Barbara, I played on this junior tour thing in Massachusetts. It was called—"

"Barbara!"

The mother has caught up to us. "Deed you pack those sandwiches for Dad in the bag?"

Barbara turns obediently to her mother. "Yes, I deed, muzzah."

"I think he's hungry for them now."

Barbara's *muzzah*, I am observing, does not seem pleased that I am flirting with her daughter. In fact, *Muzzah's* been decidedly frosty around me all day. I wouldn't particularly care about this, except for the fact that Bob hasn't been talking to either her or her husband, which means I'm never able to be alone with Barbara. Speaking of which . . . *SHIT.* Bob. I spin around and dash back seventy-five yards to my golfer, who is waiting helplessly for me on the other side of the hill, club-less and ball-less.

The holes fly by. On each green, different caddies come up to me, smile brightly at the parents, then whisper throatily in my ear, "Cannae fookin' believe it, Horovitz!" I'm the envy of the caddie shack.

But I don't feel like it.

Instead, I feel the round dwindling down, and with it the invincible, magical feeling that I had when all eighteen holes stretched before us. In a few hours, the round with Barbara will be over. It's like the caddie gods *wanted* me to meet this girl. But I'm not getting enough time to talk to her. My frustration grows. I *never* get women in my group, let alone girls my age, girls like Barbara. This is a comet sighting. And it won't happen again. I need to do something drastic. Something to impress her.

"Oh no!"

Both parents groan as Barbara's pulled 3-wood shot gallops into the Road Hole Bunker on 17. Not surprising; golfers always get suckered out left here. Barbara sighs, drops to her knees. She knows her next shot will be brutal.

Bob is floundering in the right-hand rough, but I march pointedly in the opposite direction, straight for the Road Hole Bunker. This could be my chance.

"Nat so good?" Barbara asks, walking up to the bunker.

"You know, not terrible," I say. But it is. The ball is right up near the front lip of the trap. Barbara arrives, and laughs when she sees her ball.

"Oh, deee-ah," she says.

Barbara grabs a sand wedge and sets up to hit out sideways. But I've got an idea.

"No, no. You can go straight at it," I tell her.

"Vaaat?" Barbara exclaims, as if I've just suggested playing this shot naked.

"Yeah, you can. Just swing *really* steeply, straight up and down, like this." I demonstrate with her club. "That's the secret to getting out of these traps."

"Nooooooo!" Barbara says, and gives me a doubtful smile.

"Seriously. Trust me."

There's a pause. Barbara totally doesn't believe that it's possible. But finally she nods.

"Okay . . . I veel try it."

As Barbara sets up, I watch nervously from behind. This is a huge gamble—I'd call it 20/80 odds, but I need to take the chance. Barbara takes the club back, blasts steeply down, just like I told her. The ball pops straight up, clears the lip, rolls to three feet. She spins around to me, a dazzling smile on her face. Five people standing behind the green, who witnessed all proceedings, applaud. One yells out, "Great caddying!" I nod back modestly, rake the sand trap for Barbara. Count it.

"Thank you for a great round, Oliver."

We're behind the eighteenth green. Bob hands me fifty pounds. I've already been given a ten-pound tip by Barbara's parents ("Only because of the Road Hole Bunker shot!" the mother laughs, only half joking).

"It was fun, Bob."

"Can I give you a lift back into town?"

I glance over at the Swiss Family Robinson, packing up their golf bags. "Uh, no, thanks, I've got my bike."

"Oh, okay. Well, take care." Bob walks away with his clubs. I'm left standing on the pavement. Suddenly, I see Barbara running back to put away her trolley. This is the moment.

"Barbara . . . one more thing," I say, jogging up to her.

She turns to me, smiles. "Vat?"

In the towering sunset, she looks even more beautiful than before. The moment is perfect.

"Well . . . some caddies and I are heading out tonight, later, and I'd love for you to come out with us."

Barbara looks at me. There's a pause. She opens her mouth to say something but stops. And then she says . . .

"I . . . I'm sorry, I can't. I vish I could, but I can't."

She gives me a hug and runs to catch up with her parents. I'm left standing in front of the R & A Clubhouse, alone. I shuffle to my bike, unchain it, and walk it slowly back behind the eighteenth green. Down on the green, Frasier Riddler and his golfers are putting out. Frasier calls to me.

"D'you get her number?"

All the middle-aged men in the group look up, eagerly awaiting my answer. They've been following us all afternoon.

I shake my head. "No."

There are audible sighs of disappointment from the green. Three golfers exchange money. I trudge back to the caddie shack, step inside to get my bag. Two caddies are already there.

"Well?! Did you get her—"

"No."

"Ah shit." One reaches into his pocket and pays the other guy.

In every game there are winners and losers. This does not feel like a win.

THIRTEEN

"I'm terribly sorry, but I have to cancel our gardening this afternoon."

Uncle Ken is deeply apologetic. "It's nothing *serious*, but I have to bring Bonnie over to the vet."

"No problem at all," I tell Uncle Ken, and sign on for a second spin. I haven't heard him sound this worried before . . . and this worries me.

During the past few weeks, Bonnie's real age has begun to overtake her apparent age. Unlike Uncle Ken, Bonnie is living in dog years. And suddenly it begins to show. Suddenly Bonnie is blind. Suddenly she is frightened to travel in the caravan. Suddenly she is unable to take walks. Uncle Ken has rolled with these particular punches. His gen changes drastically: He cancels caravan club trips, walks alone, spoon-feeds Bonnie her meals. It is beyond sad to see.

That evening, after finishing up my caddie round on the Old Course, I turn on my cell phone and find a message to call my parents in America. They've heard upsetting news from my aunt in Manchester. After talking to the doctors, Uncle Ken has finally had to have Bonnie put down, that afternoon. I call Uncle Ken immediately and ask if I can come by. Instead of expressing his true emotions, Uncle Ken, always the stiff-upper-lipped Englishman, invents a more "logical" reason for having me come over. "Oh, super! Do drop by. I've got a newspaper clipping you'll want to take a look at!"

"Sure, I'll be there in ten minutes," I reply warmly, not fooled for a second. As soon as I see Uncle Ken's face, it's obvious that he needs someone to talk with. I sit with him for a few hours as he recounts story after story of his bonny Bonnie.

I think that surviving those we love must be among life's worst experiences. My uncle Ken Hayward—a man of wisdom and courage who, in his eighty-three-year lifetime, led squadrons of men through countless air battles and city councils through difficult change—has just buried an aged five-pound dog. And he is distraught beyond belief.

.　.　.

"What do you think, Ollie?"

I snap to attention. Kenny is motioning for me to read his golfer's putt. We're on the fifth green of the Old Course, the largest green on the course (and in the *world*—it measures ninety-eight yards from front to back). I'm in a foursome, with three other "licensed" caddies. Among them is Kenny, the one whom I shadowed at the start of my career. Kenny's now giving me a caddie "exam."

I look at the putt. *What do I think? I think I better not fuck this up.*

The putt is a tricky sixty-foot downhill double breaker. I can't study it too long; everyone's waiting on my decision, including Kenny's golfer. My window of opportunity for study is about eight seconds. I survey the putt, look at the ridge that cuts in about halfway down, try to feel the line of the putt. "I like two cups out on the right," I say to Kenny.

"Okay," my former shadow responds in a tone that says, "Let's see how you do." Kenny relays my read to his golfer. "Two cups out on the right, sir." The exam is on.

Kenny's player goes with that read and knocks it a foot short of the hole, dead on line. I've nailed it. The caddie nods, gives me the thumbs-up sign. I nod back as casually as possible. No sweat.

August has come to the Old Course. Rain is less frequent, and the summer sun and year-round wind have begun baking the course, turning fairways and thick rough into stately shades of tan and coffee-brown. The turf is now granite-hard; the course is running like true links golf. Low, drawing drives can run out well over 320 yards; 9-irons can cover 190 yards downwind. Approach shots have to land well short of the green. Breezes off the North Sea now carry a tingle of coldness, hinting at the approaching autumn. The Thistle Golf Club has its "autumn meeting"—a tournament held over the Old Course. The New Golf Club and St. Andrews club stage their own medals. The R & A begins their preferential times.

I've been in St. Andrews for eleven consecutive months. With just a few weeks left before my return to America and my freshman year at Harvard, this unexpected "freeze" of my life is about to come to a close. The interlude of this gap year, of my caddie summer, is winding down. The curtain is falling. Life, in a sense, is about to restart.

I'm sitting on the bench at the eleventh tee right now, beside an old veteran caddie. I look out over the massive tenth green, past the eighth hole. I'm in a weird mood. I'm stoked to get to Harvard, to begin my new life. But it hits me that this summer will be hard to give up. When the sun breaks through a black rain cloud on 7 of the Old and the whole course is bathed in dramatic, glistening sunshine; when my seventy-five-year-old golfer giggles like a ten-year-old and confesses that this is the best four hours of his life—at these moments, I know this isn't just a job. At these moments, something deep inside the human psyche is tapped, something hardwired into happiness. A knowledge that I might very well be in one of the prettiest places in the world. A knowledge that I'm part of something important. At these moments on the Old, it gets no better.

Twenty feet from our bench, two trainee caddies stand up on the tee box with our four players. We hear one golfer say to the other, "You know, this is the highest point on the golf course!" The veteran caddie turns to me in disgust, leans in. "That's rubbish, he's totally wrong! Must've been some stupid trainee told him that!" I am secretly thrilled to be included in this insider complaint. Although I've been a licensed caddie for only a few weeks, the badge somehow moves me into this elite inner circle. "Yeah," I reply with equal contempt, "probably some stupid trainee!"

It is *Captains Courageous*. I am Harvey. And I have conquered the sea.

FOURTEEN

"Horovitz!"

I look up from page 3 of *The Scottish Sun*, in which today's naked girl is sharing her views on British foreign policy. Colin Gerard is standing in front of me. He's a skinny forty-year-old veteran caddie who farts a lot.

"What're yoo doin' tomorra aft'e'noon?" (*Fart.*)

Obviously, I'll be caddying. But I wonder where Colin's headed with this.

"Nothing much. Why?"

Colin slams his foot up on the bench next to me (farts) and starts lacing up his shoes. "A bunch of us caddies are playin' the Old tomorrow. We need a fourth. You wanna come?"

Does a bear shit in the gorse? "Yeah . . . I . . . Yes! Definitely!" I respond, failing at nonchalance.

"It-ull be a real caddie oot-ing," Colin laughs, and walks away to put on his rain pants and allow a blockbuster fart. I pretend to look at my pin sheet, to seem busy. But really, I'm just thinking about tomorrow. I haven't played the Old since I began caddying (one gets a weird guilt trip about skipping out on work to play golf, in front of the other caddies). This is perfect. While I swoon, a large-nosed caddie next to me coughs and peers over at page 3's naked Jen. "If she was up for it, I wouldn't say no," he remarks huskily, ending my day-dream. I'm glad he's mentioned this to me.

• • •

"The competition's going to be serious today, you know."

Uncle Ken has his game face on. I've finished caddying for the day and am now marching into the Leuchars flower show, alongside him and Henry. Several colorful tents are set up outside a church hall, where a small brass band (eighty-year-olds on tubas) bleats out enthusiastic Scottish tunes. It is pouring beyond belief.

"There's three pounds sixty, for him too," Uncle Ken cheerily announces to the bonneted, grandmotherly lady at the ticket desk. "He's my relation from America," he adds, handing me my ticket. Henry taps my shoulder from behind, points to the ticket stub. "That gets you *two* cakes and *one* cup of tea," he says, as if briefing me for a space-shuttle launch. As we wait in line, Uncle Ken and Henry saunter around, shaking hands, chatting to other gardeners' club officers. Politics meets pollen.

I've tagged along for this flower show, partially because Uncle Ken has been bugging me about it annoyingly for the past three weeks, but also because I badly want to hang with my two mates. I've got only four more days left in St. Andrews, and I'm realizing how close I've grown to them.

Inside the church hall, it is a gardener's wet dream. Table after table stretches out before us, flaunting the flower and vegetable en-tries. All are immaculately presented and labeled by category—best floral arrangement, best perennial, best cucumber. The crème de la crème have won awards and proudly sport "first prize," "second prize," or "honorable mention" ribbons on their stems. I spot a few repeat winners: Mrs. Angela Brown, for example, has a first-prize rose, and an honorable-mention collection of potatoes.

Henry rushes up to us. "Golly, the leeks at that far table are *something*." He looks impressed.

"Hamish has done well with his carrots," Uncle Ken replies.

"He always does well," Henry says in agreement. I could be at a Knicks game, the way this commentary is running. The duo leaves my side to go inspect more leeks. I watch them go. There's something totally strange about this scene, and I can't shake it. Uncle Ken and Henry both fought in World War II; both men led soldiers into battle, held real power involving life and death. These same men are now admiring leeks as one might admire a newborn baby. I consider how life can be reductive to the point where a large leek is important. But also how life needs purpose, even in the home stretch.

A commotion erupts in the hall. The tea and crumpets have been brought out. Looking slightly alarmed, the seven grandmothers carrying these refreshments are swarmed by hungry flower show attendees. Within the swarm, I spot Uncle Ken and Henry. They gesticulate wildly for me to come over.

"Hurry up, the crumpets are cooling!" Uncle Ken calls.

"Aye, lad, don't dawdle!" Henry adds.

I'm going to miss these guys.

. . .

The tee box is ours.

It's the next day, the afternoon of our small caddie outing, and all four of us have arrived on the first tee. Our group is comprised of the following: 1) my host, Colin Gerard; 2) Gordon Smith, a small, fiftyish, steadfast St. Andrean, one of many generations obsessed with two things in life: his golf and his garden; 3) Kenny, my former shadow caddie; and 4) me. I'm thrilled to have been included in this group. I'm also catatonic with fear.

Swarming around by the first tee are several other caddies waiting for jobs. They see us with our clubs, give us confused looks. This makes it even better. Today we're not playing the Old Course in a "dark time slot"—the day's final few tee times that guarantee fading light and dampening greens. Today we're smack in the middle of the afternoon. Prime time. I hope I don't whiff off the first.

"Who's playing who?"

The guys are picking teams for the match. "I'm off five," grunts Gordon.

"I'm eight, you too, right, Kenny?" asks Colin. Kenny nods, stretching with his TaylorMade 3-wood.

"Horovitz, you're a one, right?" Gordon asks rhetorically. *How does he know my handicap?* "One point eight," I correct, weakly.

The teams are chosen, Kenny and me versus Colin and Gordon. I'm hitting first. In the starter's hut, George knows that we caddies are playing and decides to announce us in dramatic fashion. "From the Uniiiited States of Ammmerica, Oliver Horovitz!" He's done a Texas accent with my name for some reason. As I set up for my drive, I glance to my right and see five caddies lined up at the near fence, watching me intently. I gulp and try to focus. *Don't screw this up*, I say to myself, *or you'll be the laughingstock of the caddie shack*. I take a deep breath, and swing. As if by a miracle, the ball shoots dead ahead, 265 yards, rips the middle of the fairway. The other caddies look impressed. I feel giddy with relief. Golf is still my passion.

"Feels good to be out, huh?"

Colin is striding down the third fairway next to Gordon. He claps his friend on the back. I'm walking behind them, to my ball (in Cartgate bunker). It's apparent that this is a rather special day for my caddie partners. Because, in reality, they're rarely able to play the Old Course. Unlike private clubs, the Old is owned by the town of St. Andrews, which gives caddies no playing privileges whatsoever. For caddies without a links ticket, then, there is a certain irony to working on the Old. Caddies know their course better than anyone but normally can't afford to play it themselves. Our round today is clearly a big deal. Kenny has even bought a new red sixty-pound Berghaus golf jacket, "Just in time for the day."

"Forrrre!"

As we head toward the seventh green, Alistair Taylor walks past us, coming down 11. He salutes us with a hilarious flourish of his cap. Also in the group is Willie Stewart—the caddie who wouldn't give me a pin sheet. Willie surveys his three friends, then looks over at me and says with tacit approval, "Ah, Horovitz is a player too." As afternoons go, this is not a bad one.

"Good move through the ball, Gordon."

We've all just driven off the twelfth tee. Gordon, Colin, and Kenny start walking ahead of me down the fairway. Kenny finishes telling a caddie story, and the others roar with laughter. I watch everyone walking past Admiral's Bunker with their clubs. Suddenly it hits me. This is exactly what these guys want to be doing with their lives. In their way, these St. Andrews caddies are living the life of their dreams. Perhaps Kenny and Colin wanted to be professional golfers, but this is the next best thing. They're doing what they love, surrounding themselves with golf. There is something pure about this. I'm reminded of dockworkers and fish packers in Gloucester, Massachusetts, who shared childhood dreams of being fishermen and now frequently say, "At least I'm earning my living on the water."

I head down the fairway. For the past few weeks I've been thinking about what it is I want to do with *my* life. Honestly, I still don't know. But this much is now clear to me. You have to do something you love. It doesn't matter what other people think—you just have to do something that you love.

"Unlucky."

Gordon and Colin murmur consolation as my second shot into 17 (the famous Road Hole) skips up, then over, the smallest green on the course. "Shit," I mutter. Any ball over the green here is dead. Kenny and I are 1-down going into this hole (a side match between him and Gordon for four beers is already over), so we have no chance of winning the match. Gordon is twelve feet from the cup in two, for birdie. When I reach my ball, it's over the road, up against the famous wall. A group of spectators look on as I survey my predicament. I'm about to pitch out away from the hole, in defeat, when Kenny walks up to me.

"Play yuh five-iron, intah the wall," he tells me.

How can I ignore this advice? I pull my 5-iron, mumble to myself, "Here goes nothing," and hit. The ball pops into the wall, ricochets back toward the green, lands in the fringe, and scuttles up the hill onto the green, eight feet from the hole. The tourists applaud. The other three caddies look at me and go, "Watson."

I suddenly remember being a kid, watching video of Tom Watson hitting from the same spot in the 1984 British Open. The others head up to the green, but I don't want to move yet. I stay by the wall. My grin is from ear to ear. Some moments in life you'll never forget. This is one of them.

FIFTEEN

It's my final day in St. Andrews. I've just finished my first round of the day and, having expected constant rain throughout the morning, decided to wear both rain suits, one on top of the other. As if the golfing gods were paying a cruel joke on me for my lack of confidence in the official Old Course caddie waterproofs, the weather is sunny and baking hot, and I, having nowhere to stash any clothing, am forced to wear all three layers of nylon around the course. (And yes, I had to carry a cart bag. And no, my player didn't allow me to put any of my clothing in his bag.)

I'm exhausted, my body feels like I'm in a sauna, and I'm hungry. I grab some lunch from Tesco and plop myself down on the caddie bench outside the shack—chicken sandwich, liter carton of orange juice, and cookie in hand. I have ten minutes before my next round and know from experience that if I scarf down my lunch in three to four minutes, I'll be fine. I've unpacked everything and have just started moving sandwich to mouth when an uncomfortably loud, high-pitched, piercing voice jolts me out of my small revelry.

"Oh my gahd, are you a *caddie*!?"

I turn and behold a fifty-year-old woman, replete with fanny pack, too-short cargo shorts, an "I ♥ Chicago" T-shirt, and a throwaway camera tied around her neck with string.

"Yeah, I'm a caddie."

The voice, by some miracle, manages to rise to an even higher pitch. "Oh my gahd! And you're *American*!" To which she adds, "Me too!"

"Really? Great." I'm not enjoying this.

Lady who hearts Chicago continues. "Can I take your picture?"

I mumble an answer in my most irritated tone: "Yeah, sure, go for it."

She snaps a photo of me glaring at her as darkly as possible. She is obviously delighted with her souvenir. As she leaves, I realize that for the first time, I actually *feel* like an Old Course caddie. I watch a Japanese golfer duck-hook his opening drive across the eighteenth fairway. It careens off a car and bounces up the road toward Uncle Ken's house—where I know he and Henry are planning an attack of large leeks for their upcoming St. Andrews flower show. I smile. And then all thoughts return to my chicken sandwich.

PART
TWO

PART

TWO

SIXTEEN

"Seriously, this is a fuckeen *disgrace.* This was an A paper!"

Dritan Nesho, one of six guys in my Harvard freshman dorm room, is working himself into a frenzy. He's sitting on our futon, wearing a rumpled gray Calvin Klein T-shirt, Wallabee shoes, and boxer shorts adorned with tiny blue and yellow fish. His paper sits beside him, marked on top in red. "A/A-."

"I'm definitely going to the government department tomorrow to complain!"

From this rant (which has brought me out of my room), I glean that Dritan has spent the better part of eight days in near-hibernation on this paper. I'm not surprised. Dritan writes all of his drafts in Albanian first (by hand), then translates them into English. Dritan is deliberate. Dritan is also the son of Albania's ambassador to the United Nations.

"Yeah, I guess just sort it out tomorrow," I say, sidestepping un-easily over the half-empty gallon of chocolate milk that Dritan has been guzzling. There's a pizza box farther along the floor that's been there for at least five days, and around it, a trail of ants are getting seriously involved. Every so often, Dritan will cull their ranks by pumping air freshener directly into their swarm for thirty seconds. It might be easier to just throw out the pizza box, but I'm not asking questions.

I head for the door. I have to get my own paper—on Stanley Milgram's 1963 obedience experiment—finished (as well as started). I also need to get out of this room. Zipping up my jacket, I throw open the door to Weld Hall. A blast of arctic December air hits me in the throat as I head for Lamont Library.

Harvard has begun. Already, I can tell that I'm in a different world. Harvard's libraries are open twenty-four hours a day—several offering free back massages to stressed-out students. Harvard's dorms house gymnasiums, libraries, grand-piano rooms, wood shops, plus tutors in every academic subject, always on call for home-work help. Winthrop House has squash courts. Lowell House has a rock-climbing wall. In Annenberg (the freshman dining hall resem-bling Hogwarts from the Harry Potter novels), waffle irons imprint Harvard's insignia onto every single waffle.

"What up, Ollie!"

I pass a group of four freshmen—two guys, two girls, heading in the opposite direction. Both guys in the group are named Alex. Alex #1 is Alex Blankfein. His dad is the CEO of Goldman Sachs. Alex #2 is Alex de Carvalho. His family owns Heineken. I think one of the girls' family owns Marriott. I do fist bumps with my classmates and keep walking. It's a little weird, all this. The kid on the floor above us, Matthew Blumenthal, is the son of Senator Richard Blumenthal (D-Connecticut), and a seventh-generation Harvardian. His room-mate is the son of Cadbury Schweppes's CEO. When my friend Alex Hubbell checked into Weld Hall for freshman orientation, everyone just assumed his family invented the telescope. (They didn't.)

I don't care about all this stuff. I'm digging in here. This semes-ter, I'm studying George Orwell's writing, social psychology, and filmmaking under Ross McElwee, who directed *Sherman's March*. I'm writing and directing episodes of Harvard's TV soap opera *Ivory Tower*—spending late-night coffee-fueled hours in an alcove with six other writers, hashing out scandalous subplots for our TV coeds (this week's episode: Haley gets seduced by her teaching assistant, Sudbay!). I'm also dating a cute girl named Vanessa from my film animation class. And I ran for student council last week. And lost. Well, technically, I was disqualified for "excessive postering." My campaign poster featured a photo of me wedged between images of Bush and Kerry, with a caption reading, "There *is* another choice. Let's put Harvard on the map!"

I see Emerson Hall up ahead. Just last week, I was there for a lecture given by the Irish poet Seamus Heaney. I've also been to talks this month at the Kennedy School with Ralph Nader and Jesse Ventura. Whenever I have free time, I've been "comping" (Harvard-speak for "trying out at") Harvard's humor magazine, the *Lampoon*. And I'm crewing on as many shoots as possible in the film department. In short, I'm doing everything an eager freshman should be doing here. Especially someone who's waited a year to arrive. I'm forcing myself into the flow. Telling myself that I should love it here.

But somehow I don't.

Truthfully, I miss St. Andrews. A lot. Harvard kids seem, quite frankly, a lot less cool than St. Andrews kids. SAT scores from high school are discussed with alarming frequency. And life is different here. I'm thirty minutes from where my dad was born (Wakefield, Massachusetts), forty-five minutes from where I was born (Gloucester, Massachusetts). Relatives are mere miles away, in neighboring Newton, Brookline, and Danvers. I'm back in my safe zone. But I miss the sense of adventure. I miss what it was like to be three thousand miles away from home, and to be an American abroad—and how cool that was to people. I miss taking Claire, my St. Andrews girlfriend, up to the Isle of Skye for Valentine's Day weekend, whizzing past lochs and Scottish wilderness. (And then privately playing back the trip's photos on my computer in "slideshow mode" over the corny *Braveheart* theme song.)

I miss every accent, every slang word, and every weird food. I miss being known as the American who has a good short game. I miss the Old Course. I miss my university friends. I miss the caddies. I miss Uncle Ken and Henry. Actually, I miss *everything* about last year in St. Andrews.

I speed-walk through Tercentenary Theater, the huge lawn with elm trees towering overhead, and climb the stairs toward Lamont Library. I think more about this school year at Harvard. Maybe I'm being crazy. I mean, this is what I wanted. This is the thing that got me through a million Saturday nights studying AP U.S. history in high school. This is the goal I jotted on all those embarrassing notes taped to my bedroom wall for motivation. And come on, I *am* happy here. I'm having fun. I'm working hard. I'm learning new stuff every day. It's just that something doesn't feel right here in Harvard Yard. Something's missing. And I don't think it's just the black pudding . . .

I didn't grow up in a tough neighborhood; I grew up in Greenwich Village. But I'm a New York City public school kid, and I grew up with other public school kids. And now I'm suddenly surrounded by legacies and crew team members from Andover and Choate and Collegiate. I'm in a world of money and privilege. A social scene ruled by exclusive Final Clubs. Are there exceptions here? Sure. Is this the Harvard of the 1950s? Definitely not. But the sense of privilege, the sense of elitism, it's all still here. And somehow I can't quite synchronize the world I'm living in with the caddie world that I just came from. I can't shake the feeling that I'm in college with the very R & A guys whose bags I just carried.

Maybe if I'd gone straight from Manhattan to Cambridge, from high school to Harvard, this might not feel so uncomfortable. Maybe if I hadn't lived as a caddie first. But I did. And it sounds crazy, but something in me changed last summer. I mean, I earned a living with my own legs and four A.M. wakeups and soaking rain pants. *I* did that. I worked alongside sturdy blokes for sixteen hours a day who didn't care what anyone else thought about their life choices, guys who just loved golf and wanted golf to be their lives. And maybe it sounds corny, but there was something so totally *pure* about that world. To me, that world made sense. And now it's making life at Harvard even more difficult to take in. Now I'm seriously asking myself, what do I want? Or more important, what the hell am I doing here?

I head inside the library. Stanley Milgram, and an all-nighter, are waiting for me.

● ● ●

March 25, 2005, Cambridge, Massachusetts. I'm in my dorm room. New England's "wintah," with thirty-six inches of snow and temperatures to freeze a grown man's tears, refuses to release its Heimlich hold on the city. I'm at my PowerBook, trying to write a two-thousand-word American public policy paper, due the next morning (word count thus far: seven).

I sigh loudly. I'm feeling homesick. Not for New York City. Not for Gloucester, Massachusetts. I'm homesick for St. Andrews and the Old Course—posters of which are both tacked to my wall. I look out my window. More snow is falling, promising a white Easter.

Suddenly there's an AOL ding. It's an e-mail from my friend Alistair Woodman, who is captain of the University of St. Andrews Men's Golf Club. He tells me the club will be marshaling at the British Open the week of July 11, covering the grandstand directly behind the infamous seventeenth, the Road Hole. Ali wants to know if I'm up for coming back over and marshaling. I've been considering a return to St. Andrews to caddie anyway, and I've got just enough caddie savings to make the trip. This seals the deal. I e-mail Ali back: "Count me in."

I log onto Travelocity, book a cheap airline ticket. I check the snow outside my window. It's kind of pretty.

SEVENTEEN

"Do you wanna keep the *Animal House* poster?"

Dritan is perched precariously on the top ledge of his desk, attempting to remove posters and Blu Tack from our common-room wall. He's sweating a little from the exertion. Stacks of books and boxes line the floors, as well as a good portion of his twenty-three sweaters.

"No, she's all yours."

I throw on some shoes, grab my folder and ID card. I shoot past my suitcases, out the door. I'm running late.

Outside Weld Hall, Harvard Yard is a beehive of activity. Futons are being carried clumsily by packs of freshman roommates. Books are being carted by parents toward awaiting minivans. Students everywhere are hugging, crying, saying good-byes. It's our final day of school, our final day in Harvard Yard freshman dorms, our first hours of summer. I'm already thinking about the Old Course.

Sprinting faster than Phil Mickelson toward a buffet, I make it to the Expository Writing building and hand in my final essay of fresh-man year ("The Later Works of Ernest Hemingway"—composed at three A.M. and unlikely to win a Pulitzer). Ten minutes later, I'm shouting good-byes to my roommates and friends and gunning it to Logan Airport. I've got a 2:40 P.M. Continental flight to Newark: the first leg of my St. Andrews journey. Everything's ready; Rick's given me the okay over the phone and I'm set to re-don my caddie bib in a few short days. All I have to do now is make it across the pond.

It might not be so easy. Instead of booking on a direct Boston-Edinburgh flight, I've selected a more circuitous route to save money. Many more legs, many more layovers. It looked painless on Travelocity, but I'm already exhausted from all-nighters analyzing *A Farewell to Arms*, and my journey now threatens a great deal of pain. After arriving in Newark (and a six-hour layover), I imagine myself sleeping through the next leg—from Newark to London Gatwick. When I board this flight (behind a man with a neck pillow already inflated around his head), I find my seat nestled between two very large, very loud ladies. A toddler with authority issues starts kicking my seat from behind and giggling. His sister yells, "Mom! Craigie's misbehavin' again!" We're held on the tarmac for two hours. Craigie keeps misbehaving. And I sleep not one second on this flight.

In Gatwick Airport, I'm treated to another six-hour layover and begin to deeply regret my thriftiness. Gatwick is heaving with sun-burned tourists leaving England (where they sunburned, I have no idea), and my terminal is a mosh pit. My flight up to Edinburgh is delayed, and upon landing, I have to maneuver myself dazedly through Edinburgh airport to the Edinburgh City Center bus. Then onto the St. Andrews bus—which, I discover, won't be leaving for another ninety minutes. I now haven't slept in thirty hours.

The icing on the haggis, however, comes when I'm finally on the Stagecoach X59 Edinburgh–St. Andrews bus, speeding down the highway at fifty miles an hour. My golf clubs and suitcase are in the lower hold, and I've (finally) passed out in my seat. For some reason, I am dreaming about horses. Mid-dream, I'm stirred by a small bump. Probably nothing more than a pothole. I shut my eyes again, wipe drool from my cheek. An elderly lady who boarded the bus with me in Edinburgh taps me on the shoulder.

"Excuse me, sir, but I think your golf clubs and suitcase have just fallen oot of the bus."

This wakes me up. I snap to attention, spin around, and, sure enough, spot my golf clubs and suitcase on the road, receding away from my view at fifty miles an hour. The baggage compartment door hangs fully open.

"Stop the bus! My stuff fell out!"

The bus driver mutters a sharp, shocked obscenity and screeches the bus to a halt. I look back and spy a gigantic semitrailer hurtling toward my clubs. My body goes numb. Semitrailer man slams on his brakes as well (the sight of a golf travel bag is instantly recognizable to any Scotsman) and the huge semitrailer comes to a groaning halt, inches short of my bag and suitcase. I let out a soft whimper. Then I tear out of the bus and scoop up my clubs from the road like a mother duck rescuing her ducklings from a hyena. I reboard the bus and take my seat among twenty glaring Scots. By the time the steeple of St. Andrews rises into view, thirty minutes later, I've fallen back into a troubled sleep, now clutching my golf clubs tenderly in both arms. It's been a long trip for all of us.

．　．　．

"Wakey wakey! Up up up!"

I open my eyes, which are seemingly glued shut with cement. I gradually become aware that I'm in St. Andrews and in the top-floor guest room of Uncle Ken's house. I toss, pull the covers back over my head, and try to force my way back to dreamland.

"Yoo-hoo! Up up up!"

No use. I sit up, yell back downstairs groggily.

"Yep! Yes. I'm up. I'm up!"

I hear a high-pitched giggle and then footsteps down in the lower reaches of the house. Uncle Ken's alarm clock duties are done.

I'm spending my first week back in St. Andrews at 4 Howard Place. The caddie flat that I'm to move into—a three-story house at 123 North Street (next door to Old Tom Morris's former home!)—won't be ready until June 3. So this week, I too have been spreading Benecol on my toast ("proven to lower cholesterol") and abiding by Uncle Ken's eight P.M. bedtime—at which point, the house is conveniently also locked. I'm not given a key.

I stumble along the top landing, lost in replays of the past. It's easy to remember myself here as a ten-year-old, waiting impatiently for Dad and my first round of golf on the Jubilee Course, or at age twelve, breathlessly recounting to Mom each of my first ninety-nine strokes on the Old Course. Uncle Ken's house is like a time capsule, a museum of the past. The rooms smell of Imperial Leather soap and Radox body wash. Bonnie's old chew toys and water bowl still sit unused in the hallway. The upstairs storage area—packed with my University of St. Andrews textbooks and spare golf balls—hasn't been touched since I left here, nine months earlier. On the second landing, my blue bicycle leans against the wall, its gears loyally oiled by Uncle Ken in preparation for my arrival. I can't help smiling as I pass by it. It's nice to know that there's a place where you matter.

"Hm hmm hm hmmmmmm . . ."

I follow the contented humming sound downstairs and find my now-eighty-four-year-old uncle in his kitchen. He's wearing a blue-and-white-striped bathrobe over an off-white wife-beater. There's a small yellow sweat towel draped around his neck, as if he's heading to the gym, or to a backup-singing gig for Wu-Tang Clan. I suspect that Uncle Ken waked up at least an hour before me, to prepare for my "wakeup call."

"I'm making scrambled eggs, then I'll have my wash-up," Uncle Ken announces enthusiastically, motioning for me to sit down at the table. "It's all go-go-go around here, you know!" he adds with a giggle. He's clearly very pleased to be lodging his caddie nephew. I take my seat. "Did you sleep well?" Uncle Ken asks.

"*Very* well," I reply. This is completely untrue. There are five spring-wound clocks in Uncle Ken's house, each displaying a slightly different time, each ringing every hour and half hour. This sequencing, I'd forgotten, allows a roughly seven-minute window between *dong*s in which to fall asleep. And I missed a lot of those windows last night. I sit down groggily as Uncle Ken scrambles eggs. On the wall to our right, I spot four calendars (all displaying flowers), marked off for today, Monday, May 30. One of them has the day circled heavily, along with the inscription "Oliver to begin caddying!" This was another reason I didn't sleep well last night.

I'm a little nervous about starting back at the shack. And by "a little nervous," I mean *absolutely terrified*. I haven't caddied in St. Andrews since last summer and, with my typical relaxed and easygoing disposition, am now convinced that I have forgotten every possible caddie skill. The run-out to Cheape's Bunker on hole 2. The delicate strategy needed for skirting Hell Bunker on 14. How to read putts. How to carry a golf bag. Suddenly the course that's barely a tee shot from Uncle Ken's kitchen, the course that I knew so well last year, seems intimidating. Scary. *If I'd stayed in St. Andrews, I wouldn't have forgotten everything.* A sinking feeling begins furrowing deep in the pit of my stomach. Caddie doomsday. The golfers that I'll be guiding today will have paid over $200 for their chance on the Old. Each stroke, each putt, will have unthinkable significance. Their game—their *dreams*—will be in my hands . . .

And I was in Boston yesterday.

What am I going to say if my golfer asks me, "What's the weather been like here the last few weeks?" That I'm not *sure*? That it was pretty nice near *Logan Airport* yesterday? I decide that if the question arises, I'll just say, "Rainy."

As I say good-bye to Uncle Ken and start pedaling down toward the course, my inner paranoia builds. By the time I reach the shack, I am a complete mess. Rick Mackenzie is there to meet me. I timidly approach the window. Although I'm returning as an official caddie, I can't help feeling like a lowly trainee again. I can almost see negative caddie-assessment cards raining down from the sky. Rick squints as I approach and gives me a look as if an alien has just appeared from under Swilcan Bridge. My panic grows. *Should I have called last week to tell him I was definitely coming back?* Rick looks me up and down.

"Ah, the American's back," he says.

I'm given a job for 10:20 on the Old. This first round will be the toughest. Once I have one round under my belt, I'll be able to at least fake my caddying for the rest of the week, until I'm fully back in the swing. But on this first round, I'm naked, vulnerable, like a penguin. Or a hamster. Or some other animal that sounds vulnerable.

But what I don't want on this first round back, above all else, is a good golfer. Simply put, a laser-accurate golfer on your first round back exposes all caddie chinks. Rusty clubbing, bad yardages, poor reads, incorrect pitch-shot-landing advice—all will be exposed by a good golfer. No, for the love of God, I do not want a good golfer today. At 10:12, I head to the first tee, nearly catatonic with fear. *I can't have a scratch golfer. I can't have a scratch golfer. Oh God, please don't give me a scratch golfer.* I meet my guy on the first tee—a tall hulking man from Canada who looks good. It's the moment of truth. I ask him what his handicap is.

"Nineteen . . . but I'm not shooting to it."

I want to hug him.

Hours have passed, and we're out on the course. Ted, a Canadian ex–football player, swings with all the grace and control of an elephant on methamphetamines. He botches his shots so badly that my (numerous) misclubs and iffy reads are hidden under a delicious veil of ineptitude. Ted's golfing buddies are all also ex–pro football and lacrosse players from Toronto. They spend the round complaining about their aching bodies and frequently popping extra-strength Advil gel tablets.

There's something else happening, though, as well.

Down every double fairway and on every double green, I pass other caddies. They squint at me from afar, as if not trusting their eyes. And then they wave at me. Shouting welcomes. Every fairway. Every green. Colin Gerard. Sandy Bayne. Scott Bechelli. His brother Bill. Dougie Saunderson. Gordon Smith. Kevin O'Donnell. Steve Jones. Graham Cowan. Willie Stewart. Big smiles. Backs temporarily turned to their golfers for the greeting. Alec Howie simply abandons his golfer and walks across the enormous fifth/thirteenth green (today, a fifty-seven-yard walk between pins) to shake my hand. I couldn't dream up a better welcoming ceremony.

Finally, on 15, I see my ex–shadow caddie, Kenny. Kenny's got a small Korean lady. He sees me, grins, does a small fist pump from the opposite side of the green. I return the pump and turn back to give my own golfer a brilliant read (inside left). He drains his putt. My freshly ironed caddie bib flaps in the wind. There's a big smile on my face. It's good to be home.

EIGHTEEN

"Are you fucking serious?"

I can't believe what I'm hearing. Greaves, Patrick, Alex Findlay, and I bang a right onto the Scores, passing a group of American golfers sitting outside the Chariots Bar, and continue on toward the pub Ma Bells.

"Totally serious. Some of them should be out tonight, I'll introduce you," Alex replies.

I've just been told something wonderful. No, way beyond wonderful. Something magical. Apparently, a new business has just begun in St. Andrews—founded by two University of St. Andrews fourth-year students named Kenda and Lauren—and everyone is talking about it. It's called Model Caddies. The idea is this: Twenty-five gorgeous university girls, mostly English, mostly with cute English accents, all with modeling experience, will be caddying on Scottish golf courses this summer. They're charging fifty-five pounds plus tip (significantly more than the thirty-five pounds our curmudgeonly Old Course lot charges) and can be individually selected, via a brochure with head shots of each girl. To advertise the program and sign up American golfers, the girls have apparently been heading to pubs in St. Andrews every night.

A seagull screeches above our heads. Alex starts texting someone.

"Tasmin should be there already."

I just met Alex yesterday. Alex is a friend of Greaves's. He's a tall and polite blond-haired English kid whose family belongs to super-posh Royal St. George's Golf Club in Sandwich and who's going into his second year at the University of St. Andrews. Alex just started his first season of Old Course caddying, and I was out with him yesterday. In fact, I saved his ass yesterday, informing him midround that sprinkler-head yardages are to the *front* of greens, not the middle.

Alex finishes sending his text message and starts chatting with Greaves about a Model Caddie. Alex knows a lot about the Model Caddies program, and with good reason. He's dating one of the Model Caddies. One of the most beautiful.

"Jesus, it's heaving."

We head down the stairs and into Ma Bells. Patrick's right, it's totally packed. People are everywhere—students, caddies, golfers, locals. A DJ blasts music from the opposite end. The bar is three rows deep; it's a great crowd for a Wednesday. As we squeeze toward the bar, I pepper Alex with more questions.

"Do they know how to caddie?"

"Except for two of them, no clue. Most haven't even been on a golf course before."

"Really!"

My attention has never been less divided.

"Yeah, they actually got thrown off Kingsbarns the other day. Some Americans paid two girls, like, a hundred and eighty pounds to caddie for them. The guys brought along beer and kept trying to kiss them." Alex waves to a friend across the bar. "One guy asked his girl to come with him to Italy for a month. He said he'd phone his wife to ask. Sounded pretty funny."

"But how'd they get kicked off?"

"Oh right, anyway, one of the girls got carried away and started doing cartwheels on the seventh green."

"Uh-huh. And?"

"The owner of Kingsbarns was in the four-ball behind them."

"Ah."

Alex and I emerge at the front of the bar, order pints of Belhaven Best. I can barely focus on counting out the money. At this moment of my arrival in town, there are twenty-five beautiful girls who are trying to caddie and haven't had any training. This is quickly sounding like a caddie dream.

Alex and I grab our drinks, and Alex spots his girlfriend, Tasmin. He ushers me over to a group of leggy blondes, introducing me to one in particular. "Ollie, this is Julia." Julia is voluptuous, with an amply curved body that screams to me from under a tightly clinging golf shirt.

"Julia, this is my friend Ollie. He caddies on the Old Course." I remember meeting Julia once last year, at a friend's flat. She seemed remarkably disinterested during our last meeting. Now she lights up.

"Wow! That's so cool!"

Never in my life have I been told by a girl that caddying was cool.

Amid the crush of music and voices, Julia and I talk for a while. I learn that Julia's one of the Model Caddie partners.

"It's pretty tough right now actually," Julia confesses. "We just need to get these girls *trained*. They're all eager to learn, but we need to teach them before they can start caddying." Julia looks distressed.

I pause for a second. And then I say what any self-respecting nineteen-year-old caddie should say.

"You know . . . um . . . I could . . . possibly . . . train you guys."

Julia's expression could light up a small village.

"Really? Ohmigod, Ollie. That would be amazing! I don't know how we could ever thank you!" Her eyes lock on mine. I hear harps . . . and flutes . . . and oboes . . . It's as if the gates of heaven have swung open. Wide open.

NINETEEN

I just moved into my new flat at 123 North Street this week (thanks to Uncle Ken, who made three trips in his twenty-year-old red Vauxhall to transport my belongings). I'm already a big fan. The flat is huge, with high ceilings, large bay windows, and easy access to Broons, the bar next door. Equally cool, I'm sharing the flat with Greaves, as well as a caddie friend of ours named Gordon Archibald. Gordy is a slightly overweight twenty-two-year-old University of St. Andrews graduate with a baby face, a 0.8 handicap, and lots of Pringle sweaters.

Gordy is on the couch when I stagger into the living room.

"How'd it go today?"

Gordy is still wearing his caddie gear. He is lying in an odd position—similar to how Julius Caesar might have lain while being fed grapes in ancient Rome. The TV is on, and I recognize the program, since Gordy watched it yesterday. It's a puzzling game show in which people simply call in to guess a hidden number, and a bored-looking host takes the calls every seven minutes or so, announcing that they've guessed the wrong number. Gordy looks very entertained.

"Yeah, it went well," I say.

"Cool." Gordy looks back at the TV. "I think the number's going to be seventeen," he announces very seriously.

". . . Yeah, maybe."

I collapse onto the other couch, exhausted. Late double rounds are draining, and climbing the two flights of stairs just now seemed like scaling Kilimanjaro. I let out a long, low groan—one that in the animal kingdom signals either intense pain, or that you're dying and your young need to go find help. Gordy looks over at me.

"Where's Greaves?"

Greaves walks in. Instead of a regular greeting, he lets out a deep "*FOOOOOOOAHHHHH!*" It's an extension of the regular golf course "Fore" shout, and it's quickly becoming a battle cry for us younger caddies in town. I turn to Greaves.

"How were your rounds?"

"How was the bubonic plague?"

Greaves takes off his shoes.

"That bad?" Gordy asks.

"My guy's iron shots *lit'rally* varied by thirty yards each time; clubbing him was impossible." Greaves opens a can of tuna fish and packet of low-fat cottage cheese that he's brought home from Tesco. Greaves is a total health nut, which is funny, considering that he chain-smokes like a steam engine while caddying. He looks over at the TV. "I think the number's going to be twelve."

"Mmmmm . . ." Gordy seems to admire the guess.

After dinner, I leave my housemates watching the *Big Brother* housemates and escape to the Jubilee. Tonight, the call of the gorse gods is too strong. I have to play some golf. This often happens. No matter how tired I'm feeling, I always seem to get sucked back to the courses at night. They're like an empty amusement park, with all the rides open and waiting. I bike to the Jube's first tee, clubs on back, and join up with a jolly American tourist. Together, we cut around the course to get in nine holes. And for these two hours, I hit the shots that I try to get my golfers to hit. I take my own reads on putts. I practically giggle with glee as I break the cardinal rule of St. Andrews caddying and allow the flagstick to drop to the ground.

At nightfall (eleven fifteen P.M.), I bid farewell to my two-hour friend, having never revealed that I'm a caddie; doing so always ends in my having to give advice on my playing partners' every shot. I pedal back toward town. Halfway there, though, in the darkness, I hear the faint buzz of bagpipes. It's coming from the middle of the Old's eighteenth fairway. I follow the tune and find a crowd of fifty people gathered in a circle. They're all golfers, probably here to play in a large charity event that's on this week. In the middle of the circle stands a gaggle of twenty bagpipers, belting out "Amazing Grace." It's a bizarre scene. I join the circle, golf clubs still on my back, and, surrounded by fifty fanatical golfers—husbands and wives, fathers and sons, business partners and golf buddies—I listen to the bagpipes. The notes float up into the evening sky above us. I have a thought: *This is better than* Big Brother. As I daydream, a man next to me turns to a tuxedo-wearing friend.

"They're called *Model Caddies*," I hear him say, breathing heavily.

TWENTY

"Ollie Horovitz and Nathan Gardner."

Nathan looks up from his newspaper (*Scottish Sun*, page 3, naked girl). He's just finished telling the twelve of us who are currently shack-side about his favorite alternative porn websites. He groans. "Just us two caddies for four guys?"

I start readying my bib. Don Stewart, a posh English thirty-nine-year-old caddie who reads Yeats and Voltaire before rounds, and should have been a philosophy professor instead of a caddie, announces, "Ah, the most enthusiastic caddie in the shack is out with the most switched-off caddie!" I'm secretly thrilled at this compliment. It's also an accurate one for Nathan—to say that Gardner is switched off during rounds is to say the Atlantic Ocean is a little moist.

It's time to go, but before we leave, Don concludes moaning about his American golfer from this morning and the five-pound tip he received. Suddenly we hear an unfamiliar voice. "Don?" Everyone turns—an American golfer (Don's) has wandered confusedly into the caddie shack, through a door left ajar. No one can believe it—golfers aren't allowed in here. The low-tipping man walks to Don and presents him with a hat. He announces, "Here's a little something extra for you; it's from our course back home. Superb layout!" Don switches back instantly, Englishly, into full suck-up mode. "Oh, that's very kind, sir! Thank you very much!" Don's golfer beams a Santa Claus smile, replies, "Happy to do it!" He exits the shack, obviously very pleased with himself. The shack door closes, and perfectly on cue, polite Don whirls around and slams the hat into the garbage can, muttering, "Un-fucking-believable." Everyone laughs. Gardner and I head to the tee.

Nathan Gardner got his degree at the University of St. Andrews. When university ended, he moved to Edinburgh and got a job in finance. "Two years of being stuck in an office, listening to your boss. No thank you." Nathan beat it back to the caddie shack, where he'd looped during university, and started caddying again. That was twelve years ago.

"Jeeze Louise, I'm nervous!" my lady pipes.

Our golfers are four women from Tennessee. Nathan does not appear happy about this. "Well, this is total scrap . . . ," he announces to me on the first tee, with only marginal effort to lower his voice around our golfers. Nathan is wearing his housefly-looking sunglasses, plus our caddie knit hat with the normal fold tucked down, so that the hat now stands about twice its normal height on his head. He does this—I am told—specifically because the caddie masters hate it. I give my golfer her line off the first. She, like everyone else, bunts a weak drive down the fairway. We start walking as a group, and I hear from behind me, "Aye, this is really top-of-the-heap, prime A-1 scrap." Nathan has officially switched off.

Gardner is famous in the shack for his on-course antics. He will frequently make up names of Old Course topographical features for his unwary golfers. "That's Henderson Hill," he'll say, pointing to a clump of grass and referencing our assistant caddie manager Ken

Henderson. Photos will then be snapped in abundance. Other exciting points of interest can include Saunderson's Creek (for caddie Dougie Saunderson, in place of Swilcan Burn), Dougie's Dip (the drop-off behind 11 green), and Mackenzie's Traverse (for caddie master Rick Mackenzie). On 18, to avoid snapping the required corny photo on Swilcan Bridge, Gardner has been known to walk away from Japanese golfers, toward the tiny maintenance bridge thirty feet downstream, and announce, "Sorry, sir, caddies aren't allowed over the main bridge." Once Gardner actually took a group of Japanese golfers onto the maintenance bridge for their historic photo, telling them that *this* was Swilcan Bridge. Somewhere on a mantel in Tokyo, there proudly sits a picture of four golfers smiling brightly while standing on top of a temporary wooden service bridge, thirty feet from the actual Swilcan structure.

"*FOOOOOOAAAHHH!*"

Nathan has just screamed extra loudly at a trainee caddie and middle-aged golfer who have wandered haphazardly into our fifth fairway in search of their golf ball. The middle-aged golfer hits the deck, certain that a ball is bound for his cranium. Nathan just wants them to move left. All four women in our group are a little shocked. "Is it safe to hit now?" one asks meekly.

"Aye, clang it out there," Nathan replies disinterestedly, then turns to me. "Looks like I'll be laying the coils of TNT now," he announces brightly. Nathan is referring to "blowing up" our golfers, aka asking them for more money at the end of the round. It's his trademark line, and whether he actually does this or not, Nathan will reference the necessity of "laying dynamite" (especially for horrible golfers) during the course of each round.

I'm getting to know a lot of the guys in the shack now, and Nathan is definitely in the inner circle. My status as a returning caddie is earning me passage into this group—away from the trainees and novices. Today it's granting me Nathan's camaraderie against our golfers. And truthfully, this is kind of thrilling.

Over the next few holes, while I futilely try to guide my golfer around pot bunkers, Nathan makes frequent trips to other fairways and opposite ends of the greens, to converse with other caddie groups, but mostly to complain about our women. As we walk, he holds his club high in the air at passing caddies. It's inner-caddie code for "My round sucks, and my golfer is shit." The club lift is frequently returned by other passing caddies—all unbeknownst to attached golfers. Nathan has a wry smile permanently etched on his face and a long drawn-out Scottish accent, always seemingly tinged with disbelief in his golfer's ability to hit new lows of "scrappage."

Throughout the round, Nathan and I chat frequently. Nathan's worldview, subscribed to faithfully, is that caddies are plagued by moronic golfers at every turn. On 10, in our golfers' backswings, Nathan continues his view espousal. "I've been asked by my golfer if they'll be using this turf for the British Open, or if they'll be planting all new grass before the tournament," he says. "I've had a golfer point out a fire hydrant behind seventeen green and ask me excitedly if that was Old Tom Morris's grave. I've had a golfer ask me how many times the U.S. Open has been staged on the Old Course. I've even had a golfer in '05, as we're walking past the scoreboards and grandstands for the Open, ask me if some kind of *championship* is being played here. It's just mind-bogglin'; you think people would do a bit a research before coming here . . . like if I was gonna go play Augusta, I might do a bit of readin' up beforehand, so I that knew the Masters was played there, kinda thing."

On the eleventh tee box, we have a wait for the group ahead. Nathan continues: "Phil Lawrie had a boy on the New Course few years ago who was taking pictures *everywhere*. Bunkers . . . tee boxes . . . bushes . . . Phil cannae understand it. Then on eighteen, the guy asks, 'So where's the Swilcan Bridge?' And Phil goes, 'That's on the *Old* Course, sir. This is the *New* Course you're playing.' Guy has nae idea what Phil's talking about. He goes, 'But this is St. Andrews, isn't it?' Ridiculous."

Nathan's gut-wrenchingly funny, and I can easily commiserate with him—I've certainly had my share of perplexing tourist ques-

tions. But during this entire round, an uneasy thought has been cir-
cling me like a vulture. Now on 11, its full force hits me. Our golfers
have paid 130 pounds each for their rounds today. This is their one
chance to play the Old Course. Shouldn't we caddies be, like, *enrich-
ing* their experience? Staring at our women chatting excitedly, it
strikes me that every golfer in St. Andrews has come here on a kind
of pilgrimage. For all of their inappropriate questions and lost balls
and fanny packs, they need to be respected as observant golfer-
worshippers. Has Nathan completely forgotten this? Or is it perhaps
that after carrying someone else's bag two rounds a day, seven days
a week, for twelve years, you become numb to this? Perhaps, after
years of semi-servitude to a richer class, you arrive unknowingly,
overpoweringly, at resentment toward your golfer. Now in my second year on the Old, I'm not sure where I stand. Or in which direction I'm headed.

"Hey, look!" Nathan's woman jolts me out of my daydream.
"Why is he holding the pin like that?" She's looking toward the
eighth green, where a caddie is vertically holding the flag above his
head, fourteen feet in the air. It's an expansion of the club lift, visible
to most caddies in the area, and indicates a golfer beyond compre-
hensible levels of horrendousness. Nathan doesn't miss a beat. "He's
probably alerting the group behind that they haven't cleared the
green so that they won't hit."

There's a pause. "Oh!" Nathan's golfer accepts this. Nathan returns his gaze to the Eden Estuary, lost in thought.

"You'd be surprised how often that happens," he adds.

TWENTY-ONE

I'm in the Jubilee Course parking lot.

It's eight o'clock in the evening, and my two rounds are done for the day. Since then, I've showered, put on a freshly ironed golf shirt, and casually checked my hair in the mirror about four or five dozen times.

Soon I hear the crunch of tires, and a blue Ford Fiesta rolls into the empty lot, pulling up at the curb. Four remarkably pretty girls get out, all sporting the height of pretty-girl golf attire. They're nervously talking, giggling, and heading toward *me*. Julia waves.

"Sorry we're late!"

Not a problem.

Julia continues. "I thought I'd come along as well tonight, to get some training in myself!"

"Well, the more the merrier!" I exclaim, instantly wishing I had said something less dorky.

It's evening number one of Model Caddie training. And the first batch of Model Caddies is here. I hand off my golf bag to a blonde named Emily. Emily is someone you would write songs about—long legs, curves that could cause coronaries, and a devastating smile. Tentatively, I show her how to use the bag's double straps.

"Just, that, arm through, you know, through that strap . . ."

"This one?" Emily giggles as the other girls watch with amusement.

"Uh, no, the other . . . yeah, that way, now slide your other hand through . . ."

"Oh, like this . . ."

"Yeah, and make sure the bag's resting just above your bu— . . . um, your, bottom."

This strap lesson finished, the five of us move onto the Jubilee Course. I guess I should get started.

"Now, the first thing is to find out your golfer's handicap," I say, standing on the first tee, surrounded by the girls.

"What's a handicap?"

"That's how good they are. The lower, the better."

"Oh."

"Yeah, a fifteen-handicap is sort of like, pretty good, for the golfers who come here."

"What's yours?" Emily asks.

"Well . . . two."

Four mouths open in awe. This is going well.

"Okay, so on each tee box, you want to describe the hole to them. On this first hole, for example, I'd say to my golfer, 'Right, we've got a par four here—three hundred seventy-two yards. The ideal line off the tee is on that green bush down there.'"

I hit a tee shot (pushed nervously right, but the girls don't notice), and we all start walking down the fairway. It's weird to be vocalizing how to caddie, but I'm trying. As we walk the fairways together, I show the girls how to pace off distances. How to select clubs. How to carry my bag (they all want a turn carrying it). The time passes in a blur. I don't think I've ever even been *alone* with four girls before, let alone on a golf course with four beautiful models. I should be totally screwing everything up right now. But somehow I'm not. Somehow, because I'm in so far over my head, I actually forget to be nervous. In fact, to my amazement, I do *well*. I make jokes. I tell my best caddie stories. I act cool (sort of). As the sun's rays stretch out over the orange sky, the girls listen attentively, hanging on my words. They giggle. They rake sand traps. This is the best Tuesday evening of my life.

Two hours later, we all gather back in the parking lot.

"Ollie, that was so unbelievably helpful."

There's a glow permanently etched on my face (either happiness or sunburn, or both). Julia continues.

"To say thanks, we're all taking you out for drinks now, Ollie. Our treat."

Emily adds, understandingly, "That is, of course, if you're not too ti—"

"*No, I can do that!*"

Broons is relatively empty this Wednesday night.

We roll in, and it's like we own the place.

"It's the golf dance!" Emily and Lorna announce, interspersing sexy grinding dance moves with unimaginably cute golf swings and overly dramatic ball watching. Sean Paul's "Get Busy" blasts from the overhead speakers.

"Here's the caddie move!" Lauren replies, and jumps up to gyratingly fake-read a putt. "How does that look, Ollie?"

She repeats, "Ollie?"

I am sitting at our table, in a zombielike state. I am unable to move or employ basic methods of human communication. I am mesmerized by what is happening in front of me, and I'm not actually 100 percent sure I'm awake. I force myself to say something back to Lauren.

"Uh, it looks . . . um . . . you know . . . k-keep going."

Emily calls to me. "Come on, Ollie!"

Oh my God. They're all motioning for me to dance with them. And my dance moves resemble a flounder flopping on a fishing boat. But I snap into action. Flounder go-time. When I reach the girls, Lauren grabs me, pulls me up close, and starts grinding with me. Emily starts dancing with me from behind. Lorna slides behind Emily and tousles my hair. It's a Model Caddie sandwich. The girls dip and grind to the bass beats. They press against me, giggling, while Sean Paul waxes poetic.

"Drinks!" Julia yells, descending the stairs with a tray of Pimm's. The girls eagerly reassemble around our table, and Julia hands out glasses.

"To Model Caddying!" Lauren shouts.

"To our trainer!" Emily adds, and the girls cheer as five glasses clink in the middle. Three forty-year-old American golfers enter the bar, glance at our table, and look at me like I just won the British Open.

"So honestly, how did we do today?" Julia asks.

"Honestly? . . . I thought you all did *amazingly*."

A chorus of "Awwwwww"s goes up from the circle. This was a slightly biased answer, I note, but I think it was also the correct one. There's a deafening synthesizer beat, and 50 Cent's "In da Club" comes crashing on—causing Emily, Julia, and Lorna to jump up for more dancing. I stay at the table, talking with Lauren. It is hard not to remember that I'm the only guy here. It is also hard not to replay in my head—at a rate of roughly thirty loops a minute—a sexual fantasy involving myself and twenty-five Model Caddies. We are all naked, carrying golf bags. Sisqó is singing "Thong Song" beside the Eden Estuary. The girls each kiss me. Then Paula Creamer floats down and gives me a putting lesson. She tells me my technique is strong, but then my name is called on the caddie shack loudspeaker by Rick Mackenzie. End of fantasy.

At the end of the night, we all gather outside Broons. As good-bye hugs and kisses are exchanged, the girls' shouts ring down North Street.

"See you soon for more training!" Julia says.

"Thanks again, Ollie!" Emily shouts. The group disperses, and I'm left standing with Lauren. It's time to say good-bye, time to go home. But I decide, in a momentary mix of bravery and stupidity, to press my luck. I mean, even if she says no, it'll still have been a good night.

"So, um . . . can I . . . walk you home?" I ask Lauren, implying more.

I know exactly what she's going to say: "Thanks, but I'm okay."

Lauren looks at me for a second.

"Yeah, that would be nice." She smiles.

It takes me a few more seconds to realize she said yes.

TWENTY-TWO

"Oh, this is marvelous. I'm very pleased about this, you know!"

Uncle Ken is gunning his motor caravan along, walking cane resting alongside the clutch. He is wearing a matching tweed jacket and cap. I'm in the passenger seat.

"It really is a super van!" my uncle continues happily.

Uncle Ken has just replaced his old caravan with this new one. It's green and large. Very large. Maybe too large, in fact. When we pass cars in the narrow oncoming lane, it's usually by a matter of millimeters. Uncle Ken is clearly excited to show me his new vehicle, but he's also eager to be testing it out. This is, after all, the maiden voyage.

"The gang is going up to Crieff this weekend, and I think I'll be joining them," Uncle Ken chirps. He loves calling the motor caravan club (mainly composed of mideighty-year-olds) "the gang." "Friday night is the big meeting. But they make you play all sorts of games."

"Like what?" I ask.

"Oh you know, the usuals," Uncle Ken says seriously. "Pass the Parcel. Squeak Piggy Squeak . . ."

Uncle Ken has a full schedule of motor caravan trips. Nearly every weekend, in fact. The "gang" is always going to places in Scotland with dramatic-sounding names. Markinch. Inverkeithing. Kirkcaldy (*Kir-coddy*). At each site, I imagine an assemblage of eighty-four-year-olds with caravans and exterior electrical outlets.

"What do *you* think of the van, Oliver?"

Uncle Ken turns to me. He's waiting for my response like a second grader holding up a finger painting.

". . . It's really, really great, Uncle Ken," I say with a smile.

And it is. We're in a movable home, a home that can whisk this eighty-four-year-old gent around Scotland, setting him down in places that he once used to fly over in jets, places that he once walked over hills and fields to get to. Even in his later years, Uncle Ken is still exploring, discovering, traveling.

"There's a wonderful tea place coming up that we can stop at," Uncle Ken announces. "It's called the Peat Inn. Their scones are rather tasty actually."

"Excellent."

"You know, I *think* it's important to *show* you these things, Oliver." Uncle Ken giggles.

I look over at him. So full of life. So full of cheer. He's become more than just an uncle to me. He's like a grandfather. Or a godfather. Or a dear friend. Uncle Ken never had children, and it's possible that I'm like the son, or grandson, that he never had. If that's the case, I'm proud to be that kid.

"Here it is, hold on tight!"

Uncle Ken snaps on his turn indicator, and pulls us into the Peat Inn parking lot, for the rather tasty scones.

TWENTY-THREE

"Crouch down like this and see if you can find any break."

I show Grace the proper putt-reading technique.

"Oh, that does help," she says, crouching down. The "visible panty line" reference from *Annie Hall* springs into my consciousness.

"Okay, now do you see any break?"

"Break?"

"You know, like, side hills."

"Oh! Let me check."

Grace is now lying flat on her stomach on the green. Oh my God!

I'm on the third hole of the Jubilee Course, and class is in session. Three new Model Caddies stand beside me: Model Caddie number one is Grace, a strikingly beautiful half-English/half-Asian brunette with piercing eyes. Model caddie number two is Sally, a stunning blonde with inappropriately sizable breasts. Model Caddie number three is Ashley, petite, tanned, with a rear end to rival J.Lo's. All three are wearing tight yellow and pink golf shirts, plus short shorts that expose endless legs. It's all I can do to keep my mind on the lesson, and my blood from pumping to specific outer extremities.

"Oh, I think I see something!" Grace has now placed her hand above her eyes, as if looking out from a ship deck. It probably isn't helping her read the putt, but it does look unbelievably cute. "Does it move to the right?" she asks.

"Cor-rect!" I say with a level of dorkiness that frightens me. I'm having trouble containing my enthusiasm out here. "How much would you say?"

"Um . . . let's see . . . inside right?" Grace asks. I get down to study the putt. I can feel the girls holding their breath for my verdict.

"Actually, that looks really good."

"Woohoo!"

Grace and Sally do a jumping high five. We're making progress.

• • •

"Nice beard, Horovitz."

John Boyne motions to his face and rubs imaginary stubble. He laughs. This is not good—I didn't think it was so obvious. I nervously return the laugh, then, when Boyne leaves, scamper into the shack bathroom to inspect my chin. I have a problem.

Of all the rules that Rick Mackenzie enforces in the caddie shack, the most surprisingly strict is the caddie shaving policy. Quite simply, caddies must be clean-shaven for work, every day. The consequences of breaking this rule are equally simple. If Rick catches you unshaven on three separate occasions, he will fire you. Amongst the veteran caddies, clearly defined facial hair is acceptable (one older caddie, Nick Robertson, looks exactly like "Fluff" Cowan with his handlebar mustache). For the rest of us, however, even microscopic stubble adorning our chins can bring serious trouble.

I arrived in St. Andrews at the start of this summer armed with my shiny electric razor. It was a birthday present from my parents at age thirteen and is the only razor I've ever used. Four days ago, it died. Like, seriously died. No replacement batteries can revive it. Worse, I haven't been able to find another affordable electric one, and I don't know how to use a manual razor. So for the past three days, I've been cautiously avoiding Rick at the window, ducking in and out of the shack after my rounds. So far, the strategy's been working.

My luck continues this morning. Ken is at the window when I pay my admin fee, and I scuttle away safely to the first tee for my round before Rick returns. At the end of the round, I collect my tip (Hawaii Five-0) and head back to the shack. I say hello to Rick at the window and ask to sign on for another. Rick stares at me for a second. His eyes tilt down to my chin. His face clouds. I suddenly realize the blunder I have just made.

"You're not going out again like *that*!" Rick screams.

My heart leaps into my mouth.

"Oh, uh, Rick, I'm really sor—"

"A shave is part of the uniform that a caddie has to wear!" Rick bellows. This doesn't seem like the clearest metaphor, but I keep the observation to myself.

Rick continues. "You'll have to go home and shave right now!"

"Rick, the thing is, um, my electric razor broke, and I can't replace it, and, um, I don't know how to use a regular razor."

Rick takes in this new information. Then he dives into the shack, reappearing moments later. In his left hand, he is holding a small, antiquated bladed razor. In his right hand, he is holding a bottle of hideous-looking green liquid.

"Shave in the next ten minutes, or you no longer work here," he says.

Desperately, I grab Patrick McGinley from the shack and drag him down with me to the Links Clubhouse locker room. There, I force Patrick to give me a brief demonstration in proper shaving technique before he has to leave for his own round. Alone at the mirror now, I decide to use hand soap in the absence of shaving foam and begin my first razor blade experience. Eight frantic minutes later, I reappear at the shack window. I am clean-shaven. I am also stinging. I am also dripping with blood from five different major areas on my face. I hand back the tools to Rick, who looks with interest at my countenance.

"You're not good with the razor," Rick announces, and shoos me away from the window, trying hard not to laugh. I am herded back into the shack. All the caddies see me. They laugh.

"What the fuck happened, Horovitz?!" Bob Perks, an older caddie with two artificial knees and two artificial hips, asks.

"Must have been pretty tough out there on the Old!" Alistair Taylor shouts.

"Jealous husband? Lion attack?" Alec says, piping up.

I give them the Scottish equivalent of the middle finger (the universal peace sign flipped around) and search for my bib under the benches. For reasons I cannot quite explain, I am extremely proud of my war wounds. I succeed in finding my bib, and pat my face with a towel. The bleeding comes to a stop twenty-five minutes or so later.

I'm about to leave for my second round when Rick walks into our room, holding a newspaper. He stands in the doorway, addressing us all. He looks angry.

"This goes for all of you. If anyone hears anything about this Model Caddie *shite*, I want to know about it!" Rick fixes us with a stare for two seconds, then storms off. Nobody moves. The suddenness of Rick's outburst has shaken everyone. Which is good, because at this moment, I am having a small panic episode.

"He's right, you know," Perks says.

"Fookin' tarts," an older caddie mutters viciously.

"You heard about this, Eck?" Alistair asks.

"Oh aye," Eck replies. "You, Horovitz?"

"Uh-uh," I say.

"Oh," says Eck.

My caddie number can't be called soon enough.

After my second round, I bike up to Uncle Ken's. I feel major relief to be going there. After this week, it's become like an island of safety, a life raft, a place where I can finally escape the Model Caddie questions.

"Have you heard the news, Ken?"

Henry is at the kitchen table, holding up the Scottish *Courier* in both hands. Uncle Ken places down three cups of Nambarrie tea for us, followed by two rock buns from Fisher & Donaldson. My uncle is all ears. "What news is that, Henry?"

"These lassies. They're carryin' golf bags. For this new business."

"Oh yes, I had heard that."

Henry points to the article. "It's all in the papers." Henry, as usual when reporting on anything, is speaking at about 30 percent speed, with lengthy pauses thrown in for dramatic effect. "And it's causing quite a stir, I can tell you."

This is an understatement. Over the past few weeks, word of Model Caddying has been spreading faster than Facebook. And it's becoming notorious in town. The St. Regulus Ladies Golf Club published an article in the *Citizen* yesterday calling the program sexist and promoting of female subservience. Letters have been written in, ranting that the program will take away work from the real St. Andrews caddies. Locals are fuming to one another in Tesco. Now, it's clear, Model Caddying has reached the kitchen table of 4 Howard Place.

Henry takes a sip of tea and continues his report. "Brochures with pictures and everything—by golly."

I'm not surprised that Model Caddies is so controversial. In such a small, traditional town as St. Andrews, Model Caddying doesn't exactly blend into its surroundings. And it's not surprising that the idea of young university girls taking jobs away from locals would stir resentment. The truth, however, is that this thinking is totally misguided. First of all, the Model Caddies don't even work on any of the same courses as the St. Andrews caddies (nor, thanks to the cartwheels, on Kingsbarns). Even if they did, one could argue that the golfer who would hire a Model Caddie isn't the kind of guy (or lady . . . but probably guy) who would want an Old Course caddie anyway. I also happen to find the idea of university students starting an international business to be pretty cool. But within this town, I have to keep such thoughts to myself.

"Did you know any of these girls at school, Oliver?" Uncle Ken asks casually.

I shift a little uneasily in my chair. "Oh, me? No. I wish, though."

Henry chuckles. "Aye, they're beauties!"

Bzzzzz. Bzzzzz. Bzzzzz.

We all jump nearly a foot out of our seats. I realize it's my cell phone vibrating (loudly) on the kitchen table. I grab it away like a murderer hiding his gun and secretly read the text message.

"Have three more eager girls for training tonight! You free? xx. Julia"

At knee level, I type back the response. "Yes."

Then I take a guilty bite of rock bun. Delicious.

TWENTY-FOUR

I am in deep.

Each night at eight o'clock, I am bringing girls, three or four at a time, around the Jubilee Course. They are dropped off by Julia, the queen bee of the group. There is a long list of Model Caddies who need training, so whenever possible, the girls want to go out on the course with me. I'm only too happy to oblige. When my friends and I decide to go and play golf in the evenings, I call up and "reserve" some trainee models to carry our bags. They are all extremely "fit" (British slang for "attractive").

Tonight Greaves and I have decided to squeeze in a quick post-supper nine holes on the Jubilee Course. Greaves has been away for a week, visiting family, and is unaware of the latest Model Caddie updates. "I'm totally shattered," Greaves complains, clearing his plate in our kitchen. "My Swede didn't hit more than two fairways the whole way round today."

I yell back from the living room, "Yeah, Gordy told me it was pretty rough."

Greaves comes in, stretching his legs. "I definitely have to pull a trolley on the Jube tonight."

Not looking up from my bowl of pasta and cheese, I respond. "Maybe not."

Greaves seems to sense implication behind my overly cocky comment.

"What the fuck are you talking about?"

Before I can answer, there's a honk from the street. We go to the window and spy two extremely pretty Model Caddies getting out of Julia's car. They walk toward our flat.

"They're gonna caddie for us."

Greaves's mouth drops opens.

"They need training."

Dazedly, Greaves hurries out of the living room to collect his clubs and apply hair gel. I hear him murmur from the hallway, "Somebody fucking pinch me."

The great tragedy of American boyhood was not knowing that nine-year-old girls also wanted to be kissed.

At least that's my excuse.

In truth, my natural ease around girls can be nicely illustrated by a few key moments.

Second grade. Her name was Christine Azzizodon—an adorable brunette with red hair clips. She was amazing. During class, I would stare at her endlessly (fortunately this was the second grade, before the phrase "pervert" had entered our vocabulary). Toward the end of the year, I decided that I would give Christine a present. Without telling my parents, I bought a purple silk scarf from a local clothing store with my allowance, put it in a small box, and added a note, written in my large block handwriting, with the following message: "I love you so much, Christine, I really do."

The next day, at the end of class, I handed Christine the box. Fourteen minutes later, on PS 41's asphalt playground, Christine tracked me down.

"I don't love you, I only like you!" Christine announced. Then she tossed back my present. "And I don't like the scarf."

Boyhood continued, and a few years later, in fifth grade, I was ecstatic to go to PS 41's Spring Fling Dance with my crush, Jennifer Baumstein. The dance went well—four fast dances, one slow dance— and I considered the whole night a big success. This outlook was altered slightly a few days later, when my twin sister, Hannah, informed me that "Jennifer said she only went to the dance with you because she felt sorry for you."

Mine was an adolescence of lean romantic success. High school wasn't much better. So when I shipped off to St. Andrews (still answering, "Yeah, of course!" a little too insistently when anyone asked if I'd gotten laid before), I was hoping desperately that something was going to change. That my luck with girls would get more, well, lucky.

It's Friday night, and I've got the evening off from Model Caddie training. I'm at a dinner party that my friend Miles is hosting in his flat on Hope Street. Ten St. Andrews students are here, and I'm sitting at the dinner table next to a pretty girl I haven't met before (and who is not exactly moving mountains to change this fact). The overcooked chicken is served, and conversation turns to our summer jobs. Most of the students are working in pubs or restaurants to earn money for the school year. It comes up that I'm caddying.

The pretty girl suddenly turns to me.

"Wait, what did you say your name was again?!"

"Oliver."

"And you caddie on the Old Course?"

"Uh, yeah."

"Oh my God! You're 'Fit Ollie'!"

There's a pause. I'm unsure that I heard this correctly.

"Excuse me?"

In a whisper, the girl continues. "I almost did Model Caddying. A lot of my friends are doing it. They've all been saying, 'Ooh, we all want to go and get *trained* by Ollie!'" She concludes her little speech with a casual final remark, one that will in turn mark the happiest moment of my young adult life.

"That's what they call you—'Fit Ollie.'"

Twenty-five

I'm at Castle Sands beach. It's the same beach where on May 1, all St. Andrews students charge into the North Sea, naked. It's also a pretty good spot for sunbathing. Just not at this particular moment, because it's three o'clock in the morning.

"Throw another log in!" Alistair yells.

Twenty of us are sitting in a semicircle, facing a crackling bonfire. Our group is a collection of students, locals, and a few tourists who have happened upon the bonfire. Several bottles of champagne are passed around, "borrowed" from Ma Bells by a bartending friend of mine with limited employee-establishment loyalties.

"Right."

I chuck a medium-size log into the fire. Several burning embers dislodge and rise into the darkness. I plop back onto the sand. I'm exhausted after a late double this afternoon, and I'm happy to be off my feet. I'm happy for another reason, as well. Sitting next to me on the sand is Model Caddie Grace.

To my surprise, Grace came with me to the beach after Ma Bells closed. Her friends called it a night and went home, but Grace wanted to stay out later. Now, to my greater surprise, Grace is laughing at my jokes . . . smiling brightly at me . . . giving me her full attention. She takes a sip from the Moët bottle. She's wearing a yellow hoodie and short shorts, and her knees are pulled into her body. Her silky dark hair falls over beautiful eyes and perfect cheekbones.

"Is New York a fun place to live?" Grace asks, looking directly at me.

"New York? Oh yeah, it's great."

"I really want to visit—is it true you see the *Sex and the City* people everywhere?"

I look at Grace. "Absolutely true."

Alistair and a waiter from the Grill House begin wrestling in the sand. Others cheer them on. Grace and I start talking about Times Square, and the night continues like this, with the sounds of waves crashing and kids laughing and no one caring how loud we are. Our beach is one hundred feet below the road, wedged between sheer cliffs and North Sea—we can do what we like.

At four A.M., when the first rays of sunlight gasp over the North Sea and the fire begins to putter out, I walk Grace back to her flat. It's just outside the West Port arch, opposite the Whey Pat Tavern. It's either the champagne or the having been up all night, but I'm feeling weirdly calm.

"Thanks for walking me home," Grace says sweetly.

"No problem." Neither of us move.

"Can I tell you something?" I ask.

"Sure."

"I think you're extremely cute."

"Can I tell *you* something?" Grace asks.

"Yeah."

Grace pulls me right up to her, stands on her tiptoes so that her face is inches from mine.

"I think you're a great trainer," she whispers.

123

TWENTY-SIX

I'm finally learning the Old Course. I mean, really *learning* it.

Caddying out here, going around twice a day, eavesdropping on caddies like Jimmy Reid and Alec Howie and Bruce Sorley (one of only five people in the world to have caddied competitively for Tiger Woods), you start unlocking the Old's secrets. If the pin on 2 is cut left, you *must* be long and left to carry the mounds. If the pin on 2 is right, you can't be short; otherwise you've got a minefield of humps to negotiate. Each hole has its dangers. Each hole has its truths. On the par-3 eleventh, you have to play for the heart of the green, to the left of Strath Bunker. The eighteenth green is always one club more than you think.

There's something about caddying for other golfers that forces me to examine the course like I never have while playing. Stripped of the attention to golf swings, I'm free to think about the humps and the hollows. When I run fifty yards ahead of my golfer to forecaddie his approaches into the fifth and thirteenth, I see bounces and incoming shots for the first time. My golfers are playing this course once, and each shot is their one chance on the hole. But for me, the shots are part of a long-running series. Patterns form; common mistakes become obvious. Every day, mini-epiphanies strike. I realize that being slightly long on almost every hole (except 11 and 17) is preferable to being short, since it gets you past the mounds protecting most green fronts. And soon I've learned the cardinal caddie sins that must be avoided. There are four that particularly stand out: 1) Winding up in Swilcan Burn on the first hole. (It's the only water hazard on the course, so you *have* to give golfers enough club to get over.) 2) Driving into the Seven Sisters bunkers on the right of the fifth. (Sure, if your golfer slices, there's nothing you can do, but there are *miles* of room left, so they have no business being right.) 3) Going long on the par-3 eleventh. (Short is fine. Long is screwed.) And 4) going long on the seventeenth hole. (Road. Wall. Death. Short right is the play.)

As the weeks pass, I find myself memorizing all the different pin locations. I catch myself excitedly perusing the morning pin sheets before rounds, analyzing which will be the easy ones (the twelfth hole cut on the lower tier) and which will be the "fookin' crazy" ones (the thirteenth hole cut long right near the bunker, the sixteenth hole cut right up front). I can look at the third-hole pin—cut twelve yards on and nine yards left—and *know* that the approach shot should land five yards past the front edge, so it funnels down to the hole. I can see the pin and remember where the putts will break from similar lines on previous rounds. I'm starting to experience the same pride as the old guys in knowing my course. And the more I know, the more I *want* to know.

• • •

I'm meeting more of the Model Caddies.

Training is picking up, and my name seems to be spreading around the group. I pass girls on the street now who stop and introduce themselves. Girls who are Model Caddies. Girls whom I'd never have had the courage to go up to on my own. I meet new Model Caddies outside Tesco, along South Street, on the way to the Old Course. It's like a secret society. And I'm getting initiated.

• • •

"Come on! Let's run!"

I'm heading to a party. Actually, an after-party. Emily, one of the prettiest Model Caddies, is with me.

"It's just around the corner, they live across from the KFB," she announces breathlessly. Emily is wearing my blue caddie hat on her head, backward. She is skipping down the damp street—a blaze of thrillingly fitted jeans and intoxicating energy. She looks even sexier than usual. Sally, another Model Caddie, prances along behind us, holding a giant stuffed panda bear.

I run to catch up with Emily. We pass the KFB—a late-night "chippie" that is a staple among St. Andrews students, offering such delicacies as black pudding, haggis, and deep-fried Mars bars (which, famously, move through you very quickly). This area of town, just down the hill from the all-night garage and packed with student flats, is known as "the badlands." Along with Hope Street and Greyfriars Garden, "the badlands" is after-party central.

"Here we go, this is Ashley's place!"

Emily motions to a house that has music escaping from all windows. Under the orange glow of the streetlamps, I can see that the door is ajar. Emily leaps through it. I follow.

Inside the flat, it's a typical St. Andrews student after-party. People sit on the living room sofas and floor, drinking wine from the bottle. Others are dancing in the middle of the room. A few are tipsily playing a golfing video game on what looks like a replica of the Old Course. In the hallway, an impromptu cricket game is taking place, with proper equipment and knee pads. A fish tank sits on the left side of the room, with two people standing beside it, pouring vodka into the water.

"To the kitchen!"

Emily leads me through the living room maelstrom as if leading troops on a battlefield. We reach the kitchen and uncork a bottle of white wine that's sitting on the table.

"What a place, huh?" Emily says, offering me a glass.

"Yeah, it's nice!" I reply.

In the background, I can see Sally dancing in the living room— alone—with the panda bear.

"I'm so glad you could come with us tonight!" Emily says. Her English accent is outrageously cute. Her low-cut top tilts casually downward. I'm in way over my head.

"To this summer!" Emily says, offering a toast.

"To this summer!" I say back, and we clink glasses.

There's a happy pause. And then suddenly I kiss her. It's totally not thought out, totally uncalled for. I just can't *not* try to kiss her. I really like her. And I've missed too many moments like this before in my life. I've arrived home at the end of too many nights kicking myself for what might have been. Even now, I'm half expecting to strike out. But Emily melts into the kiss. It's just us in the kitchen, and the kiss lingers, grows more passionate. She tousles my hair, brings her body up to mine. All party sounds fade out, and the world narrows, as it always does during a first kiss. Emily's eyes, her lips, her perfume. All my senses scream. It's the best feeling in the world; the first moment of discovery that the person you like, well, likes you back. After a length of time that I lose track of, Emily and I break from the kiss, both out of breath. We smile at each other. I have a thought: *I don't want this summer to end.*

TWENTY-SEVEN

"What a fookin' disgrace!"

Alec Howie is reading a paper in the shack and muttering disgustedly.

"Aye, mental, isn't it?" Stevie Zamora says in agreement, holding a copy of the same paper. "I've never seen anything like it!"

My St. Andrews caddie peers, to put it mildly, do not like the Model Caddie program. Every day, caddies put down the venture. They call it "ridiculous," "a fookin' catastrophe," "slags with bags." This is not partial dislike. This is venomous, visceral. And it's not a case of simple rivalry either—I think the reasons are more complicated. My shackmates seem threatened by the Model Caddies' youth, beauty, and sexiness. They seem offended by the flippancy with which a group of female students have decided that they can do this job too, a job many St. Andrews caddies have spent their lives perfecting. The very *notion* of Model Caddying seems to challenge my shackmates' identities. Obviously, a nerve has been touched here. To even side with the Model Caddies in a discussion is dangerous.

"Did you hear, Mackenzie made three of 'em cry last week?" Scott Bechelli announces. "They came down to talk to him about workin' on the links, and he absolutely went crazy!" I heard about this. For Rick, that was probably flirting.

"Horovitz, what do you think?" Alec asks.

"Oh yeah, it's a total joke," I say, scoffing with sizable disgust. Alec and Stevie both nod. There have been moments of greater bravery in my life.

I'm dating Emily. The night at the flat party has turned into many more nights together, and I'm now firmly entrenched in the Model Caddie program. And I won't soon forget my moments with Lauren or Grace before her. In short, I'm living the life of my dreams. But it's becoming painfully clear that I have to be careful. If Old Course caddies find out about my involvement, I'll be in danger. And if word gets back to Rick that I'm training this rival program—on the very courses from which they're banned—I'll be instantly fired. My St. Andrews summers, just like that, will end.

I have other worries as well. Glorious as they are, the training rounds themselves are often punctuated by moments of danger— when rangers, golfers, and other caddies suddenly appear from other fairways or along cart paths—and all semblance of training has to immediately cease (in these moments, I take back my bag and pretend that I'm playing golf).

I look over at Stevie and Alec on their bench, still reading the article with disgust. There's no doubt—what I'm doing in this anti–Model Caddie town is illegal. It's potential suicide for my caddie career and my caddie friendships. I sense that my heart—and other body parts—is leading me toward danger. But I'm having too much fun to give this all up. I can't stop now. Why should I let these guys end my good fortune? As long as I keep the operation quiet, I tell myself, I should be fine. In fact, lately I've come to adopt a slightly heroic view of my circumstances. I am in a spy movie, leaking secrets to the enemy. Or I'm in *Romeo and Juliet*, caught between two warring families. I have to admit, the whole notion of this situation is kind of exciting.

Stevie Zamora keeps reading the article's final paragraph.

"Says they've got some kind of trainer, too . . ."

TWENTY-EIGHT

I've gotten a text from Emily.

The girls need me.

Apparently, the Model Caddies are doing a deal with *Golf Punk*, a self-styled "urban golf" magazine. *Golf Punk* will be putting on several events during the British Open in the Gin House, the home pub of the University of St. Andrews golf team. The nights are going to be huge. Paul Casey and Ian Poulter—both sponsored pros—will be attending. A giant marquee and Old Course golf simulator will fill the outside beer garden. And roaming around everywhere, smiling and advertising *Golf Punk* magazine, will be Model Caddies, dressed as "Bunker Babes." Sounds remarkably good.

I meet Emily outside the Gin House at eight P.M., where she explains the problem to me.

"Everything seemed fine at first, but now the *Golf Punk* guys are being utter assholes! They want all of us there every night, and they're paying each girl less than they originally said! Isn't that terrible?"

"The bastards . . . ," I breathe.

Emily continues anxiously. "We're meeting both *Golf Punk* directors here in a few minutes to go over the details. The girls want you here as well, Ollie, to represent us." Emily looks up at me with big, adoring eyes. "Can you do that?"

I look straight ahead, catching my reflection in the glass doors of the Gin House, and lower my jaw. I'm like Bruce Willis. Only more powerful.

"Yes," I announce dramatically. "I will help you."

At the back of the Gin House, waiting for us, are the other Model Caddies. All of them. Together, the twenty-five girls create an image that is almost too perfect to behold. As a group, they seem even leggier, even more pouting, even more beautiful. There isn't enough space for all of them in this room. Girls stand by the wall, girls lean on stools, girls sit on other girls' laps to share seats. It's like a photo shoot for *Elle* magazine. Or a caddie version of *Playboy*. As I enter, a chorus of "Hi, Ollie," goes up.

"Uh, hey," I say back meekly, and take a seat. Julia walks up to me.

"Thanks so much for coming, Ollie!" she says.

"I'm here for whatever you need," I say, closing my eyes slightly so that I look cooler.

"They'll be here soon," Julia says. "I've told them you're one of our advisers."

I take a seat in the middle of the group and await the Punks. Minutes later, they arrive. Two guys in their thirties with brown blazers and South London accents. They look like they mean business.

"Let's cut to the chase," the taller guy says. "I thought we had a deal."

"We did have a deal," Kenda replies, "and then you changed it!" Other Model Caddies voice agreement.

"Look," the other man says gruffly, "we don't have time for all this hassle. The terms are going to stay put, or we'll get other girls."

"Which won't be hard," the tall guy adds.

"All right, that's it!" I am shocked by the force of my own voice. "You can't talk to them like that."

Both men turn to me.

"Who the hell is he?" the shorter guy says to Kenda.

"That's Ollie. He's one of our advisers."

The guy looks at me. "Okay. Well, I advise you to stay the fuck out of this."

A wave of discontent slams through the room. "Don't talk to him like that!" Emily shouts.

Thanks, Mom. I should say something back, but I don't know what that would be. These guys are intimidating. And I'm not good with conflict. I feel like I'm in fourth grade when Mark Lewis dumped water on my shorts and everyone thought I peed. Or in fifth grade, when I repeated a line to a bully that my dad had told me to say—"I'm not listening to you, because I know your mom dropped you on your head as a child"—and I got pummeled.

Silence now. The room is at a standstill. I look at Julia and at Emily. They expect me to do something. Everyone does. I realize I can't wimp out. Suddenly I have an idea. I decide to channel someone I know; someone who wouldn't back down from this. I pretend I'm Rick Mackenzie.

I turn back to the man and stand up threateningly.

"Sorry, mate. If you want Model Caddies at your event, you gotta go through me."

The man is silent a moment. He just stares me down. Then, reluctantly, he nods. "Fine."

I'd like to thank the Academy.

* * *

"What's your number today?"

Greaves hits his putt, draining it on the left edge.

"Eighty-seven. You?"

"One hundred and nine."

"Fuck."

I take the putter. We're standing on the side putting green, located just behind the shack. It's for golfers, but as long as no one's there, caddies are (sort of) allowed to putt on it. I make a few practice strokes with the communal caddie shack putter, which, in typical shack form, has several pieces of hardened chewing gum stuck to its back edge.

"Yeah, I'm pretty sleepy this morning."

Greaves and I start moving around the putting green. We're wearing our caddie waterproofs and caps. We play each hole as a par 2, keeping track of our over/under-par scores. Holes are played in clockwise fashion, except when cute girls pass by; then we immediately switch to the hole nearest their path. Greaves lights a cigarette, makes his putt with the cig in his mouth.

"So I've been thinking."

"Yeah?"

"About the Model Caddie stuff. You really gotta be careful, mate."

I clean up my three-footer for a par. "How so?"

"I dunno. Rick's been ranting about them. He kind of sees them as the enemy."

"Yeah, I bet."

Greaves continues. "Seriously though. If you get caught, you're, you know, fucked."

"Thanks."

"I'm just saying."

I take back the putter. Greaves is right. He's totally right. Every day it feels like I'm closer to being caught. But for the first time in my life, I have an "in" to a world of beautiful women. And I like it. A lot. I'm not going to back out now just because I might get caught. Hell no. This is my moment.

"I hear what you're saying, Greavesy. I'm being careful," I say.

"Fine."

I line up my six-foot putt for the win. But I'm thinking about Emily.

The ball stops halfway to the hole.

"You okay, mate?" Greaves asks.

"Yeah, fine! Why?"

. . .

I'm training three beautiful Model Caddies on the Jubilee's fourth hole.

"When you get to a tee box, use your course guide to point out the trouble off the tee. It's easier that way."

I take out my course guide, and the three model caddies crowd around me like seven-year-olds at a *Harry Potter* book signing. Helen is carrying my golf bag, and the other girls, Lorna and Sue, hold notepads to transcribe my lesson. I begin my dictation.

"On this hole, I'd say something to my golfer like 'Okay, this is a par four, three hundred forty-seven yards, and left is better than right off the tee. That bunker you can see down there is a good line, since it's out of reach for us today.'"

Pens busily scratch away on notepads. I'm loving this. With a smile on my face, I look over from the girls to our fairway. What I see makes my smile vanish.

Coming right up to us—in the fairway beside ours—is an Old Course caddie.

"Shit!"

My exclamation startles the girls, and everyone looks up. I frantically grab my golf bag back from Helen and start walking ahead, pretending to be playing golf for myself. But it's no good. The caddie has seen everything. And anyway, let's be real, this doesn't exactly look like regular golf course activity. *Shit! Shit! Shit!* It's nine o'clock— I can't believe there are still guys out this late. The caddie walks up to me. He looks at me for a second, then looks at the Model Caddies, before turning back to me. Finally he speaks, quietly but firmly.

"I didn't see anything."

He starts walking away. I'm frozen in place, unable to say anything back. After a few steps, the caddie turns again.

"And neither did Davie last week."

. . .

"Morning, Dougie."

It's a sunny Tuesday morning, and I've pitched up at the caddie shack window. Dougie passes me, holding up four fingers ("Fore!"), and walks to the Old's first tee. I've got a booking on the New Course at 9:42 (small New Yorkers with large wallets) and need to pay my fiver before I head down.

Rick comes to the window.

I smile and hand over my admin fee. I'm thinking about whether or not to buy a cheese sandwich at the Links Clubhouse. The sandwiches there taste pretty good. And I'm a little hungry. Yeah, I'll probably buy a sandwich. Rick clears his throat. "Oliver, I have something to talk to you about."

"Sure, what's on your mind?" I ask. For some unexplainably stupid reason, I cannot imagine what Rick is getting at. The caddie master stares at me for a three count. Then he begins.

"Oliver, I'm going to ask you a question. Are you training Model Caddies?"

Before I can blink, Rick adds an addendum. "If you are, you'll have to leave right now."

My heart seizes. *Stay calm. Stay calm!*

"No, Rick, I'm not training them," I reply as coolly as I can sound. Rick receives this information without averting his stare.

"Your name has come up twice now in connection to them."

Thunderclap.

My mind races. *Shit! Shit!*

"Rick, I'm not connected to them." *Total bullshit! What do I do?*

Rick considers this statement. He slowly nods. "Okay. I'll take your word for it. But if you *are* training them, it *will* come back to me. And if you're passing on information from the caddie shack to others, you'll be hearing from our lawyers!"

I stumble away from the window. This last part of Rick's statement, regarding the lawyers, is probably bullshit (I doubt the caddie shack is, like, litigious), but the part about firing me seems real enough. It suddenly hits me that I shouldn't have lied outright to Rick. That sets me up for disaster. It'll be too easy to be proven wrong, and then I'm screwed. I need a workable explanation. Suddenly I have a plan. I run back to the window.

"Rick, there's something I should tell you," I hurriedly begin.

"Yes?"

"I'm currently dating one of the Model Caddies, and this might be why my name has come up in connection to them."

Rick doesn't say anything. I decide to throw my loyalty at Rick's feet.

"However, I feel bad about implicating us with Model Caddies, Rick. And I'm prepared to end the relationship, if you think it's necessary."

I look up at Rick. He is obviously delighted by this display of dedication. He shakes his head vigorously.

"Oh noooooo, Ollie, that won't be necessary!"

I walk away from the window again, leaving a very pleased Rick. I exhale like a deflating balloon. I've dodged a bullet. For now, I'm in the clear. But then it hits me—and hits me hard. I can't bear the thought of what almost just happened. I can't possibly give up my caddie life. It's become a part of me, a part of my life. And just as suddenly, I realize what I have to do. If I have to choose between Model Caddies and my fellow caddies—if it's one world or the other—then my loyalties are with the shack. I will not be like Fredo in *The Godfather*. I've made up my mind. I will never take sides against the family again. Ever.

• • •

"Julia, I can't do this anymore."

We're walking along North Street, out toward the North Point café.

"Oh no! Why?" Julia looks extremely upset.

"It's not you guys. It's nothing *you* did. Really. It's me . . ."

I feel like I'm breaking up with twenty-five Model Caddies.

"I don't understand. What's the problem?"

I stop for a second on the street. "Well, I . . . I got caught."

Julia's eyes widen. "Shit! Really?"

"Well, almost caught. Rick heard a bunch of rumors, and he pulled me into his office yesterday."

"Oh, Ollie! I'm so sorry!"

"No, it's okay. I think I talked my way out of it. But I've been thinking a lot about this. I just can't risk it anymore. If I had to stop caddying here . . . I dunno . . . I'd . . . this just means too much to me."

Julia looks at me with understanding. "I'll tell the girls. You've already helped us so much."

Soon we're hugging and parting ways, and I'm walking back down the street, to change clothes for another caddie round. I know what I'm walking away from—but I know I have to do this. My caddie career depends on this. And somehow, deep down, I'm proud of my decision.

. . .

Emily's leaving.

A lot of them are. The Model Caddies haven't been getting enough work, and many are apparently heading home—to London, Edinburgh, Manchester, Glasgow—for a few weeks with their families before school starts up again.

It's evening, and Emily and I are sitting at the end of the pier, down by East Sands Beach. The sun is setting, casting shimmering gold onto the waves of the outer harbor. Emily and I dangle our feet over the pier's edge, looking out onto the North Sea. Neither of us is really addressing the inevitable conclusion.

"I think I'm moving to London after school," she says.

"Oh, nice."

"Yes, I think I'd like it there. When do you start back at Harvard?"

"Three weeks."

"Wow."

"Yeah."

There's an easy silence. We both know it's time to head back.

"I'd love to see you again you know, sometime," I say.

Emily smiles. "I would too, Ollie."

And then I kiss her, and as we stand up, I know this will be the last time we'll ever see each other.

•   •   •

"Two more spitfires came through the clouds—it was a real dog-fight, you know! That's when Neil's plane was hit."

Uncle Ken takes a swallow of carrot and coriander soup. As usual, he's ordered a "half portion," followed by an amusing insistence to the Grill House waitress that he'll "gladly pay for the full portion." He's also perused the menu, as usual, for a lengthy period of time, before settling on the exact meal he always gets—Scottish Tay salmon, then vanilla ice cream for dessert. A giggle ends his order, and our waitress leaves the table, giggling herself. Uncle Ken turns back to me.

"It was '44, wintertime, and we were behind enemy lines. Neil's navigation was out, and he was losing fuel, so he really had no idea where to go."

Uncle Ken takes a sip of house red. It's in his normal amazing way, throwing back his entire head, as if bracing his whole eighty-four-year-old body for the sip. Tonight is our final dinner together at the Grill House. And Uncle Ken is sharing World War II RAF stories.

"Neil was really in trouble. He was going down. But then out of nowhere, a plane from a different squadron appeared. The pilot flew right up to Neil's wing and stayed with him, wing to wing, guiding him all the way back to base. Saved his life."

"Wow!" I say.

"After the ordeal, Neil spent ages trying to get a note to the mystery pilot, to thank him for saving his life. Weeks later, he got a reply from the pilot. And it said, 'No need to thank me. Was only doing my duty.'"

Uncle Ken sits back and smiles. A waiter comes to clear our bowls. The man knows to move quickly, since Uncle Ken has to be home by six thirty. That's when his favorite TV program, *Antiques Roadshow*, starts.

"How are things, Ken?" the waiter asks.

"Oh, very well, thank you!" Uncle Ken replies, beaming.

By now Uncle Ken and I have become firm regulars. Uncle Ken is greeted with huge smiles by the staff, who have come to adore his giggle, his happiness, his tweed jackets. They always save us the seat by the window. Uncle Ken and I have come here a startling number of times. Thus, Uncle Ken has at least twenty or so Grill House frequent-visitor cards. These give you a free bottle of wine on the fifth visit and a free meal on the sixth visit. We always manage to misplace them after the fourth visit, so by now we'd be due for many, many free meals. My uncle never seems to mind.

"It's all go-go-go once you're off, Oliver," Uncle Ken says. "The gang is going to Dunfermline this weekend, then Perthshire the weekend after."

I smile. And then I lean into the table. Because even amid the bustle of other diners and the noise from the kitchen, we're in our own world, and I don't want to leave it just yet. Because as I've grown to love St. Andrews, I realize I've also grown to love Uncle Ken. And as Uncle Ken starts telling me about an upcoming caravan trip to Loch Lomond, and how beautiful he finds the area, all I can think about is how much I'm going to miss my friend.

. . .

"Horovitz. Where the hell are you?"

Patrick's text message bleeps from my phone. There are eight more texts from other caddies just like it. I shoot back the same reply—"Packing!"—then continue feverishly throwing clothes into my suitcase with remarkable speed and disorganization. Patrick texts me back: "We're all at the Raisin. Get involved."

This is my last chance to see the boys; I don't need any more prodding. I leave my packing half finished and rush out to join my friends.

The Raisin is located on the end of Hope Street; it's a pub sporting the smallest pool table in St. Andrews. When I walk in, I find Iain, Rory, Swedish Olle, Jono, Ross, Chris, and Russell already there. It's not hard to spot them; they're the seven most sunburned people in the room. Greaves and Gordy soon arrive, and together, we order the largest bottles of Moët champagne available (with the caddie wads of twenties and fifties all stuffed into our wallets). Loudly, we begin our toasts.

"To the shack!" Patrick yells.

"To St. Andrews!" Jono replies.

"To Ollie!" Greaves yells.

"To Tiger Woods!" Iain adds.

"To Rick Mackenzie!" Olle shouts.

Pitchers of Tennent's lager are bought. Patrick yells, "See these away, boys!" and as is customary, we down our pints.

When the pub shuts at one A.M. and we all spill out into the street, someone offhandedly suggests that we play the Jubilee Course one final time. Somehow, in our inebriated states, this sounds like a great idea, and we all run to our flats, grab our clubs and caddie jackets, and charge down to the course, copious beers in hands. Using cell phones to illuminate greens just enough to grab serious and accurate putt reads, we stage a competitive, boisterous, eight-player match in the pitch-dark, making our way out impressively far into the back nine. Astonishingly, we lose only one ball the entire round.

At four A.M., we say our good-byes in the middle of Market Street, clubs still on our backs, grins on our faces. My head is spinning, and I've got to be up in four hours. I'm not even close to finished packing yet. In my immediate future, I've got a Carnoustie-difficult wakeup, an endless trip homeward, and sophomore-year Harvard classes to choose. But for now I don't care. For the moment, everything is perfect. Everything is glorious. Everything just feels right. A seagull screeches overhead. The traffic light changes unnecessarily in the empty street.

"See you next summer!" I shout over my shoulder.

"You better!" the others reply.

And as our motley crew of caddies parts ways in Market Street, the seagulls now beginning to awaken from their roof perches, we all let out one final caddie chorus that echoes down toward North Street, reverberating back to the shack:

"*FOOOOOAAAHHHHHHHH!*"

PART
THREE

TWENTY-NINE

"So, Ollie, what's your project idea?"

Robb Moss, my Visual and Environmental Studies 50 professor, is staring across at me. His hands are tucked into his vest jacket, and behind his beard, there's a hopeful smile. Next to Robb sits his teaching assistant. She's eagerly clutching a notepad and pen, poised to capture my every thought.

"Ummmm . . ."

She could be poised for quite a while. I have zero ideas.

It's April. I'm in the middle of Robb's office, in the middle of Harvard Yard, in the middle of my interview for next year's VES 51b: Non-fiction Video Projects. In my opinion, this is the coolest class in Harvard's film department. Each May, fifteen students are given high-end video cameras, thirty hours of tapes, and the freedom to shoot a documentary over the summer on any subject they want. When school resumes in September, the ten best projects are chosen. If yours makes the cut, the rest of the semester runs like a buildup to the Sundance Film Festival. Professional filmmakers are brought in. Working editors drop by for one-on-one cutting sessions. Sound technicians eagerly discuss ways to improve your film's soundscape. For a film student, it gets no better . . .

I should have prepared better for this interview.

"Well . . . uhhh . . ."

Robb continues. "For example, Mishi's heading to Jerusalem for the summer. And Sam Ellison's going to Mexico City to follow the presidential election. And I think Stephen Black is making a film about his grandfather in Poland . . ."

"Gotcha . . . ," I say, nodding my head, now fairly certain that I should've had a project idea *before* showing up to this interview. I seem to be the only applicant without a fully thought-out proposal.

"So what are you thinking?"

I rack my brain for potential subjects. I need to throw *something* out here now. At least as a placeholder . . .

"Well, I could do a thing on Old Course caddies."

I look for a reaction. When there isn't one, I nervously continue.

"Like, you know, I could maybe shoot in St. Andrews, and on the Old Course, and around the caddie shack. So, um, it'd be about the daily lives of caddies, and their rounds, and—"

"I *love* this idea!"

Robb looks thrilled. Beside him, the teaching assistant is excitedly machine-gunning notes down on her paper. "This is excellent! Are you sure you can get permission?"

I think about this for two seconds. About Rick. And the caddies. And how insanely hard that's going to be.

"Absolutely no problem."

"Great! Really great. That's . . . Hey, Alfred!" Robb calls outside to Alfred Guzzetti, the wise white-haired patriarch of Harvard's film department, who has just wandered by Robb's door.

Alfred pokes his head in. "Yes?"

"Listen to this. Ollie's going to be making a documentary this summer about the Old Course caddies in St. Andrews."

Alfred lights up. "Oh! I see," he says. "That sounds excellent!"

I smile brightly. And behind my smile, there's a single thought: *How the hell am I going to deliver this?*

. . .

They call sophomore year the "sophomore slump." But so far, it ain't bad. My roommates and I have moved into Eliot House, an idyllic dorm along the Charles River (where the crew team rows daily, at five A.M.). Eliot House is like a Winslow Homer painting crossed with a Wordsworth poem, on a heavy dose of Zoloft. Students lie on blankets in the inner garden reading their schoolbooks and eat lunch on the white marble veranda. Each spring, there's a *Great Gatsby*–style ball called the Fête, featuring a live jazz band and chocolate fountains. Leonard Bernstein lived here when he was a student. Also James Joyce's grandson. So did Ted Kaczynski, the Unabomber, although that's less widely publicized.

It's been seven months since I left St. Andrews, but it feels longer. Like, half a century longer. Truthfully, St. Andrews has never felt farther away. The Dunvegan and the Pilmour Hotel, the putting green behind the caddie shack, Margaret Squires's bookshop, and Uncle Ken's kitchen—they all feel like Peter Pan's Neverland . . . a place that maybe, just maybe, never actually existed.

Nothing feels totally real right now, as I dial the caddie shack from my Eliot House dorm room.

There's a ring, then two UK-ringtone rings. Then Rick picks up.

"Caddie department. Rick Mackenzie speaking."

I feel a shiver of dread race down my spine. And then I feel my hands begin to shake. And then, with the same level of bravery I usually display in front of Rick . . . I hang up the phone.

Well, that went great. I take some deep, wheezing breaths to calm myself down. Then, hands still shaking, I redial.

"Caddie department, Rick Macken—"

"Rick! Hi! It's, uh, Ollie Horovitz!"

I've spoken. I guess I can't hang up again now.

"Mmmmmm . . . hello there, Ollie. Are you coming back this summer?"

"Yes, definitely, Rick! I can't wait! But, I . . . I have a question for you."

There's a pause on the other end. "What's that?"

"Well, I have this little thing I want to do for my film class. It's nothing really, just a short documentary about the caddies."

"A short what?"

"Uhhhh . . . a documentary, a very small little video, just—"

"You're making this for television?"

"No! Noooo . . . just my film class. I'm a film major at university now, Rick. This is a requirement for my degree." I stammer away, trying to think of how I can relax Rick. "It's just going to be seen by the class."

"And it would focus on what?"

I consider this for a second.

"The romance of caddying. And the problems of being an effective caddie master."

"Hmmmm . . ."

I keep at it. "Obviously I'll be caddying full-time, Rick, and I'd only film when I was finished for the day, or before caddie rounds. But it's really important for my film degree . . ."

I wait for Rick to say something. When he doesn't, I add meekly:

"So . . . what do you think?"

There's a long pause on the line. And then Rick delivers his final verdict on my summer.

"Well . . . I suppose I can make that work."

The young trainee caddies. Sunburned and smiling.

In the shack

At the Dunvegan, with Big Eck and his mate Bruce Sorley (one of five people in the world to have caddied competitively for Tiger Woods)

On the sixteenth green, locked in thought over this crucial putt to get back to 26 over par

June in St. Andrews. I'd like to point out that on this same day, it was 97 degrees in New York.

With Greaves; both (finally) official caddies

With Uncle Ken, dressed for the occasion, at the Himalayas Putting Green

Please, don't ever do this.
Just . . . don't.

Rick Mackenzie, our
caddie manager

Lydia Hall, warming up before
our round in the 2007 Women's
British Open qualifier

2007 Caddie Outing. I'm
third from the left, or five
left of the guy holding the
goblet of wine at 9 A.M.

Guiding Huey Lewis to greatness at the Dunhill Links Championship

The Stuyvesant golf team. As you might glean from this photo, we broke a lot of hearts in high school.

On the eighteenth tee of the Old Course. Not a bad office.

On our third round of the day (at 9 P.M.). This is what happens when you decide to do "The Treble."

At the Dunhill Links Championship, with Huey Lewis, Tico Torres's caddie, Tico Torres, Michael Douglas, and Andy Garcia

Standing between Henry and Uncle Ken, during an important flower-scouting operation.

"Fa fook's sake!" Alistair Taylor. A man of wisdom and many f-words.

Our team, outside the shack

Model caddies, getting some ink

Jimmy Bowman, my documentary subject. Caddying doesn't get much more old-school than this.

Ken Henderson and Robert Thorpe, working the window in the caddie shack office

Jimmy Castorphin, an
Old Course legend

Malcolm Dewer, aka Big
Malky, aka the Tay Seal

THIRTY

"The use of approved portable electronic devices is now permitted."

Our head flight attendant—a tall man with a crisp Continental vest and excessively floral tie—is working the intercom.

"Ladies, gentlemen, good morning. I mean, uh, good evening . . ." (He's tired.) "Drink service will begin soon, followed by dinner. There will also be a light snack as we approach the United Kingdom. For now, though, we'd like you to sit back, relax, and enjoy this six-hour, sixteen-minute flight over to Edinburgh, Scotland."

I look about the cabin from my seat, 8C. All around me are older guys dressed in full golf attire—golf shirts, golf vests, Titleist hats—as if they might all be called upon to hit emergency bunker shots while on board our flight. One sixty-year-old guy walks past me to the bathroom wearing a Titleist backpack. I didn't know Titleist made backpacks.

"Would you like something to drink?"

A friendly-looking stewardess is peering down at me. Even though I'm twenty years old and look seventeen, it's worth a shot.

"Sure, can I have a beer?"

The stewardess smiles. "Of course, honey, what would you like?"

Count it. Our plane is pointing toward Scotland; all alcohol rules are out the window.

"Do you have Belhaven Best?" I ask brightly.

"Uh, no."

"Tennent's? Stella?"

Her smile fades. "Budweiser. Or Coors Light." We're not in Scotland yet.

Around us, the interior of our cabin (decked out in a soothing toddler blue) bounces and pitches around with just enough turbulence to remind me that yes, I am still thirty-six thousand fucking feet up in a shaking airplane.

"Budweiser, thanks."

The stewardess sets the can down, moves to the next row. I take a sip, glancing across the aisle to my right, where a middle-aged American lady with tartan socks is eagerly filling out a workbook called *The Super-Colossal Book of Sudoku*. The dorkiness factor on board is high tonight.

I should get some sleep. I press the seat-back button on my armrest and accidentally slam my seat back into the knees of the seventy-year-old man behind me. He lets out a cry of pain that is very earnest and very loud. I apologize—ignoring the glares from Sudoku lady (I've decided I dislike her anyway)—and readjust my seat. Up by the galley, the head flight attendant is beginning to relax. I hear him telling another attendant how he met his wife (also a flight attendant) three years ago on a New York–to–London leg. I put on my eyeshade. The hiss of our engine has turned more gentle now—a soft purr in the cocoon of our cabin. As I settle back in my seat, my thoughts fly to St. Andrews. My old friends are welcoming me back.

And then my thoughts darken. I remember that I am obliged to film a caddie documentary before the end of the summer, or I possibly won't get my film degree. I don't know what I was thinking when I pitched the idea to my film-department professors, but I did—and they loved it. And the caddies will hate it. And Rick Mackenzie will be an unmovable obstacle. Guaranteed.

Under the eyeshade, I have a headache.

. . .

There's something about your arrival into St. Andrews. On the bus from Leuchars Station, the homecoming happens in stages. It begins with the outermost reaches of the St. Andrews Links, when farms and hay fields suddenly give way to the fifteenth tee of the Eden Course and you are instantly seeing locals striking with 5-irons. Excitement builds as you speed past the driving range and then the back side of the Old Course Hotel. And then suddenly you are clear of the hotel, beyond the playing fields, and *boom*, you are staring *right* down the eighteenth fairway, at the Royal and Ancient Clubhouse, and stately Hamilton Hall, and Swilcan Bridge, and the final sloping green, and *there*, in the very center of it all, are the caddies, leading golfers down the first fairway, on rounds much like rounds in the year 1520 . . . and when you see this, when you take it all in, it's as if time has stood still since your last visit, as if life here has just rolled along unchanged inside a Scottish snow globe, untouched by the intervening period of dramas in your life and in the world. Just golf and divots and clouds and sky. And as I stare out this window now, down the first and eighteenth fairway, at caddies that no one on my bus knows I recognize, at a town where almost all my small teenage victories have played out, it's no different. I'm here, and my golf clubs are here, and a whole glorious summer now stretches out in front of me . . . and as I keep looking out the window, I realize that I am crying.

Ten minutes later, after forgetting that cars drive on the left side of the road (and narrowly avoiding three serious collisions with tiny

Vauxhalls), I arrive on the doorstep of 4 Howard Place—oversized suitcase, golf case, backpack, and camera bag strewn haphazardly on the sidewalk behind me. I press the doorbell. The same ring bounces around the house.

Henry answers the door.

"By golly! It's the American lad!"

Henry's wearing a dress shirt and tie, a beige sweater, and his customary tweed coat and cap. He ushers me in and begins briefing me as if we're receiving cannon fire from the trenches.

"Ken's told me to wait for you 'ere. The local shops are all out of rock buns, so he's off to Dairsie to find some for you. Should be home in an hour."

Only Uncle Ken would drive all the way to Dairsie to get me a rock bun. Only Henry would stand guard for him. I smile and make two labored trips back outside to bring in my bags and the twenty-five pounds of film equipment, dumping everything in the hallway. I'm exhausted. Henry leads me into the living room, where he turns, very seriously, to other matters of business.

"I hear you lot been gettin' some torrential rain this month. It's in all the papers."

"Oh right, well, those are in the Midwest."

"Seventeen inches, in some parts. Terrible business, these rains."

Henry shakes his head gravely.

"It's actually been pretty nice in Boston," I offer.

"Oh aye?"

Henry is obviously very excited to see me, and to get full reports from America. And I'm excited to see him. The only thing is, the heating is on extremely high in this living room (Uncle Ken always has the furnace on at full blast, even in summer), and I haven't slept in nineteen hours. As the minutes pass and Henry updates me on gardeners' club inventories, I become sleepier and sleepier. I sink deep into the sofa cushions.

"The marigolds are putting on a great show over by the Bute."

"Mmmmm . . ."

"And the wee pansies are really shooting up now."

"Ahhhh . . ."

My answers transition from sensible replies, to murmured sounds, to occasional head nods, to very occasional head nods. Until suddenly, I am not hearing Henry, or seeing Henry, and . . .

Uncle Ken's giggle wakes me.

"Hello hello! Hee hee hee!"

How long has it been? I look at the clock. I've been asleep for five and a half hours. Off to my side, Henry is stretched out in Uncle Ken's easy chair, watching golf on TV. I'm in eighty-five-year-old-hangout land.

"We didn't want to disturb you, Oliver, but I think you should go upstairs and lie down for a bit."

Ninety-one percent of my brain is still asleep. This seems like a good idea.

"Yeah."

"But first, come outside and have a quick look round the garden. Oh, and your rock bun is on the table."

I smile and tell Uncle Ken, "Okay."

I don't tell Uncle Ken that I've been waiting to hear him say that for the last nine months.

*   *   *

Two days pass. And St. Andrews is buzzing with the start of summer. Along the streets, packs of fourth-year giggling girls carry buckets of water, racing to soak their friends upon completing their final exams as university students (it's a St. Andrews tradition—years ago, champagne was used, and social status was measured by the quality of the champagne, with snobs tossing Bollinger).

Up at Uncle Ken's, I'm all moved in. My clothes are unpacked. My golf clubs are unpacked. And my camera equipment is, I suppose, also unpacked (this was done, slowly, last night, with all the eagerness of a captured spy unwrapping his blue suicide pill). Now all film essentials are laid out in neat piles on my bed. I've inspected the camera, the shotgun microphone, the lavalier clip-on microphone, the headphones, the tripod, the four Sony camera batteries, the battery-charging unit, the thirty-five Sony MiniDV tapes, checking them all for in-flight damage. Everything's perfect. My confidence level, meanwhile, has more dings in it than the Road Hole shed by the seventeenth tee box. I'm terrified about how Rick and the caddies will take to the documentary. And I can't stop thinking about the high expectations I've set back at Harvard. For the past month, I've pitched the idea (perhaps a tad overenthusiastically) to everyone in Harvard's film department. A few of my professors bragged to golfer friends that their student was making a caddie doc on the Old. This was all bonny in the safety of Harvard Yard, three thousand confidence-striking miles from St. Andrews. But now I'm actually here. Now this thing is real. Now I'll have to shoot this film.

• • •

"*FOOOAAHHHHH!*"

A blue Mini speeds past me, the passenger window cranked open. Two caddies wave out at me and honk.

"Need a caddie?" the guy in the passenger seat, Jamie Patterson, yells out the window.

"I can't afford you!" I yell back.

"No one cannnn!" Jamie cackles evilly as the car speeds away.

I keep walking.

It's my first day back on the links. I'm trudging down North Street, toward the shack. And simultaneously, I'm having the same winning thoughts as on opening day last year. *First round back. Forgotten everything. About to make a fool of yourself.* I pass the Dunvegan. Pass 1 Golf Place. Pass the Quarto Bookshop. As I walk, I obsessively recheck all caddie materials, to make sure everything's in order. Caddie yardage book. Caddie towel. Chewing gum to offer other caddies in the group. I pass the back side of the R & A, beside two club porters smoking cigarettes, and hesitate for a moment before rounding the corner. On the other side of the building lies my third caddie season, and an entire film I have to shoot . . . which no one knows anything about. Once I turn the corner, there's no going back.

I turn the corner.

Outside the shack, I see an ocean of torn blue rain pants and faded blue caddie bibs. The shack is out in force this morning. Nervously, I wander down the path. *All* the caddies turn.

"Ollie!" Alec Howie shouts, and breaks into a smile.

"The boy is back," Dougie Saunderson calls out.

"Ach, not another body doon at the shack!" Nathan Gardner shouts, grinning.

I arrive at the window, suddenly relaxed, as other caddies now—John Rimmer, Gordon Smith, Mark Eglinton—come up and clap me on the back. All smiles. I'm beyond touched by this welcome. Rick appears at the window. Sans smile.

"Mmmmm. So you're wanting a job here again . . . ," he says grimly, as if we never had that phone conversation. Or as if, last season, I'd lobbed a petrol bomb onto the eighteenth green.

"Yes, Rick, I—I do."

Rick pauses, weighing the matter and hiking up the drama to final-round British Open levels. *Oh my God—is he going to say no?!*

"Well . . . ," he says at last, "I'll allow it." He shoves some paper at me. "Fill out these forms. The new waterproofs are sixty pounds. I'll need that money now."

Lovely seeing you again too, Rick.

There's no time to overthink my caddie master's warm welcome. At 10:40 A.M., I'm thrown onto the Old for my first round back. (I determine that it is possibly not a good idea to remind Rick about the caddie documentary just yet.) In my group are four American dentists . . . and three trainee caddies. I survey this scene and observe, with a small measure of delight, that I'm the veteran caddie in the group. Out on the course, the welcoming ceremony continues.

Davie Coyne waves his flag at me from the second green. Colin Gerard gives me a big high five as we pass in the third and sixteenth fairways. John Boyne doffs his cap overdramatically on the fourth. Susan Squire and Nick Robertson do a coordinated team dance from the other side of the sixth green. On every double green, in every double fairway, caddies squint at me from afar, then march over to welcome me back. Each hole, my happiness level soars. Each hole, my confidence level soars as well, and my green reads and club selections begin to sharpen. My caddie "chat" is returning. I lead our group in sightseeing, pointing out bunkers, course features, town history, flaunting my experience over the trainees. It's all coming back.

"What's the line on this one, Ollie?"

My golfer, Mike, is gazing down the thirteenth fairway from our tee box.

"Well, I'd start this on the right edge of the St. Andrews Bay Hotel. With our draw, it should funnel left nicely. But give it another minute or so—that group in front still has to clear."

"Okay. Sounds good!"

Mike returns to chatting with his buddies. "I can't believe some people don't take caddies!" I hear him confide to his friends. That phrase never gets old for caddies out here. I'll have to try to work that in for my documentary.

I turn back down our fairway, proud of how quickly I've regained my form. Just like riding a bicycle. As I daydream about the caddie documentary, I can feel the other trainees watching me, waiting to hear my advice before giving theirs. They're looking up to me. Learning from me. Loving me. Since we have a little more wait time, I decide to go rewet my caddie towel. I stride over to the ball washer and casually insert my towel into the washer hole. It's an old caddie trick, providing just enough soapy water to dampen your towel for ball wipes, and usually eliciting awe from your golfers. The trainee eyes follow me. I'm the center of their attention, and I'm loving it. I press the handle down on the washer, then go to remove my bib. It doesn't come out. I've rammed in my towel too deeply. Eyes widening, I try again, less casually now. Still nothing. It's totally stuck. Worse, with my towel clipped to my caddie bib, I am now suddenly *attached* to the ball washer . . . ten horrifying feet in front of where my golfers will tee off.

"Okay, I think it looks clear to go now!" Mike announces to his friends.

Fuck!

Desperately now, I try to free myself from the ball washer. No luck. I perform a series of increasingly frantic lunges and thrusts—all unsuccessful. My golfers are oblivious to what's happening.

"We're starting a new press here, boys. On that building, Ollie?"

"Uh . . . yep!" I squeak back from the ball washer. *SHIT! Why is this not coming out?* I try another tug. Nothing. It's too late. Out of hope, I turn back down the fairway and have to desperately act as if I've *planned* to stand here—*ten* feet in front of my golfers. The first ball whizzes by my head. The other trainees, having observed this entire scene, begin giggling.

Not all the kinks have been worked out.

• • •

"Good strike, Ollie."

Greaves lights a cigarette, slots his Cleveland driver back in his bag. My drive's heading slightly right, but it should be fine. The eighth hole opens up a lot down the right side. I pick up my tee, then my Guinness can, and stroll over to my blue University of St. Andrews bag. We're on the New Course, and the setting sun is peeking out behind plush purple clouds. We've both done double rounds today. This is our reward.

"How'd your exams end up?" I ask as we start heading down the cart path.

"English and history went all right. Classics I nailed."

"Nice."

"Thank God they're over."

Greaves adjusts his backward cap, takes a drag on his cig. I can't believe he's about to be a senior. It feels like the last time I was in St. Andrews, we were barely freshmen. Time can move so fucking fast sometimes.

"It's good to have you back, mate," Greaves says. "Gonna be a great summer."

I nod in agreement. "Until the Rotary tournament starts up again."

As nice as this evening is, as much as I've waited for this over the winter, my mind keeps drifting to the caddie documentary. I haven't told Greaves about it yet. Actually, I haven't told anyone yet in the shack. If Rick thinks that I'm here for anything besides caddying, I'll be in trouble. And by "in trouble," I mean "fired." So I've decided today to not bring up the subject of the film, *at all*, for my first week back. Instead, I'll pound out the doubles and remind Rick that I'm here this summer—first and foremost—to caddie. It is, I think, the only way I can make the project work. But it's not easy. I want to tell my friends, to recruit them for advice, especially Greaves. But for the moment, I'll just have to continue keeping it a secret in the shack.

"I'm thinking about journalism after uni, by the way," Greaves says. "Maybe try to work for Sky Sports, something like that."

"Nice! That would be sweet."

"Yeah. I think so. Any ideas on your end?"

I pause, then point to the rough. "Oh good, my ball's sitting up. I might be able to reach the front from here . . ."

* * *

"Alistair Taylor. Oliver Horovitz."

I arrive at the window for our round assignment, followed by Alistair. Ken takes our fivers. "Nine twenty-six," he says to us. Then as we walk away, he adds, "On the Jubilee." Alistair recoils as if he's been pricked by a gorse bush.

"Fa fook's sake! That's four times on the Jube this week!"

"You're the Jubilee king, Alistair!" Sandy Bayne yells gleefully from behind us. Sandy's wearing a woolly blue jumper with a thick turtleneck, which, combined with his set of gleaming false teeth, makes him look slightly like a crazed sea captain. *This*, I wish I were filming this for my documentary.

"Aye, you'd think I'd done something to upset the golf gods!" Alistair grunts.

"You workin' the Boyd Quaich tomorrow?" Sandy asks, referencing a junior tournament on the Old, famous for slow rounds and stingy tips.

"The Boyd Quaich? I'd rather push sticks inta my eyes," Alistair responds. He motions to me. "Cummon, Horovitz. Onward to hell."

Caddies don't like working the Jubilee Course. The rough is jungle-thick, so anything less than a good golfer makes life on the Jubilee distinctly unjubilant. The holes also don't share fairways, à la the Old Course, so you won't pass caddie friends on each hole with which to commiserate. Worst of all, there's no food cart.

Our golfers this morning on the Pube-ilee (as it's sometimes referred to in the shack) are from Minneapolis. My guy is a short, pudgy man in his forties. On the first tee, he tells me that he's an 8-handicap. On the second tee, he tells me that he reached for an Aleve last night, but confused it with his Viagra, and thus couldn't get to sleep. "They're both blue!" he explains. I wish I hadn't heard this story. Alistair's golfer appears more normal but also less skilled. He three-putts the first two holes, from distances of seven and five feet, respectively.

"Oh no! Not again!" the golfer moans on the second occasion, and taps in the remaining two-inch putt (it lips in). "Sorry, Alistair."

"Nae bother, boss," Alistair replies, and slots the putter back into the bag. "Three-puttin's like wanking. You're disgusted when you do it, but you know you're gonna do it again."

Alistair is in his tenth year on the Old Course. He's remarkably skinny, with graying sandy-colored hair (his nickname in the shack is "Smithers," from *The Simpsons*). Alistair tends to wear plaid corduroy shirts under his caddie jacket and *Top Gun*–esque aviator sunglasses. A deep guttural laugh is never far from his lips. He has a kind smile. When I take a picture of him once and show him the photo, he remarks, "Christ, I didn't know I was that ugly a bastard!" Alistair lives in Dundee, commuting each day into St. Andrews. During the winter, when caddying goes into hibernation, he has another job—delivering roses for a friend's flower store in Dundee.

"Valentine's Day's a nightmare. It's fookin' *heavin*' from sunup to sundown," Alistair says as we trudge to the third tee. "One of the worst days of my life."

"How about Mother's Day?"

"Worse."

We reach the tee box. "People must be happy to see you, though."

"Ach, you'd be surprised. One eighty-year-old lady ran ootside in her dressin' goon last month and screamed to me, 'Get those roses away, mah son never calls me!'"

I find the idea of Alistair Taylor delivering roses to old ladies in Dundee rather comical. But also kind of cool. And it's not exactly out of character. Alistair, along with Dave Lindsay, serves as a kind of watchdog for the younger caddies. He looks out for us. Includes us in conversation. Makes sure we're okay. There's a tenderness to Alistair. It makes me want him in the documentary. It also makes me wonder what he did before caddying. As I'm meeting more of the old-timers down here, I'm learning that many had long-term careers before starting at the Old Course. John Robertson was a certified public accountant. Randall Morrison worked as a manager for Compaq. David Lindsay was a career Royal Navy man, seeing action in the Falklands War. But I haven't heard what Alistair did, until now. I'm a little surprised by his answer.

"I was a male nurse in psychiatric wards for twenty-five years."

"*Really?*"

"Over in Australia and in Europe. Aye." Alistair lights a cigarette. "You had to be rotated around every two years. And you could only do a year in the anorexia unit, 'cause it was too depressin' for the workers."

After twenty-five years of service, he found the stresses of the job too much; the wards were too draining, so Alistair retired. "Of course," he says with a grin as our golfers arrive on the tee box, "this was a nice calm place to retire to, with all these other sane people in the caddie shack!"

I'm learning other nicknames in the shack.

And wondering how I could insert them into my film.

Jimmy Reid is "Hot Dog," because of the shape of his mustache. Don Stewart is "the Dynamite Kid" (or just "the DK") because of his propensity for "blowing up" his golfers. Dave Lindsay is "the Badger," because his hair resembles that of a badger. Dougie Saunderson is "One One Five," as that appears to be the only yardage he knows to give on the course. John Rimmer is "Dr. Rimmer," because he has a PhD in philosophy. Alec Howie (also known as "Big Eck") is "Volcano" or "Vesuvius," because of his temper. Jim Napier is "Doctor Who," for his resemblance to the UK show's main character. "Caddie Longlegs" and "Top Shelf" are the same (very tall) caddie. Skinny John Henderson is "Skeletor." Malcolm Dewer, more commonly called "Big Malky," is the "Tay Seal," because he claims to have once swum across the river Tay for a pint. Grant Fisher is "the General," because of his name association with the Civil War general (a dot that I embarrassingly failed to connect until this summer—figuring for two seasons that it was because Grant owned a funny general's hat or something). James McHugh is "Scruff." David Coyne is "Coynie." Jimmy Bowman is "Boozy." David Hutchison is "Loppy." And Kenny Brown (a very quiet caddie from Kirkcaldy) is "Cartgate." This last nickname might be my favorite. While backing up on the third green a few years ago to give his golfer a line, Kenny back-stepped directly into Cartgate Bunker. When his golfer, unaware of this development, turned around asking, "Hey, Kenny, which way does this break?" there was no Kenny. Kenny was five feet below, lying stunned on his back at the bottom of Cartgate. The name never went away.

Caddies love using these nicknames. They delight in them. It's as if by using the nicknames, the caddie community is strengthened—each member of the cast of characters labeled and cataloged. Ready for easy inspection. Because of these 160 guys, you couldn't ask for more colorful characters. Each caddie has quirks, a larger-than-life Old Course persona. And as I look around at the guys in the shack now, I imagine a sequence in my video as an homage to Scorsese introducing the wiseguys in *Goodfellas . . . Fat Andy, Freddy No-nose, Pete the Killer, Nicky Eyes, Jimmy Two-times . . .*

"Horovitz, what's your number?" Scott Bechelli calls to me from his bench.

A lot of the nicknamed are in the shack right now, because it's a ridiculously slow day.

"Seventy-six," I yell back.

"Sandy, you'll be oot with Horovitz," Scott announces.

"Me, Patrick, Scruff, and Horovitz—the da-ream team!" Sandy shouts.

I don't really have a nickname in the shack, but I notice that caddies have been simply calling me Horovitz. I think it could be because people in Scotland enjoy the unfamiliarity of my last name (they pronounce it different over here—like *Hoh-lo-vitz*, really quickly). Or maybe it's because I'm the only Jewish caddie.

"Duncan, where *you* been the last two weeks?" Willie Stewart barks at another caddie while collecting a coffee from the KLIX machine. "Ah've barely *seen* you."

"Ach, just the usual blur . . . grass and flags, grass and flags," the caddie responds with a grin. He starts speaking with John White, an old caddie famous in the shack for always asking his golfers, "So, are you enjoyin' ya-shelves then?" at precisely the wrong moments, such as during violent downpours when his golfers are clearly soaked and miserable.

"Colin Donaldson, Neil Gibson," the shack speaker blares. Colin and Neil stand up.

"Watch yourself, boys—lotta danger out there," Big Eck says, motioning toward the Old Course and her golfers.

I settle back into my seat with a shack coffee (white, no sugar) and the *Sun* (naked page 3 girl). It's fun being here, in the shack with the boys. Especially on crowded days like this one. Every ten minutes, more guys come off the course and back into the shack—each immediately launching into some version of "Fa fook's sake!" upon reentry. A steady wave of fresh faces and wide grins and tales of terror. I know that any of these guys would make an amazing subject for a documentary. This excites me. And terrifies me. Each moment that I think of the documentary, I think of Rick firing me and of being sent home without a job . . . without money . . . without the film needed for my film degree.

Paddy Buist enters the shack, fresh off the eighteenth green, folding up his caddie bib. He's a former kickboxing champion and current member of Scotland's leading AC/DC tribute band. David Coyne's in right behind him, off the same round.

"Ya won't believe this one," Coynie announces in his thick Scottish accent. "My guy asks me on the third hole what part of *England* ahm from!"

All Scottish caddies within earshot moan. For Scots, this is the equivalent of tossing scalding tea into their eyes. (As legend has it, if a Scotsman was in a room with an Englishman, a German, and a Russian, and had only two bullets in his gun, he would shoot the Englishman twice.) Coynie takes off his rain pants, exposing a phrase tattooed on his left calf that is the classic caddie motto: *Show up. Keep up. Shut up.* He coughs loudly. "Ah says to the guy, 'Nae part. If it were up ta me, I woulda built Hadrian's Wall twelve feet higher!'" The Scots grin. The few English caddies in the shack shift uncomfortably.

I look around me. Caddies often complain about having to wait in the shack for long periods between rounds. And it's true, hour-plus waits can suck. But caddies clearly enjoy the camaraderie of this room, being here and hanging with their friends. The thing you forget is, it's a Wednesday afternoon, and we're here, sitting among sixty comedians, shooting the shit and talking golf. It's a pretty good office. And sitting here now, among these guys, I realize that I'm happier than I've just been during the entire school year at Harvard. I only wonder if—now that I'm accepted here—I really want to jeopardize everything by trying to shoot a documentary.

"Oliver Horovitz," the shack intercom blares. No other caddie names follow.

"Ach, Horovitz, you're by yourself!" James McHugh announces with commiseration.

I grin at McHugh, grab my bib, gulp down the last of my coffee, and shuffle toward the shack door. On my way out, I glance at the clipboard. Someone's pinned up the headline of a newspaper article, which they've cut out from the television section.

The headline reads, NEW SEASON OF HAWAII FIVE-O BEGINS.

THIRTY-ONE

I'm on the Scores, with my camera.

Specifically, I'm on the Scores, in the garden of a church. Filming a cat.

What the hell am I doing?

For the past week, I've been shooting around St. Andrews. Sunrises. Sunsets. Seagulls in the air. Buses on the street. Anything but what I'm *supposed* to be shooting.

"Meeeaooowww."

The cat slinks across the grass, in front of my camera. It pauses, gives me a puzzled look, as if to say, "I am *not* going into the final version of this thing, right?"

Enough. I sigh and, from my sprawled position on the grass, click off the record button. I peer at the time code: 47:06:31. Brilliant. I've just shot forty-seven minutes tonight of absolutely nothing. I stand up, wipe off my trousers, and grab my camera. This is ridiculous. I need to start shooting at the shack. Otherwise, I'm going to be showing my class twenty-nine hours of cat moves . . . and editing the world's most boring nature documentary ever conceived.

I head out of the garden and make a left down the road . . . in the opposite direction from the Old Course.

The truth is, I'm terrified to get started. I mean, really started. To face the caddies and my caddie master. To endanger what I already have—my friendships with the other caddies, my place in the shack. Am I being paranoid? Maybe. I don't know. But I do know that I don't want to upset Rick.

Give it a few more days, I tell myself as I head toward a row of red roses—and press record.

. . .

The e-mail message in my inbox is simple.

> *Dear 51b Students,*
>
> *Please update me as to how the projects are progressing.*
>
> *Thanks,*
> *Robb Moss*

I reread the e-mail for the tenth time, my heart beating slightly faster than a cardiac version of "Flight of the Bumblebee." How is my project progressing? Well, let's see . . . I haven't shot a single frame of meaningful footage yet. My camera bag is actually, at this moment, at the back of my closet, underneath three dirty golf shirts and two cataclysmically smelly golf shoes. And worst of all, I haven't brought up the subject of the film again to Rick.

It's not that I don't want to get started. I really do. Every day, things are happening in the shack that would be so great on camera. But I know that if I upset Rick, if I anger caddies in the shack, I'll have a problem. The thing is, though, I already have a problem. I've sold this idea to my academic adviser and gotten Harvard's film department excited about it. I've arranged my film courses around this. If I somehow back out of this film now, I'm going to screw up my degree track for next year. I feel trapped. Perhaps I should just be honest with Robb. Tell him what's going on. Man to man. The truth. That I haven't shot anything. I think about this for a second, then tap "reply" on the e-mail.

Hey Robb,

Progressing really well.

Ollie

. . .

"Over a little more! Oh yes, that one!"

Uncle Ken points decisively up to the top of the rosebush. He's speaking loudly . . . because he's eight feet below me . . . because at the moment, I'm perched precariously on top of his 1940s wooden garden ladder.

"This one?" I'm leaning out so far to the right, I'm not sure I can keep my balance much longer.

"Let me see. Oh no, not that one. No, further right."

I stretch out even farther. This is becoming alarmingly acrobatic. "*This* one?"

"Hang on a moment . . . Oh yes, we'll have that off." With a final lunge, I snip with the clippers. The deadheaded petals fall to the plant bed below. Count it. I make a frantic move back for the ladder, and safety, as I hear below me a cheery "Hee hee hee." Uncle Ken is, as my Scottish friends would say, "loving it."

"I see a couple more behind this branch, Uncle Ken. Shall I cut them off?"

"Okay . . . Okay," Uncle Ken answers in a funny, resigned way, as if I've just asked him for an ice cream cone before finishing the roses. I pull myself in for my next deadheading target as below me,

167

my great-uncle potters about the lawn, inspecting the pansies, pulling back the pink daisies, digging out a dandelion here and there. Doing his bit.

"Be careful, you know, Oliver," Uncle Ken calls out. "I don't want you falling into those rose thorns!"

"I'll be okay!" I mumble back from the midst of the thicket, which prompts another giggle from my gardening partner. We've been out here for an hour now, working away together as the wind dies down and sunlight streams in lazily over the lawn. It's Scottish summer at its best—not steamy, but perfectly pleasant, sunny, still. Sparrows chatter overhead. Bees dart between flower petals. The outside world doesn't matter. This garden doesn't know old age, or sickness, or digital videotapes. It's just flowers, and green beans, and standing beside your great-uncle.

"Now then," Uncle Ken announces, looking at his wristwatch, "do one more deadhead, then I want to see the weather program quickly, and we'll shoot off for the Grill House."

"Sounds good." I look over at my eighty-five-year-old great-uncle, once a much-feared RAF squadron leader, gunning down Nazi plane after Nazi plane. Now he's leading a crew of one (me) deadheading roses. I think about what's important in life—about spending time with the people who matter. Your dad on a golf course. Your great-uncle and his green beans. But I also think about courage. And how facing my fear of this film project is nothing if Uncle Ken can bravely face old age, and face it with a giggle. I've made a decision.

I reach up and snip off the last rosebud. Then I call out.

"Hey, Uncle Ken?"

"Yes, Ollie?"

"I've got something to tell you."

Uncle Ken walks over. "Yes, what is it?"

"This summer, I'm going to be shooting a documentary about caddying. For my film class."

Uncle Ken considers what I've said, then puts in his twopence. "Oh, that sounds exciting."

"Yeah, I'm going to ask Rick about it tomorrow. But later in the summer, could I maybe film you and Henry?"

Uncle Ken picks up a garden spade. "Yes, yes, of course. That would be super." I feel better. I've got one subject at least. Although my mentors in the film department will probably notice if my caddie documentary features only Uncle Ken and Henry eating rock buns, and no caddies. Uncle Ken starts walking for the house and calls back to me, putting things in perspective.

"Come along, though, we've got a six fifteen reservation at the Grill House, and we *cannot* be late."

THIRTY-TWO

"Uh, Rick, can I speak to you for a second?"

I hover nervously by the window. The shack phone is ringing off the hook, and Rick looks angry. This might not be the best time. Actually, this might *really* not be the best time.

"Yes . . . what is it?" Rick responds with a frown deeper than the Atlantic. It's too late to back out now. I glance around and see that there are twenty caddies near the window. I don't particularly want to have this conversation out in the open.

"Actually, Rick, can I speak to you for a second, in your office?"

Rick looks me up and down. "No. Not right now. *No!* We're too busy." Rick closes the window and leaves me standing outside. A little embarrassed, I back-step to the fence, as Rick now reopens the window. Three and a half seconds have passed. Perhaps fewer.

"Okay. Now I can see you."

I troop into the shack, but instead of turning left for the caddie room, I make a right, into the office. It always feels wrong to be in here. Illegal. This is Rick's territory. And as a caddie, you're usually inside only when you're in trouble. When you're in danger.

Rick closes the door. "Yes? What is it?"

I take a seat, determined to not let my voice tremble.

"So, um, Rick . . ." My voice is definitely trembling. "I know that I mentioned to you . . . earlier . . . that I'd be shooting a documentary for my film class. About caddying . . ."

Rick isn't saying anything. I take this to be a good sign.

"And I just wanted you to know that I was hoping to start filming a little bit around—"

Rick cuts me off. "Mmmmmm. See, this is what I was afraid of . . ." He sits up. *Oh shit.* "You're not here to caddie. When I agreed to take you back this year, I agreed to take you back as a caddie . . ." Rick's voice is growing louder, angrier. "I expected a bit of commitment, but see, this is too much . . ."

My eyes are Battle of the Bulge bulging. Am I about to get sent up the road? "No, Rick, I *am*—"

"*No*, you're always trying to interrupt me, mate, and talk around everything, but I don't like where you're—"

"Rick, you don't understand—"

"Oh, I *do* understand! I thought long and hard before I agreed to take you back, mate! After your affair with the blonde who tried to caddie illegally, it was clear . . ."

I have to say something. Anything. This is crazy.

"Wait, Rick, *please* let me finish. I was about to say that I wanted to film *you*, first of all. To show how much you've done here. You're an important part of this documentary."

There is silence. My whole body is shaking now. I'm terrified. Finally my caddie master breaks the silence, and speaks.

"Well, I might be able to do Tuesday."

• • •

I'm getting more respect from other caddies in the shack. When I ride my bike down on some mornings, a whole bench of seated guys will nod. Even the more veteran caddies have begun taking an interest in me. Using me as a resource for various questions about America or other cultural issues (yesterday, I got a text from caddie Craig Robertson, with the message "hey ollie what does mozzletoff mean in jewish?").

Like anyplace, perhaps, the caddie shack rewards experience. Not that being on my third caddie season is anything to give out prizes for. But it ain't nothing. I'm realizing, too, that no matter how good a caddie you are, being in your first or second season means that guys will be less friendly to you. Even for older guys, age on its own isn't enough down here. Sixty-year-old guys will be called out in the shack by twenty-one-year-olds, for mistakes like yelling, "Get up!" to a ball that then airmails the eighteenth green (this happened).

For any caddie, actually, mistakes made on the course are remembered, and discussed endlessly. Famous misclubs don't die easily in the shack. People are still talking about how "Big Malcky gave his golfer a three-wood on eleven, doon-wind, and the ball was still rising as it went over the green!" Such airmails are referred to in the shack as "cuckoos," as in, "You should've seen Dougie's golfer cuckoo the fookin' sixth green yesterday!" For his part, whenever Nathan Gardner witnesses a "cuckoo" on the course, he will just keep walking, silently flapping his arms like wings.

It's always amazing to me that here, among grown men and women, clubbing and putt reading are the currency by which you win respect. In a theater troop, you get jeered for forgetting lines. In an orchestra, you're in trouble for missing the high notes. In the Old Course caddie shack, simply put, you get shit for misclubbing. Even yesterday, I gave my golfer too much club into the second green. He thinned it slightly, and also pulled it (I swear to God), but it was still way too much club. As we walked beyond the green, to our ball—twenty yards away—I prayed that no one on the back nine would spot us. My prayer didn't work. Up walked Jimmy Reid and David Coyne, on the sixteenth green. "Great clubbing, Horovitz!" Coynie yelled. "Keep that seven-iron out, sir, ya'll need it agin!" Jimmy sang to my golfer. I knew that this story would get back to the shack. I wanted to bury my head in Hell Bunker.

• • •

I look over my camera equipment. It's time to shoot my first subject: Rick Mackenzie.

Since I haven't brought up the documentary to the other caddies, filming Rick first seems like the obvious way to start. Even if I don't use his footage, filming Rick first will still be a good way, I think, to calm him. To maybe even get him on my team. So now I'm down at the shack, with Harvard's Sony PD-170 video camera, headphones, and a fresh box of mini-DV tapes. And now, the thought that I'm actually going to be *alone* with Rick, filming him for a caddie documentary, is hitting me for the first time. *What the fuck am I doing?*

"Um, Rick, are you ready?" I ask at the window.

Rick sees me. "Oh yes! Yes. Just give me a second!" I haven't seen this side of my caddie master before.

Rick comes striding out of the shack office, in a fresh blue vest. He looks very happy.

"Where shall we shoot? Did you have a spot in mind?"

"Umm . . ." I trot behind Rick, catching my reflection in the shack window as I pass. I notice (with sizable pride) that my headphones, plus the external microphone on my camera, make me look kind of professional.

"Well, over here might be nice, beside the putting green."

Rick surveys the spot. "With the R & A in the background. Good thought. The lighting will be strong there."

I notice that other caddies have begun staring at me and my camera equipment, wondering what the hell is going on. I still haven't told anyone yet that I'm shooting the documentary. I didn't want to until I first filmed Rick, until it was safe to let the secret out. Other caddies are coming out of the shack now—staring, motioning for others to join them. Yeah. It's definitely out now.

"Um, can we do a . . . levels check?" I ask nervously, framing Rick in my viewfinder, totally aware of how conspicuous we look to everyone around the shack. But Rick is in a different world—his own—and he is rolling.

"Sure . . . Okay! . . . One . . . two . . . three . . . testing testing testing . . . one . . . two . . . these workin' for you?"

"Uh, yup, those are good," I reply uneasily. Where did he learn all this shit?

"All right then, just cue me in—I'm ready when you're ready."

I take a huge breath to calm myself, to slow everything down. Because it's almost too much. The caddies glaring at us confusedly; Rick in front of me, waiting for his cue; American golfers staring from the putting green. All attention is on me. I've just opened Pandora's box. I've started something I won't be able to stop. To these guys, I'm no longer just a caddie in the shack. I've got a fancy camera, and our boss out in front of me, and whatever the hell this all means, I have the unmistakable feeling that the rules down here have just changed. I swallow hard and click the red button. We're rolling.

"Okay, so what's your favorite part of the job, Rick?" I ask, feeling faint.

"Mmmmm . . . well, I suppose it would have to be satisfying the caddies, believe it or not, rather than the golfers," Rick replies. He's still rolling. So are the eyes of several stunned caddies, who are watching this entire spectacle unfold from the benches. Rick sees them and loses his train of thought.

"And they all think it . . . at the um . . . hold on, can I start again? They've just been giving me the ole . . . ." He mimics their backward "peace" sign, the Scottish symbol for "fuck off."

"Sure, Rick, let me just refocus," I reply as Rick lets out a little grunt at having to wait. "Okay, go for it," I say.

"Well, okay, well, I'll change that last bit—what I love about the job . . . what I *love* about the job, is meeting new people. I've always been interested in people; I'm a kind of people's person, you see."

"What would you say is your greatest achievement as caddie master?" I ask. I'm not exactly serving the hardest-hitting questions.

"Wow . . . my greatest achievement . . ." Rick takes this in. "That's actually a difficult question. It's a very *good* question, but it's a difficult one, because there is *so much* . . ."

An hour later, Rick and I walk back into the shack. The interview went really well, I think, apart from when I accidentally stopped the sound during an important part of Rick's achievement speech.

"Got everything you needed from that?" Ricks asks. He seems *very* pleased.

"Absolutely, you were great," I say, swooning. "We got a lot of good stuff."

Rick nods. "Mmmmm . . . I just tell the story how it is, and people seem to like it."

Caddies are still staring at us as Rick opens the door to his office and starts walking inside. It's clear that filming Rick first has done the trick. I've gotten him excited about the project. Now it's time to ask my big question. "So, Rick, as we were discussing earlier, I'll be filming around the shack, with the other guys too, between rounds and everything . . ."

Rick turns, faces me. "Absolutely, Ollie. Whatever you need."

My caddie master smiles, closes the office door. I feel relief. And I feel anxiety. Rick's on my team. I just wonder if I'm still on the caddies' team.

THIRTY-THREE

"Can I help?"

The lady in the striped hat motions at me. I've just entered Fisher & Donaldson bakery on sunny Church Street, for a yum-yum. And I'm immediately in a world of delicious smells, funny ladies in funnier striped hats behind the counter, and rather odd prices. Forty-six pence for the apple tart, fifty-three pence for the potato scone, thirty-seven pence for the "supper pie." It's as if some lady in a back room (wearing a funny striped hat) actually calculated out all these prices on the basis of sugar content or how many raspberries were used.

"Yeah, hi. Can I have a yum-yum, please?'

To adopt a Scottish brogue for a second, yum-yums are what *ahm all aboot*. It's a small pastry with glazing on top. A delicacy that melts in your mouth and makes you quite sure that the icing is infused with liquid ecstasy. For sixty seconds after each yum-yum bite, I'm in a trance—minus the glow sticks.

"That's fine. One yum-yum. Anything else?"

I have a thought. "Oh, can I also have a rock bun, please?"

Striped Hat Lady looks distressed. "Ooh, ahm not sure if we've got any left. I'll just have a wee hunt." She pops off into a back-room pastry netherworld, on her wee hunt. As I wait, an elderly lady behind me talks to her elderly friend. "Ah made a wee quiche yestah-day, so ahm joost gonna have tha for ma lunch." "Oh ayeeeee!" her friend replies enthusiastically. I'm at a meeting of the Funny Old Scottish Ladies Association.

There's a noise. Striped Hat Lady emerges from the back room, looking forlorn.

"I'm sorry, we're all out for today. I can put you on the rock bun reserve list, though, if you'd like." Somewhere out there, a war is being fought, a health care bill is being debated in Congress, and here I'm about to go on Wednesday's rock bun reserve list. "Yeah, that would be great," I say with a smile. I'm about to give my name when the lady stares at me.

"Say, are you Ken *Hayward's* nephew, by any chance?"

I nod. "Yeah, I am."

The lady beams. "Oh, I thought you were! That's lovely! He speaks about you all the time!" I half expect her to hand me a secret rock bun stash from under the counter.

I leave the bakery to smiles from all the old ladies. I take a bite of yum-yum and head up Church Street to grab my golf clubs. Away from the shack, I've forgotten about the implications of my filming Rick, about what this all might mean. Instead, I'm just happy to be in St. Andrews.

*   *   *

"Hey, guys!"

I stroll up to a group of caddies, all sipping shack coffee by the fence. It's a beautiful morning down at the links. Sunshine and (thank God) zero wind.

"How's it going, boys?" I arrive at the caddie group and offer up a smile. None of the caddies acknowledge me. I'm a little confused by this. I figure they haven't heard me, so I try again. "Everything going good?"

Joe McParland turns to me viciously. "What the fook was up with that camera?!"

Shit.

"Oh yeah, that. I was about to tell everyone." My heart starts to pound. "I'm doing a small thing for my film class, and I was hoping to shoot around the shack a little bit."

"What, of *Mackenzie*?" Neil Gibson growls.

"No! No . . . that was just so, you know, so Rick wouldn't be—"

Joe cuts me off. "I'll tell ya one thing, that fookin' camera better not be pointed at me."

Neil elaborates on this point. "Or me. If I see that pointed at me, I'm knockin' it outta your fookin' hands."

My morning is changing. *What's going wrong? Did filming Rick first send the wrong message? Should I have told people first? Am I about to get into a gang fight?* As my mind races, I try to calm the situation.

"Okay! That's fine, that's totally cool! I won't film you guys. No problem!"

"Yeah, it *better* not be a problem. You see what I'm saying?" another caddie barks.

And with that, the entire group of older caddies turn their backs to me. It is a stunning, definitive move. I try to think of something else to say. But I've got nothing. Instead, I turn and stumble away.

It's scary when the shack turns on you. It can happen light-speed fast. Especially with the velocity at which news spreads down here. One altercation on the course, one bad decision to not check above the sixth tee before driving, and it'll get back to the shack faster than caddies to the food cart before its seven P.M. departure. My hope, though, is that if I start filming in the shack, with different caddies, and just get people *used* to the camera, then I'll be okay. But I need to start soon. Right now, the caddies who've heard about my project seem to view it the same way they saw Model Caddies—worthy of scorn, of scoffing, but also somehow threatening.

. . .

It's Thursday morning. I'm going to try to film in the shack tomorrow morning, so I'm doing a double today. I'm currently heading down the first fairway of the Old. Fifty yards to my right is the Himalayas putting green. And on the green is the Ladies' Putting Club. Composed largely of women between the ages of seventy-five and ninety-two, the Ladies' Putting Club is one of the most serious golf games in town. The focus of the club is weekly putting tournaments on the Himalayas (a stern sign by the entrance reserves the green on Thursdays from ten to eleven). Here elderly ladies, usually carrying handbags, often wearing pearls, stage brutally competitive matches. Most are deadly inside ten feet. There are handicaps in the tournaments. Tea breaks. Also modest prizes (usually, a golf ball or a pen). If you get a hole in one, you win a free golf tee.

The ladies are out in force today, since it's ten thirty in the morning. As I walk, I can't help imagining them in a scene for my documentary, and I point out the group to my golfer, a Spanish guy, from Barcelona. We reach his drive and now have 142 yards left to the pin. "Eight-iron!" I say, and hand him the club. "Good!" he replies, then shanks his ball directly toward the Himalayas and the thickest cluster of grandmothers. "*Oh my God! FOOOORRRRE!*" I scream desperately, then watch in horror as more old ladies hit the deck than at social hour on a cruise ship. "I think we should just . . . leave that ball," I whisper to the Spaniard after we quickly play another shot, into the burn. "No, I need! Is Pro V1!" he responds. I wince, then hastily make my way onto the putting green to retrieve our ball—forty formerly sweet old ladies now glaring at me, milliseconds from revenge by handbag.

* * *

The shack isn't usually silent. But it is now.

I'm holding my PD-170 camera, training it on several caddies in the shack, waiting for something to happen. Nothing's happening. Everyone's gone quiet. Switchy, Stevie Martin, and Mark Eglinton are sitting uncomfortably on the front bench. Meroë Wilson, wearing an orange visor with shades perched on top, is silently playing solitaire behind them. James McHugh ("Scruff") is in the corner. A couple other caddies sit on the back benches. It's early morning in the shack. The old TV (locked behind a glass cabinet—you have to ask for the remote each time to change the channel) is softly sputtering out UK music-video noise. It should be relaxed in here. But there's an obvious tension inside the room. And I know it's because of me. Everyone was laughing and joking when I walked inside ten minutes ago, but the second my camera emerged, the mood changed. The caddies shut down. Maybe I'm pushing this project too fast. I get up close on Stevie to film. Stevie sees the camera in his face and quickly turns to me. "Easy, Tiger," he growls. More guys come into the shack now, bursting with laughter . . . and then instantly stopping when they see me and my camera. I'm killing the mood. Intruding on the morning. Some guys get up now and simply walk out of the room. This is not what I was expecting.

It's now my first official day shooting inside the shack. I've made sure that none of the same caddies from yesterday are in here right now. I mean, there are 160 guys down here; *some* of them must be okay with being filmed. My goal for today, and for this whole film, is to be a fly on the wall. Unobtrusive. I don't want to make a flashy documentary full of on-camera interviews and narration. I don't want to insert myself. I want to show the real shack, the real caddies. I want to just stay in the background, observing, allowing the caddies to forget that I'm there. Just a fly on the wall . . .

Yeah, right.

If I'm a fly on the wall, right now I'm a three-hundred-pound-elephant fly. And I'm even more uncomfortable than I'm making the caddies. All of a sudden, I'm an outsider again. The American kid with his fancy school project from his fancy school. What the hell was I thinking, deciding to do this? By showing up this summer with a camera, aren't I just distancing myself from the other caddies . . . undoing all the work I put in over the last two years to earn a place here? In this highly closed world of the shack, am I about to screw everything up? A gruff caddie on the far bench whom I don't recognize, and who up until now has been quietly reading his paper, suddenly answers this question for me.

"Turn that *fookin'* camera off!" he snaps.

I hear grunts of approval from around the room. I turn off my camera. Slink out of the shack. This is not what I wanted.

THIRTY-FOUR

I'm sitting out by the pier.

I'm here because I'm feeling lonely. Which is not a great move, because sitting on a pier by yourself isn't, like, the best antidote for loneliness. But I really just need to get away from the shack for a while, to think. In front of me, the North Sea swells smack into the left side of the granite pier and roll gently off, their force slackened, heading toward East Sands Beach. Out in the surf, about ten Scottish surfers sit on their boards, waiting for the biggest wave of the day—a wave the height of a deck of cards. Three riders grab the wave, ride it for two seconds. They exchange high fives, seem pumped. Whatever works.

As I lean against the top of the wall, I can't help replaying the events of the last few days. Rick. The stares. The back-turns. The "Turn that fookin' camera off." I guess I've kind of brought this on myself. No, wait, I've totally brought this on myself. I didn't *have* to bring over this camera and shoot this thing. I didn't *have* to create all this tension for myself. I could have just caddied this summer. Played golf. Worked. Made money. Now, though, this film might not even happen. And worse, it feels like I've violated some unwritten code in the shack. That I've lost the trust of the other caddies. Maybe, by switching on my camera, I've also just switched myself back from caddie to outsider.

My phone beeps. It's a text message, from Greaves. "Heard about the film (!!!) Lots to discuss. Golf on Jube later?" I think about this, then shoot back, "Okay," and start walking back down the pier. But I'm not feeling any better. I have no idea how this film is going to play out. And that terrifies me.

. . .

I'm outside the shack, hovering near Jimmy Reid. It's almost time for my caddie round, but I've got a question to ask him. After what happened in the shack, it's clear that I need to film caddies individually, to avoid mob violence. And Jimmy Reid would be great.

"Hey, Jimmy, I'm not sure if you've heard, but I'm making a caddie documentary this summer, for my film class. I was wondering if I could interview you for it?"

Jimmy looks at me.

"No."

. . .

It's later in the afternoon, and I'm caddying on the New Course. I arrive at the seventh tee box to dump my golf bag. Another group is already there, waiting. In the group, I spot Loppy.

"Hey, Loppy, I'm shooting a documentary about the shack this summer, and I was wondering if perhaps you'd like to—"

"No."

. . .

I'm back in the shack after my round. I see Neil Gibson.

"Hey, Neil, I—"

"Fook off!"

THIRTY-FIVE

I'm out on the Old, caddying for a rather large man with a 14-handicap. He's from Hershey, Pennsylvania—where he works for, not surprisingly, Hershey. There is no mistaking where his loyalties lie. As we walk down the tenth fairway, he tells me, with deadly seriousness, "You know, Oliver, nothing can really take on the milk chocolate and almond bar from Hershey. Nothing."

We're on the twelfth tee when I see another caddie coming down the seventh fairway. He's striding alongside his golfer, taking short, busy steps, his eyes fixed dead ahead on their ball. He looks as if he's in the British Open and *seriously* in the hunt. It's Jimmy Bowman. I forget about my own group for a second and just stare out, across Admiral's Bunker, observing the old caddie in his office. As he walks, Jimmy pulls out his pin sheet to check the flag position. Then he glances over in our direction and waves. Suddenly it clicks.

I want to film Jimmy Bowman.

It's not just that he's the longest-serving full-time caddie in the shack. Jimmy is the real deal. The wrinkles, the hand-rolled cigarette constantly dangling from his lips, the faded caddie jacket. You look at him, and you see the golfing history behind his eyes. I've also been out with Jimmy on a bunch of caddie rounds now, so I think he respects me as a hardworking caddie—a (reasonably) nice kid who tries his best. Or maybe he just doesn't know what to make of me. Last time we were out together, Jimmy came up to my golfer on 14, after I'd told him to aim down the fifth fairway, and said to the guy with a smile, "Every sentence outta Horovitz's mouth ends in '*cool!*'"

All these thoughts are sprinting through my head as I catch Jimmy on the eighteenth green this evening, at the end of his caddie round.

"Oh, I'd heard you were doing a film," Jimmy says when I breathlessly mention my documentary. There's not much time for elaboration—Jimmy's golfer has just bladed his pitch shot over the eighteenth green and is now waiting there . . . needing Jimmy, a pitching wedge, and a prayer. I have to act fast. Hurriedly, I ask the question I've been waiting all afternoon to ask. I ask it point-blank . . . ish.

"Jimmy, can you . . . uh . . . would you . . . um . . ." Then I just blurt out, "Can-I-film-you-for-my-documentary?"

Jimmy considers this question as he keeps trudging up the Valley of Sin with his golf bag. I watch him go. I realize suddenly that I am desperate. I need this guy. I need someone who caddies to support me with this film, to get into my corner of the ring, to make me feel like I'm not just single-handedly pissing off the entire shack. But I'm sure Jimmy's going to say no. Everyone else has. And Jimmy certainly doesn't need to do anything like this. He's got nothing to prove. And it's not his manner to be showy. He'd never brag to anyone that he's caddied for presidents, even though hanging in the Links Clubhouse locker room is a picture of him standing beside President Clinton. And he's done much bigger things—interviews for ABC, British Open TV specials . . . actually, I wish I hadn't bothered Jimmy with this question at all. But now I've asked, and it's too late, and having reached the top of the green, the old caddie turns back to me, finally, and delivers his answer.

"Aye," he says softly, "that'd be okay with me."

THIRTY-SIX

I'm out on the Old with two cousins from New Hampshire. The men are best friends, raised in the same house from the age of three. They have matching New England accents, and matching red and blue plus-fours in a reverse color scheme that is slightly embarrassing to be walking alongside of. Clearly neither man has taken a caddie before. My guy, Jim, a forty-year-old redhead, keeps thinking I'm giving him a high five whenever I reach to take his golf club (resulting, each time, in five to seven awkward seconds of hand-fumbling). On the first tee, when I ask his handicap, his face falls, and he says, "Fourteen," with such a look of guilt that I have to counter with "No no, don't worry, that's fine!" Jim has been wanting to play here for fifteen years and has finally made it as part of his cousin Robert's fortieth-birthday present from his wife. Being on a golf trip is clearly a big deal for Jim and Robert—neither makes a lot of money, neither has left the country before. Jim informs me, on the second hole, that he's been checking the St. Andrews weather every morning for the last four months.

The weather today, as usual, changes every five minutes. Lashings of cold rain are followed by heavenly patches of bright sun and warmth . . . which quickly slip back into downpours (an older, unhappy caddie whom I pass in the fifth fairway mutters to me, "On an' off, like a hoo-er's drawers!"). Despite the conditions, the cousins begin well. Jim shoots a 39 on the front. Robert shoots a 40. On the tenth hole, Robert tees off first and hits a booming drive down the middle. I'm about to give Jim a line when Robert speaks up. "Just so you know, I'm going to replace my ball when I get up there. That ball was just for a friend. I hope that's okay." He delivers this message with near-ridiculous formality, as if he's clearing up a ruling with an official in the British Open, or as if I might disqualify him for this infraction.

"Oh, okay . . . who's the friend?" I ask, a little confused.

"Ernie."

"He couldn't make the trip?"

"Actually he passed away last year. He always wanted to play St. Andrews, so our friend wanted me to hit one drive here for Ernie." I'm stopped cold by this statement. When we arrive at the ball (271 yards away, Robert's best drive of the day), Robert picks it up and casually replaces the ball with his normal Pinnacle gold. I ask if I can see the Ernie ball. It says "Ernie 2005" on it and has a picture of the friend's bearded, smiling face. It's official: Ernie has now driven one on the Old Course.

At the end of the round, we shake hands in the fading light, and the two men do a little huddle. Robert walks up to me. "Uh, Oliver?"

"Yeah?"

"We were just talking, and um, we'd like you to have Ernie's ball."

I pause for a second. I thought they were just going to ask me which restaurant to eat at. "Really? Are you guys sure?"

Robert nods. "Yeah. Definitely. If you don't mind. It would mean a lot to us if you'd take it." I look at the men, so ridiculous in their cartoonish clothes, but also totally sincere. They seem almost fragile in their surroundings. I'm reminded of the runner in shorts and a singlet last year who ran up to the Old Course starter as we were teeing off and handed over a putter, saying, "My dad passed away sixteen years ago yesterday, and he always said when I finally made it to St. Andrews, to give his putter to the Old Course starter." I'm reminded of the summer when I saw what looked to be, from a distance, cigar ashes on the first tee, and learned they were actually the ashes of a son's father. I think about what the Old Course means to golfers, how important St. Andrews is for so many people. I look at Robert and Jim, and the golf ball Robert's holding, decorated with Ernie's face. "Of course," I say. "I'd be happy to." We shake hands again, and I pocket the Ernie ball in my waterproofs. Then I turn away and start walking—just quickly enough so they won't see my face starting to crinkle up.

. . .

"Thas quite a camera setup."

It's the next day. I'm behind the shack, in front of the putting green. Beside Jimmy Bowman. As I hold my camera, Jimmy sits against the shack wall, sipping his coffee. He's wearing a gray plaid golf shirt. His white wavy hair is wild and unbrushed. He's just come off the course from a round. Jimmy looks tired but pleased. Another round in the books.

I press the record button and think of an opening question that won't make me sound moronic. "So, Jimmy, how many caddie rounds do you do a week?" I ask.

"Well, this year only, uh, six. I used to do ten, twelve. Up to last year." Jimmy speaks slowly, thoughtfully.

"And what year is this for you?"

"This'll be thirty-three this year," Jimmy says. "Long time," he adds with a smile.

"How old are you now, if you don't mind me asking?"

Jimmy nods. "Seventy." I note that he looks older. "Gettin' on. Just about time for retiring, let the young guys take over for a change."

"Do you find it a lot harder caddying at seventy?"

"Oh aye, oh definitely. Well, your legs go, your knees go. Back goes a little bit. You get older. The bones . . ." Jimmy trails off. "You know, the spirit's willing, but . . ." He laughs. "But the bones are not."

Jimmy Bowman came to St. Andrews originally as a milkman. He transitioned to caddying, and has been looping on the Old for over fifty years. He's now part of the nine-man "senior list," a kind of semiretirement group for the old guys, with reserved daily times (and featuring men like Wee Eck, who tends a farm during the winter, and gentle Jimmy Castorphin, who's looped for Bob Hope and Rita Hayworth and has been caddying here since the 1960s). Jimmy Bowman has caddied on the Ladies European Tour and in four British Opens. He's caddied for Ryder Cuppers and top amateurs. He can call yardages with laserlike accuracy, know if a forty-foot putt breaks an inch or an inch and a half.

All this, and Jimmy Bowman has never once hit a golf ball in his life.

We continue for twenty minutes, Jimmy sitting by his pink bicycle, me sitting cross-legged on the ground, filming. I almost don't believe it's happening. Being on camera isn't a nuisance for Jimmy; he seems actually to enjoy talking about the old days. And listening to him, preserving what he's saying, feels important. A story that deserves to be told. Three caddies pass us now, as I'm filming, on their way to the New Course. I see one of them glance at Jimmy, then nod in approval.

"Have the type of golfers who come over here changed?" I ask, wrapping up our first interview. It's almost time for my 3:10 booking.

"Oh, they have improved. Yeah, a lot. Definitely changed a lot. A lot for the better." Jimmy grins, then adds a final thought. "They tip better too."

* * *

Filming Jimmy works.

Somehow the mood changes in the shack. Knowing that Jimmy has gotten involved seems to have made other caddies more comfortable with the idea of this film. Guys are asking me about it now. People seem interested in what I'm going to film, what shots I've gotten so far. Gradually, I can feel the tide turning.

. . .

A week passes. I'm back in the shack, filming.

This time, the shack isn't silent.

Three caddies are sitting on the benches in front of me, earnestly discussing a fellow caddie, nicknamed "Coach."

"We're on six once, and his guy's just made, like, two birds in a row, and I hear him whisper real creepily to his guy, 'Oooooh, Jim, yeh playin' so good, it's got me *buzzin!*'"

The others laugh as another caddie adds, "Ah was with him on the twelfth tee once, and he says to his golfer, trying to be to'ally clever, 'Okay, on this shot, ahm givin' yoo *full artistic license!*' . . . which is just another way of saying you can go left or right!" The third caddie has a story too. "I was oot with him one time, and he says on a putt, 'Aye, this is just left edge,' and his golfer is silent, so he points to a spot a foot right and says, 'But over here would work too if ya want!'" The caddies roar with laughter. Behind the camera, I have to stifle my own laugh.

It's undeniable—the caddies are growing comfortable with my filming. Having Jimmy Bowman in my corner is a big reason. But I also think that the constant sight of me down here, with my camera, must be helping too. Since Jimmy signed on, I've been making a regular habit of it. Filming, then caddying. Caddying, then filming. Grabbing for my camera whenever I've got a free moment in the shack. And slowly—*slowly*—it's getting easier. Slowly it's become a fact: Horovitz is filming this summer. And the idea that the old caddies are actually acknowledging this—it's beyond thrilling.

Suddenly I've got an identity down here. I have something that *I'm* doing, that *I'm* carving out for myself. And as the three caddies now switch topics to discussing the official caddie waterproofs ("We should get a deal with Zero Restriction or Galvin Green—these jackets are pish!"), and as other caddies around the shack exchange snipes about golfers, I realize that I am *loving* shooting this film.

"Okay, lads, keep it clean, keep it clean . . ."

Rick has walked into the room.

All laughter immediately ceases. Everyone stiffens. Everyone realizes they're instantly in danger—like a herd of gazelle unexpectedly greeted by a mountain leopard.

"Mmmmmmm . . ." In a kind of awkward sweep, Rick has begun walking around the room—"casually" throwing away newspapers, switching off the TV, tidying up. It's clear that our caddie master is acutely suspicious about what is being said on camera, so he's keeping tabs on the filming. But he's also hyperaware that he's on camera right now himself. A bizarre situation is thus playing out, in which Rick has a smile tacked on his face and is feigning chumminess—while barely concealing a scowl.

"Interestingggg . . ." Rick has stopped at the caddie notice board and is apparently checking something out. There is literally no reason for him to be looking at this, since he wrote and put up all these notices himself. "Okaaaayyy . . . that's good . . . ," he says as I hesitantly pan my camera back to the three caddies. As tense as the caddies currently appear, as on edge as Rick is, I am by far the most freaked at this moment. I have no idea how to handle this situation. I frame a close-up of the three caddies, then realize that Rick has moved directly behind my shoulder. He's off camera right now, and he's no longer saying anything. He's just watching. The caddies being filmed realize this too. Everyone in the room goes silent, not sure how to react. It's a caddie Cuban Missile Crisis. Rick puts down a caddie yardage book on the table, in frame. "Mmmmm . . . hone in on the caddie yardage book," he says. The joke's weaker than tissue paper, but everyone feels obligated to laugh. This is becoming unbearable. Suddenly, I'm saved by a . . .

Beep beep.

My battery's about to run out. "Gotta change batteries!" I announce loudly, entirely for Rick's benefit. "This'll take a while, sorry, everyone."

"Mmmmmmm . . ." Rick seems satisfied and walks out of the room. His office door closes three seconds later, prompting the loudest sighs of relief I've ever heard emanating from caddie throats. I weakly put my camera down. I note the tremendous power a camera can have over people. Once again, I have a headache.

THIRTY-SEVEN

"We've got young Oliver here, filming Henry and myself, talking rubbish."

Uncle Ken giggles his giggle. Then he puts down the phone. "That was Pat McClaridge, of the caravan gang." As my uncle leads me into the kitchen, he smiles brightly. "Busy morning here, you know! I've got the plumber upstairs! I've got *Henry* here!"

Henry is here indeed. He's sitting at the end of the kitchen table, cup of tea at the ready, digestive biscuit in his left hand, his long legs stretched out under the table. He looks *very* comfortable.

"Your lot, your president, he was speakin' over the television last night."

The kitchen table is packed with essential items for a St. Andrews Saturday morning. Biscuit tins. Newspapers. Chocolates. And, it seems, a never-ending replenishment of cups of tea. I once read a George Orwell essay arguing that the British Empire is held together solely by cups of tea. Orwell certainly got it right for this corner of the empire.

"And I was at the church yesterday, for the funeral, and what a lovely service it was," Henry says. "There were eight hundred of us in the church."

As Henry speaks, Uncle Ken (drinking tea) pores over the St. Andrews local paper—*The Citizen*. The two are in their "casual" clothes—sweater-vests over dress shirts and ties. Outside, a symphony of seagull calls leaks into the 4 Howard Place gen meeting.

"That was the young lad, he was only sixty-seven. And he shook hands with me the day before he died. Died out on the golf course."

"Terrible, really," Uncle Ken remarks.

The two dapper gents chew biscuits together in silence for a few moments, thinking of another fallen friend. Then Henry changes topics, to something less grim.

"Does this thing do sound as well?"

No, Henry. I'm making a silent movie of you eating biscuits. "Yeah. It's got sound and everything," I reply.

Henry shakes his head at Uncle Ken. "By golly, I'm blowed. The things these young lads know." Henry takes a deep satisfied sip of tea as Uncle Ken nods his head and giggles. Behind the camera, I know that this is important. Preserving this tea session forever. Because in my head, I want to make these mornings with Uncle Ken and Henry last forever.

After our shoot, I head from 4 Howard Place down to the shack, with my camera. I'm passing behind the eighteenth green when I look down and see David Coyne (Coynie) and James McHugh (Scruff) on the green. They were first out today at six thirty A.M. and have raced around in three hours and twenty minutes. Both of them see me and see my camera. They smile widely, give me the thumbs-up. Then Coynie yells up to me, past his golfers and past the rest of the group. A big, roaring yell.

"Spielberg!"

The caddies grin, wave, then turn back to their putt reads as ten American tourists beside me give me very confused looks. I keep walking, but now I've got a whale-wide grin plastered on my face. It feels as important as getting my badge. It feels like another rite of passage. Finally, I've got a shack nickname.

. . .

Over the next few weeks, "Spielberg" sticks.

Whenever I'm filming by the shack. Whenever I'm caddying on the course. Whenever I'm in town buying a yum-yum. The call is always the same. "Spielberg!" Then, following the shout, an accompanying hand signal of a camera being cranked (slightly anachronistic, sure, but I'm not complaining). "Horovitz," my former not-really-a-moniker moniker, is gone, and I now hear myself being referred to as Spielberg, completely casually, as if that were my real name. "The number's at sixty-five right now—that'll be Scotty, Joe, and Spielberg out next," Alistair Taylor will say, calculating inside the shack. "You should've seen me and Spielberg's golfers just now— neither of us were on the same fairway all day," Greig Stanfield will announce. "You'll need tah autograph a copy of the DVD for me," Colin Gerard tells me seriously as I pass him in the shack.

There's something bizarre, and awesome, about all this. I mean, I'm only making a thirty-minute video for my film class. *Jurassic Park IV: St. Andrews* this is not. But for the caddies, this is enough. In the shack, in the context of this world, this little video makes me "Spielberg." And maybe this *is* a big deal. Maybe this is a start. Maybe if I can tackle this film and succeed, then I'll have proven that I can make a film in any environment. That I can be a filmmaker.

THIRTY-EIGHT

"Spielberg!"

David Field, a younger caddie from Guardbridge, is waving to me from the middle of the first fairway. "What's up, Dave!" I yell back as I walk up the path from Granny Clark's Wynd to the shack. Alistair Taylor, also in the group, grins at me and does the camera-cranking hand motion. It's a perfect morning, warm and windless, and as I get to the window—thoughts of a pleasant caddie round and postround filming in my head—I'm gloriously happy.

Rick is there to greet me.

"Mmmm . . . Oliver, step into my office," Rick says, frowning.

My body goes cold.

"Uh, what is it, Rick?" I ask, stepping inside and trying to sound innocent—even though, wait, I *am* innocent . . . what the hell is going on? Rick shuts the office door, turns to face me.

"Mmmm . . . I don't like where this is heading," Rick says.

"You're filming the wrong caddies. You're getting the wrong things. I'm receiving complaints."

Complaints? What complaints Rick might be receiving, I have no idea. In fact, I'm pretty sure that he's made this part up. But I know better than to question my caddie master by now.

"Here's what's going to happen, Oliver. I have a new rule. On the links, you must remain five hundred feet from golfers and caddies at all times."

". . . Wait, what?"

The implications of this new rule have hit me.

"You can film from outside this distance," Rick concedes, "but if I catch you any closer . . ." His voice trails off.

Five hundred feet. A number that Rick's probably made up in .500 milliseconds.

"But, Rick! That's . . . that's not . . . there's no way I can film from that—"

Rick throws open the door of his office. He rises to his feet, so that he stands twice my height. "Any closer, and there are going to be problems."

I rise and trudge out of the office. Rick slams the door shut.

There are already problems.

THIRTY-NINE

"Seven-iron, stay down through tha ball."

Jimmy Bowman picks up his bag, steps back to five feet. He's done his bit. Now only his golfer can screw it up. Refocusing with my camera, I film Jimmy, from the side. I'm standing two feet away—which is, give or take, 498 feet, in violation of Rick's 500-Foot Rule. But after a week of trying to abide by my caddie master's policy, in which I've recorded nothing but footage resembling Eastern European spy video with bad binoculars, I've decided to take the risk. I move in slightly on Jimmy now (new distance violation: 499 feet) as the old caddie watches his client.

"One forty-two you said, right, Jimmy?" asks the guy, a soft-spoken fifty-year-old from Wisconsin.

"Aye, one forty-two flag."

Jimmy takes a long drag on his cigarette. He looks confident, in a way you can be only when you're 100 percent sure 7's the right club. It's early morning, and a thick curtain of fog hangs over the course. Everywhere I look on this fourth hole, we're encased in white. It's kind of dreamlike. There's no wind, no noise. Only a sudden dull *thud*.

"Shit!" Jimmy's golfer exclaims. His shot was skulled. Badly.

"Nae bother, that'll be fine," Jimmy announces, and picks up his bag. Then he looks over at me and adds privately, "Sort of."

Jimmy and I have become tight.

It's a funny bond, that of filmmaker and subject. The weeks of shooting have made us close, given us a private window into each other's lives. We don't say a huge amount to each other on the course—I know enough to let the veteran caddie do his job. But Jimmy likes a chat, and if we're walking between shots and we're behind the golfers, we'll talk. Jimmy tells me about his daughter, about life in the town before the hotels and the tour groups. He tells me about knowing Uncle Ken. Which is cool, because he actually reminds me of my uncle anyway. Sure, Jimmy's fifteen years younger. And he's fifteen light-years gruffer. But like Uncle Ken, Jimmy's a fighter. Jimmy doesn't quit. Jimmy does what he wants. That's why he's still chugging along at seventy, in a profession so physically demanding that you've done well if you're still going at forty. A profession that doesn't make your body strong, as people think, but in fact wears your body down, makes you look fifty-five when you're forty, and eighty-five when you're seventy.

"You doing a round Sunday?" Jimmy asks me as we walk to the fifth green.

"Yeah, eleven forty-four on the Jube."

Jimmy nods. "Me too, I'm in that group."

"Cool."

We share a few moments of silence, both kind of happy that we know someone in tomorrow's group. I've stopped filming, and for the moment we're just walking together as two caddies. It strikes me that all those caddie rounds I did in Bass Rocks for member-guests and club championships at age twelve—caddying for Mike Butter with his pink shorts and two gloves, or Richie Burke with his directive to stand in the sixteenth fairway while he hit 3-irons at me to warm up—that all this was somehow being stored away for the future, when it would let me get to know guys like Jimmy.

"How's the rest of the film turning out?" Jimmy asks.

"Really well, Jimmy. I think I've got almost everything I need now."

Jimmy nods. "Oh well, that's good. It's been fun, this, you know."

"Yeah. For me too, Jimmy," I say. And it has been. Really fun. I'm almost finished with shooting now. I kind of wish it were just starting again.

Up on the sixth green, Jimmy studies his golfer's putt as if it's to win the British Open.

"Left-edge on it, John," he says at last, decisively.

"Get my first one today?" John asks with a warm smile. He knows that he won the caddie lottery with Jimmy this morning.

"Yeah, give it a chance," the old caddie replies. There's a short wait for John's friend to putt out, so Jimmy continues an earlier story.

"Aye, 2000 Open was nice, because it was right before my fortieth wedding anniversary."

"Oh great! So you've already had your forty-fifth . . ."

"Well, no—aye, yes," Jimmy says, calculating, then remembering. "That's right. Twenty-second of July. Forty-sixth wedding anniversary today."

Behind the camera, I'm shocked. I didn't know it was Jimmy's anniversary today either. John grins and shakes Jimmy's hand.

"Congratulations. I don't know how you do it."

"Oh well, neither do I sometimes." Jimmy smiles. There's a nice beat, before John looks at Jimmy and adds a thought.

"I lost my wife two years ago, and I miss her terribly."

Now it's Jimmy who's shocked. "What, an illness or something, John?"

John nods. "Breast cancer."

"Oh, that's a bad disease," Jimmy says, unsure of what to say.

"She was just getting into golf. She'd loved it," John says sadly.

"Bad disease, that," Jimmy repeats. And then the two men speak simultaneously for the next five seconds, not knowing how else to act:

"If you catch it early enough, some of the time . . ."

"Yeah, we caught it early . . . but we just didn't get any breaks with it."

"It's a bad disease that, bad disease . . ."

In front of the camera, golfer and caddie both fall silent, together in the fog. Behind the camera, all I can do is keep filming. As I shoot, I think about why John suddenly decided to share this information with us. I wonder if he wanted to have the memory of his wife preserved on video. Or maybe it's more simple. Maybe being out here in a strange country, in a strange wilderness of gorse and fog, makes a person vulnerable, unguarded. Maybe with Jimmy, John felt motivated to share what he's been dealing with the last two years. I think about John Updike's short story "Farrell's Caddie," and about the weird and wonderful relationship between a golfer and the caddie. I watch as Jimmy and his golfer continue to speak privately. I don't disturb them. I'm happy to have been here with them. And I hope that being out here on the Old with Jimmy, for the visiting American, was in some way, cathartic.

The round is finished. And for the last time on the Old Course, I switch off my camera. With any luck, I should be able to get straight out this afternoon, for my own caddie round. I head back toward the shack and approach the window with my camera equipment.

Rick is there.

"I want to talk to you, Ollie."

Shit.

"Meet me behind the shack."

Oh SHIT.

Meekly, I head toward the side of the shack. What's going on? Has Rick caught me filming up close? Has someone tattled on me? Am I about to be forced to destroy the tapes? I arrive at the North

Sea side of the shack, beside the pull carts, where Rick already stands. My caddie master begins speaking.

"Oliver, I'm not happy. I'm not happy at all."

I have to interject. "Rick, first of all—I need to apologize if I've upset you. This wasn't my intention. I just needed to film on the course up close for a few rounds. I'm really sorry." I put out my hand for a handshake, but Rick doesn't take my hand.

"No, mate, you always do a handshake, but you keep having goes at the caddie shack!"

My caddie master is furious. He points at me.

"I want to tell you something, Oliver. You're going above and beyond this. But this is me, this is what I do. I started from *shite* in there, and I've made this what it is. You have your life, I have my life. *This* is my life—it's not heaven, but I'm very proud of it."

He looks at me. "Just remember that."

It is a moment of honesty. A moment of truth. And it catches me completely off guard. I'm still not sure what exactly triggered this talk—if Rick actually heard that I violated his rule or not. But it doesn't matter. In this instant, I suddenly understand how much of Rick's life is tied up in the shack. I understand why he agonizes about how it's portrayed. For the first time in my caddie life, I don't see Rick as the fearsome caddie master, a source of danger. I look at him now, in his blue Links Trust vest, and see a man, proud of his world, and proud of his work, trying to avoid the pot bunkers like everyone else. Rick, for a camera click, has removed his armor and revealed himself. He hasn't fired me. He's letting me back. But he's shown me why he protects his world so tightly, and why this in itself deserves respect. It's not often in a twenty-year-old's life that an adult tells it to you straight.

Just remember that.

I nod at Rick silently. I don't think I'll ever forget it.

FORTY

I've got only two days left in St. Andrews before I have to head home. Once again, time has flown by with frightening speed. I've now shot twenty-nine hours of footage for my documentary, and I'm confident that I've got enough to edit into a film. But today, there's one more event I want to shoot before I hang up my camera case. An event that I couldn't possibly miss . . .

"Where the fook's the bus?"

A caddie named Big Jezzer, sporting a bushy blond goatee, is standing outside the British Golf Museum. He's got a Ping visor on backward, Oakley shades, bright red shorts, knee-high white socks, and a huge red hiking pack stuffed with enough alcohol to kill a sperm whale.

"On its way. Nice ooootfit!" Switchy remarks, striding up. Switchy has iPod earbuds in both ears and a TaylorMade R7 cart bag with the name SWITCH OFF stitched into the bag's front.

"Anyone see Williams last night?" Mark Eglinton asks from behind Switchy.

"Uh-uh," Colin Donaldson says, pitching up in bright pink shorts.

Eglinton looks pissed. "I'm supposed to caddie for him, but he's not answering his fucking mobile," he explains. Tom Murdoch turns to Eglinton while sucking a cig.

"I saw him last night."

"What sort of state was he in?"

"Fucked."

"Fucked?"

"*Fucked.*"

Eglinton considers this.

"Fuck."

It's the annual St. Andrews Caddie Outing. A caddie tradition dating back to the 1980s, which caddies look forward to the entire summer. The tournament is eighteen holes, net stableford, and is typically held at a different course each year—usually because we're not invited back by the club for a second time.

It's a stormy morning down by the links, with fresh gusts blowing off the North Sea—cloudy, chilly, but no rain . . . yet. We're on the curb beside Links Road, tucked behind the R & A Clubhouse, a flop shot over the building from the Old Course first tee. It's like no-man's-land down here, totally empty. But all around us, the caddies are starting to assemble. Trudging in from every side. Caddies who are playing. Caddies who are caddying for other caddies. And me, with my camera. This is the first summer I've been in St. Andrews late enough to take part. So I'm filming—and kind of wishing I were playing.

"Bechelli was trying to get Magoo to caddie for him," Jezzer says to Switchy as he uncorks a bottle of wine. It is eight o'clock in the morning.

"Class. He could'a filled him up with drink."

"I don't think he drinks, does he?"

"No, he drinks—he drinks the cheapest whiskey ever in the history of the *planet*."

Irish James McHugh ("Scruff") shows up now, looking worse for wear. In fact, he looks like he's had zero sleep. I'm starting to see the drawbacks of holding a caddie outing on a Sunday morning. "Spanners!" McHugh manages weakly—a classic Irish insult—as the others laugh. Loppy shows up now, with a big smile and a bigger bottle of gin. "This is just for the first two holes, Switchy!" he sings. Everywhere I point my camera, there are caddies and golf bags. Guys taking practice swings with their wedges. Others inspecting each other's iron grooves. The mood is upbeat, cheery, and children-on-Christmas-Eve excited. The caddies are about to finally play, ourselves.

"Everybody off!"

Our semi-luxurious River Tay coach travel bus stamps to a stop and unloads caddies dressed for battle into the Alyth Golf Club clubhouse. The first tee time is 10:10, and caddies move to the putting green for some preround putts. I follow with my camera, recording it all. Sandy Bayne has brought along a fake golf ball, which he is tricking other caddies into using, then laughing uproariously. Switchy is off to the green's far end, sternly stroking Slazengers through a 3-iron and 4-iron laid down to create railway tracks. He holes every one.

"Everyone get in for a picture, eh, boys?"

It's photo time. Everyone lines up for a picture on the first tee. And, for perhaps the first time all summer, I witness a group of caddies smiling. Everyone's happy. Today *we're* the main event. *Our* swings are the ones that matter. As I film, and as the group waits, a caddie nicknamed Canada struggles with the camera. He tries to take the photo but switches the camera off instead. The caddie crowd erupts into jeers. "*Cummon, ya spanner!*" McHugh bellows, looking more fragile by the second. Finally Canada sorts out the camera, and the caddie picture is snapped. Fittingly, it's with every caddie holding his club in the air.

Several hours later, I'm on the porch overlooking the eighteenth green. I've been filming all over the course, moving between groups. A few groups have now finished, and those caddies sit porch-side with pints of Magners cider, watching the final pairings arrive. It's time for perhaps the most important part of the day.

"Heeeeeere's Scotty!" Eglinton shouts from the porch, channeling Jack Nicholson in *The Shining*, as Scott Bechelli and his group appear in the distance on 18. Scott Bechelli is wearing a bright baby-blue and yellow Old Course golf shirt, bright white trousers with baby-blue back-pocket flaps, and a striped belt and visor. He looks ridiculous.

"Bechelli looks like Jesper Parnevik," Coynie says.

"He's playing like Parnevik too—he's all over the place," McHugh adds.

"What d'ya reckon?" Switchy says, getting down to business.

"I'll go for four blows," Eglinton says.

"Right, then, I'll take a pound that he gets three or less in," Switch says.

"I'm in too," says McHugh.

"And me," Sandy Bayne shouts.

The betting has begun.

Everyone now turns his attention onto Scott Bechelli as he plays from the bunker, completely unaware that anyone (everyone) is betting on him. "Come on, skull it!" McHugh shouts supportively. "Chunk it!" Sandy adds. Scotty hits and leaves it in the bunker. Cheers go up from the Magners gallery.

"This one coming out?" Eglinton asks the group as Scotty sets up for his second attempt.

"It's coming out, but where it goes, nobody knows," McHugh answers. These guys are like sports commentators. Scott tries again and leaves it in the bunker once more, prompting more shouts. "Five was a good bet here, Switchy!" Coynie yells.

"The Boyne getting up and down from here," Jezzer announces, creating a new bet on John Boyne, who's about to play a forty-yard pitch shot into 18 green, from the left rough.

"There's no *way* he'll get up and down from here!" Eglinton says disgustedly, as if someone's just offered him money to shoot his own puppy.

"Ten to one, two pounds on," McHugh replies, meaning if Boyne gets up and down, McHugh would win twenty pounds; otherwise Jezzer wins two. He and Jezzer shake hands.

"Ten to one, that's a good price!" Coynie says.

"I'll take a pound on that as well," Sandy announces.

"I'll put in three," says Eglinton, and suddenly there's sixty quid (120 dollars) riding on this up-and-down.

"Come on, Boyne, we got a bet on ya!" Coynie calls from the railing. Clearly trying to block out this distracting commentary, Boyne hits, and slams a low-running pitch shot up to six feet from the hole. Then he makes the putt, dead center. Everyone cheers. Boyne simply bows for the gallery. John Wayne should be this cool.

After lunch (in which I receive groans for requesting a vegetarian option), everyone assembles in the clubhouse function room, for the prize-giving ceremony. Scott Bechelli has been around to all the different golf shops in St. Andrews and has gotten most to donate prizes for the caddic outing. He's done well. The table is literally overflowing with prizes—bags, balls, clubs, head covers, golf towels, a tartan wallet from the Links Clubhouse, and, of course, a cornucopia of different types of alcohol, capstoned by a corpulent bottle of R & A whiskey, donated by the Royal and Ancient themselves.

I set myself up to film as, standing behind the table, Switchy and Scotty serve as co-MCs.

"We'd like to thank everyone for coming out and supporting this," Switchy says, to big applause from the room.

"It's been great to see some new faces too," Scotty adds. I pan around the room, realizing with delight how comfortable the caddies seem in front of the camera. It's taken all summer, but they've accepted this now. They like it.

Neil Gibson wins first place and gets first pick from the prize table (he grabs a golf bag). He also receives the 2006 Caddie Tournament Trophy, which he promptly drops and breaks, eliciting a chorus of "Way-hayyyyyy"s from the crowd. The prizes keep coming, going further and further down the list, until everyone, it seems, will win a prize. There's a closest-to-the-pin prize. There's a shortest-drive prize. A jar of jam for the jammiest (Scot-speak for "luckiest") shot prize. And a drunkest-caddie prize (going to an old guy who can barely stand up). And now, Switchy looks directly at me from behind the table. He throws me an Old Course bag tag.

"And this is for Spielberg, for being the cameraman," he announces with a grin. Everyone cheers and claps. I hold up the prize in front of the camera, then wave back to the crowd while filming. I have a thought: *I'm going to miss it here.*

FORTY-ONE

"We're making very good time, you know!"

Uncle Ken pulls the old red Vauxhall into the new M8 fast lane. We overtake a station wagon as if it were going backward, even though the station wagon's doing seventy miles per hour. It's seven thirty A.M. Tuesday. We're heading to Edinburgh Airport. And Uncle Ken is *not* taking any chances with tardiness.

"I just want to make sure that you get there in time, so that you can have *something* to *eat*," Uncle Ken continues happily, veering sharply around a corner. He's wearing a plaid green button-down, red tie, red sweater vest, tweed coat, and tweed cap. The driving outfit.

"Yeah, that sounds like a, uh, good plan," I say, terrified about our current speed.

"If we're lucky, we should be there before eight." *If we're lucky, I'll make it to the airport alive.*

Uncle Ken volunteered last week to drive me for this final trip.

We'd agreed to meet outside my flat at seven this morning, to leave enough time for my eleven o'clock flight. When I came downstairs at six A.M. though, for some Fruit n' Fibre cereal, Uncle Ken was already waiting in the car outside, tweed cap and all. He'd been waiting since five thirty A.M. Operation: Oliver Drop-off is clearly a serious mission.

"Henry sends his best regards, by the way."

"Oh great, thank him for me."

"He said that he hopes you won't be affected by the droughts they've been having in Nevada."

"That's very nice of him."

Henry had apparently wanted to come along as well this morning, to scout out the gen at the airport, but Uncle Ken wouldn't let him ("He'd be too much of a distraction," my uncle explained as we left St. Andrews).

Outside our window, the miles between us and the home of golf are building. It feels weird to be leaving. It feels too soon.

"The gang's going up to Kelso this weekend, by the way," my uncle says. "It should be a super turnout, I think." Always looking ahead. Always optimistic.

The sign for the airport approaches, and after a few (sharp) turns, we pull up outside the departures terminal. I unload my bursting suitcase, golf clubs, backpack, and camera bag onto the curb. Uncle Ken climbs out of the car. He's not one for showy displays.

"Well, all the best on the journey!" Uncle Ken says.

"I'll give you a call when I land . . . so you know I've gotten home safely," I say.

"Super. I've got some newspaper clippings that I'll need to send you," my uncle replies. Then he does the giggle. I smile at him.

"Thanks for everything this summer, Uncle Ken."

"Oh, pleasure! It's been super, you know."

"It really has."

We do a big hug.

"I'll be back next year, I promise," I say.

"I hope so. That would be excellent."

And, for the first time that I can remember, I notice that my uncle's eighty-five-year-old eyes are wet. Suddenly all I want to do is hug Uncle Ken again. All I want to do is jump back into his car and plant green beans with him in his garden until the sun sets in the sky. All I want to do is tell him how much he means to me, and how much I love him, and how much I'm going to miss him this year. But I don't. Instead, I watch as Uncle Ken climbs into his car, and wave as the little red Vauxhall putters away, off into the distance toward St. Andrews. Then I turn and pick up my golf clubs and head into the departures terminal for my flight.

Another St. Andrews summer has come and gone . . . and so have I.

FORTY-TWO

"Paging passengers Lewis and Harper. Lewis and Harper. Last call . . ."

Around me, in the departures lounge, people are racing to their gates, to flights that are moments from leaving. I'm slumped down on the floor, camera on my lap, camera bag to my left, and box of thirty-two full tapes beside me. I promised myself I wouldn't do this yet, but I'm thinking about St. Andrews, and missing it already, and *fuck it*, how can I not? At random, I choose tape number seven, slot it into the camera. The door mechanism retracts shut. I open the LCD screen. Rewind to the middle of the tape. And now, for the first time all summer, hands trembling, I examine what I shot.

Tape seven begins playing.

. . . There's Dawn, giving her golfer a line on the sixth tee. Her golfer looks terrified.

I watch for ten seconds. Then I pop in another tape.

. . . There's Rick, speaking in front of the Royal and Ancient Clubhouse. Looking *very* happy.

Another tape.

. . . Here's Jimmy with his Arkansas golfer on the third fairway. The golfer swings, skulls into the gorse.

Another. I keep going . . . changing tapes and fast-forwarding with an increasingly feverish pace. Even now—in Edinburgh Airport alongside American tourists, barely an hour out of St. Andrews—the scenes I'm watching seem pulled from a different planet. A different era. Already, they seem like lost artifacts.

Another tape.

. . . The shack, early morning. Caddies are playing cards.

Another.

. . . The caddie outing. A picture is being taken on the first tee. All the caddies are lining up.

Another.

. . . Uncle Ken and Henry, drinking tea in the kitchen. A perfect Sunday morning. Two best mates, whom I now pray can just weather the winter.

I keep watching . . . switching . . . the sounds of the airport fading into the distance. As I watch, I feel proud. *I* shot all this—*I* did this. All these moments, all these St. Andreans' lives—they've been captured. I'm bringing them back with me. I switch to another tape. Press "play." Another. And another. I've started now, and I can't stop. It's addictive.

It's wonderful.

* * *

Outside my window, Scotland is getting smaller and smaller. New York is drawing closer—563 miles every bumpy hour. I settle back into my seat. I'm happy. I'm exhausted. I should get some sleep. I close my eyes, thinking about what just happened this summer . . . and what's changed since the last time I was on this plane . . . and where this is all headed . . . as a flight attendant's voice comes on the intercom . . .

"The use of approved portable electronic devices is now permitted."

PART
FOUR

FORTY-THREE

The party in Kirkland House is wicked good.

Everywhere that there could be people drinking, there are people drinking. Bedrooms. Common room. The bathroom. Wu-Tang Clan blasts from dorm-room speakers, slamming into a competitive game of beer pong being staged in the middle of the common room. Two floors above this, in the same entryway, is the dorm room in which Facebook was invented.

I zigzag through the hallway, finding my coat, saying good-byes to friends.

"Where the *hell* are you going?" Daniel Ross-Rieder yells. He's a junior from New York City, an English major and ardent Knicks fan, who's currently wobbling like a dreidel.

"I gotta go somewhere."

Daniel takes my exit as a personal affront. "*What!?* It's only three A.M.!"

I look at my watch. "It's ten P.M."

Daniel stares at my watch, clearly seeing three of them. He processes this updated information, realizes that it helps his argument. "Right! Exactly!"

I head for the door.

Outside, the weather's turned sour again. Whoever said April is the cruelest month didn't spend December in Boston. Zipping up my jacket, I turn left out of Kirkland House and start walking up past the MAC Quad.

I pass muddy Mount Auburn Street, then Au Bon Pain—where scenes from the movie *Good Will Hunting* were shot. I cross Mass Ave, make my way through Johnston Gate into Harvard Yard. In the dark, Widener Library looks down on me like a sleeping giant. It has huge white columns, imposing white steps—the kind of building that says, "Don't take this the wrong way, but better people were here before you."

Hustling now to beat the cold, I swipe into the back entrance of Sever Hall and arrive inside the dusty basement corridor that is Harvard's Film Department. I walk down the empty corridor, each cupboard-sized room I pass holding a Steenbeck editing table. Banging my fingers to warm them up, I open the inner-basement door, then room B-22, and arrive at the back of the room. I take off my coat, switch on the far computer monitor. With a momentary buzz, the screen flickers to life. It's Jimmy Bowman, on the fifth green of the Old. I grin. Then I get to work.

The last three months have been a blur. I'm back in school mode, studying French literature, since I've decided to study abroad in Paris this spring. I'm also shooting a film for my fiction film class called *The Bar Mitzvah*. It's about a boy who drops the Torah during his bar mitzvah, causing everyone in the synagogue to have to fast for twenty-four hours.

But most of all, I'm editing my caddie documentary. It was accepted into VES 51b back in September, and each week now, I get to present clips to nine other students, all working on their own documentaries. Then the whole class discusses, in total seriousness, how much Rick Mackenzie should be in the film . . . if there's enough time on Jimmy . . . which caddies have the best screen presence. Each week, we talk about Uncle Ken, and Henry, and where the tea sessions should be placed. It's as if I'm sharing another world with my friends. As if seven of my peers are suddenly as invested in the Seven Sisters bunkers as I am. Plus, hearing my Harvard professor remark, "Well, the Uncle Ken giggle is my favorite part of this scene"—well, that's kind of awesome.

The caddie documentary screens in January, as part of the Harvard Film Department fall screenings. It's a packed house, and as the lights go down, I'm more nervous than on my first day of caddying. The room goes silent. The title credits go up. And then suddenly two hundred audience members are inside the caddie shack as Grant Fisher tells Willie Stewart, "He was a good player, like, but the fucking Canadians can't tip." There's a pause. Then the audience laughs. (Thank God.) I sit in the middle of the theater and watch everyone as they watch the caddies. Slowly my terror begins to subside. Slowly I realize that I am *loving* this.

"Come on, *hook*!" Jimmy Bowman is barking at his 19-handicap golfer's ball, midair, as if they've got the back-nine lead at the Open. "Hook round, ya bastard!" A collective grin goes up in the audience. From my seat, I keep watch over my film as intently as Jimmy his ball, silently mouthing every word of dialogue, silently cueing every character and moment out onto the screen. I watch and I listen, and I know, without a doubt, that I've stumbled onto something I love.

Twenty-five minutes later, as the end credits roll and applause fills the theater, classmates arrive at my seat. "Awesome, Ollie!" "Uncle Ken's the man!" "I love that you had to subtitle everything . . ."

From across the room, in the professor's section, Robb Moss gives me a big thumbs-up. Pete and John, the head equipment guys who rigged up my camera gear, both bellow, "Olliiiiiie!" I nod back as casually as possible, once again. No sweat.

Mid-January arrives, and I arrive in Paris for my junior semester abroad. I'm living in the Sixth Arrondissement, with a funny French family called the Brochots. Bénédicte, my host mother, is the quintessential French mother. She wears colorful scarves, plays tennis in the Jardin du Luxembourg, and loves asking me questions about my favorite foods. If I give the "correct" answers, she clucks contentedly. Bénédicte and her husband, Dominique, share their city with me, as well as their mutual obsession with the American TV show *24* (despite not understanding any of the English dialogue).

I enroll directly in Paris university classes, via my study-abroad program, CUPA. CUPA has forty-nine students . . . forty-one of them girls. Excitingly, this is a normal ratio for Paris study-abroad programs (my friend Richard Ross's program is made up of thirty-one girls . . . and Richard).

Outside of class, I bag an internship at a French TV show, *On n'est pas couché*, the French equivalent of Letterman. I cram into late-night film screenings at the seemingly hundreds of cinemas in my neighborhood and explore Paris one baguette after the other. And midway through the year, I shoot a short film about an American boy studying abroad who meets a French girl and screws everything up. I title my film *How to Blow a (French) Kiss*. And this is how I meet Sylvie.

Sylvie is an actress. She's nineteen years old, French, studying at Le Cours Florent. She's funny. And beautiful. As soon as I meet her, I instantly forget every word of French that I've learned. Sylvie plays the female lead in my film, and I direct her, while simultaneously trying not to think about how I'm falling for her. A week after the shooting's done, I invite her out for dinner. I tell her that I like her.

She tells me that she likes me too. And we start dating. If only life were always this simple.

The rest of the semester plays out like a dream with French subtitles. I show the film at Action Christine, a movie theater near my apartment, and invite all my friends. I go to picnics on the Pont des Arts. I ride on friends' Vespas. But mostly I spend as much time as I can with Sylvie . . .

.   .   .

"Will you be in St. Andrews all summer?"

Sylvie and I are sitting in a café on boulevard Saint-Michele. It's a late night in early June. The night before my flight back to New York.

"Yeah, until August. You'll be here, right? In Paris?"

Sylvie giggles. "Of course. You have to come visit this summer!"

"I know. Definitely! Scotland's only like two hours away." I can't believe I have to leave this girl now. This feels too soon. This feels like a mistake.

"I'm so sad you're going," Sylvie says as I lean in toward her.

"Me too."

We kiss. And this makes it official: I do not want to leave Paris.

.   .   .

I fly to Newark Airport, train it back to Manhattan. I lug my suitcases down Sixth Avenue as around me, businessmen flock from offices to Starbucks, and Starbucks to subways. Carefully caffeinated routes of a New York evening.

It's my twin sister Hannah's graduation ceremony at Vassar College. That night we all drive up to Poughkeepsie, in upstate New

York. The next morning Hannah walks to the stage, gets her diploma. I cheer loudly, trying to drown out Paris-related thoughts. And then I'm back in New York City, packing for Scotland, and packing for my final caddie summer. I'm heading back toward Sylvie.

FORTY-FOUR

I've sorted out my St. Andrews digs early this year. Greaves already has a full flat, as do John Williams and his family on Market Street, but after some frantic transatlantic Facebook messaging, I've managed to bag a room through my friend Miles Glickman. Miles is a graduating U of St. Andrews fourth-year from Philadelphia who is five foot seven, Jewish, and has slept with more girls at the University of St. Andrews than any other guy I know. Miles is headed home this summer, but he has a friend, a half-English/half-Danish graduate student named Will. According to Miles, Will is 1) a hunting enthusiast, 2) very tall, 3) the owner of a flat with spare rooms this summer. It's because of 3 that I'm now standing in Will's living room, panting slightly from the stair climb.

"God, the fish are absolutely *loving it*."

Will Skjott is in his red plaid flannel pajamas. His six-foot-three-inch Nordic-looking frame is reclined out on the sofa, where he is perusing *The Economist* through thin-framed spectacles and directing my attention to the nearby fish tank.

"I just ordered this floating kelp jungle. Look—they're totally getting *involved*!"

I'm on the top floor of 12 Howard Place—eight doors away from Uncle Ken. It's a student flat, and a large one, with enough bedrooms to qualify it as an Ikea showroom. Will and his parents bought the flat (and the fish tank) when Will was a second-year at the University of St. Andrews. That was back in 2004, but he's still here, doing a master's degree. Perhaps because he realizes that my golf clubs and suitcase are still in my arms, or that I haven't slept in nineteen hours, Will presses himself off the couch and moves toward the living room door.

"Your bedroom is over here. I think I've moved out all my shotguns already."

"Okay . . . thanks."

I follow Will to my bedroom. It's huge. Easily twice the size of my dorm room this past year. There's a large bed. Large closets. And a large window, looking out onto the large garden, in the middle of which is a . . .

"Wait, is that real?" I say to Will in disbelief.

"Oh, yeah. That's exactly to scale."

In the middle of the lawn, complete with golf balls and a rake, is a perfect Road Hole Bunker replica. "The R & A member downstairs had it built. You can probably hit out of it at some point, if we ask nicely." If I needed proof that St. Andrews was a golf-obsessed town, I've just helped my case.

There's a shout from upstairs now as someone bounds down the staircase and into my room. Will points toward the bounder. "Ollie, this is Chris Hill. Hilly's living here this summer too." Hilly is a shade over six feet, marathon-runner skinny, with blond hair and a friendly Northern English voice.

"So you're our new flatmate!" he says.

"Yeah."

"Fucking loving it!"

And with that, Hilly jumps up, grabs on to the bedroom doorway paneling with his fingers, and does several pull-ups in quick succession. He comes back to earth with an ear-to-ear grin and shakes my hand. "I hear you're a keen golfer," he says. "I play off six, we'll have to get a game soon!" I nod, still a little flustered by all this activity. Will looks excited. "I know, we'll all go to the driving range tomorrow. Then we can make fajitas and get some beers in after!"

I've just met my two flatmates.

FORTY-FIVE

Uncle Ken looks older.

I don't want to notice it, but I do. His fall on the sidewalk, back in November, has taken its toll. My best friend looks frail, tired. As Uncle Ken closes the door behind me, I see that he now owns a cane.

"I have to use this wretched thing now whenever I'm up. Doctor's orders!" Uncle Ken says as he motions me down the hallway. "This getting-old business is horrid, you know!" he adds with a giggle.

I follow my great-uncle down the hallway, past the living room, and past the bathroom—where inside I spot a newly installed handicapped safety bar, plus an extra-high toilet seat. It's the same house, but the modifications are mounting.

"I've had my cleaner, Joan in, and her son, young Michael, has been around," Uncle Ken adds over his shoulder. We arrive in the kitchen, where there are several newspaper clippings ready for handover.

"Now, these are for you," Uncle Ken says, as if handing me supplies and a uniform for military training. He passes me an article on the Modern History Department; an article about the town driving range; an article about my old dorm, St. Regulus Hall. All cut out by my uncle, all loyally stored for me. "I'm not *sure* if these will be useful, but I thought you *might* want to *see* them!"

I smile. "No, this is great, I'll definitely check these out." Next to the clippings, I spot a certificate from Dundee Medical School. Uncle Ken's been a volunteer "patient" there during student exams for years. He still goes—even though, at eighty-six, he's well past their age limit.

"What's this certificate for?"

"Oh, that's for the last one I did, back in April." Uncle Ken speaks brightly. "It's all very strict, you see. You go in, and get briefed on what role you're going to play, and then a medical student comes into the room, for their exam. They poke you and prod you, and ask, 'Does this hurt?' or 'Does that hurt?' and you have to *yelp* and *moan* and play your part!" He looks at the certificate for a moment, rather proudly. "I think I was 'Stomach Ulcer' last time."

"Oh, nice."

"Cup of tea?" my uncle asks.

"Sure, that would be—"

Before I've even finished answering, the kettle has been switched on. Over here, tea questions are rhetorical.

"I've got a rock bun for you too," Uncle Ken says happily, carefully unfolding his Fisher & Donaldson paper bag. "I had one reserved for you specially." He takes out two tea mugs from his cupboard as he hums contentedly. "Henry phoned earlier, to see if you'd arrived yet. He said he hopes you weren't affected by all the brushfires in America last month."

I take my rock bun. In front of me, behind Uncle Ken, the garden stretches out in a brilliant sea of yellows, greens, and reds. The upstairs grandfather clock chimes. Suddenly it doesn't matter that Uncle Ken looks older. It doesn't matter that he has a cane. He's still here, and now so am I, and now we've got our whole summer together. And as I stand in the kitchen, eating my rock bun, with the seagulls squawking outside, my new flat eight doors away and the summer stretching out before me full of possibility—life at this moment makes perfect sense.

FORTY-SIX

Alistair Taylor is the first one to see me.

"Fa fook's sake! Horovitz is back!" he shouts at me as I walk down the path toward the shack. Alec Howie comes outside now too and yells, "Ollie!" Dougie sees me. "The King of Bad Reads returns!"

It's a normal day in shack land. Everywhere I look, I see guys I haven't actually spoken to all winter, but whose images I've edited and reedited a thousand times on my computer, dissected and analyzed in Harvard's Sever B-41 classroom every Tuesday and Thursday. It's weird to think that a whole winter has passed here. I think we all have some inner belief, deep down, that whenever we leave a place, everything just kind of stops until we return. That when we leave a small town, or a country, life just . . . pauses. It's a nice thought, but of course, it isn't true. Life keeps moving. People get older. At least the eighteenth green's in the same place.

More caddies spot me now. Charlie Little and Gordon Smith

both grin at me from the bench. Nick Robertson waves. Colin Donaldson smiles. Jimmy Bowman nods to me as he cruises past on his
bike, coasting the last few yards with both legs on one side like always. And now Rick comes to the window . . .

"Mmmmm . . . Oliver . . . a blast from the past . . . ," he murmurs.

What is it with Rick and warm welcomes?

"Hi, Rick, I'm here to caddie," I say, and hand him two passport
photos.

Rick takes them, looks at me. "I didn't expect you to come back,"
he adds.

There's a pause. How do you respond to this? "Well . . . I'm
back," I say. Apparently, this is a good enough answer, because Rick
has me fill out several forms, then makes me buy the new caddie
waterproofs. I'm filling out the forms, listing my name, address, and
passport number (why do I have to give my passport number?), when
Rick leans out the window and calls the next caddie up. "Jordan
Douglas . . . ," he says. Jordan, a twenty-year-old caddie from Cupar,
is already near the window, leaning by the fence. When he hears his
name, Jordan jokingly staggers from the fence over to the window
while emitting a low groan. Rick glares. He is not impressed.
"Mmmmmm . . . Jordan, that's not good enough. Go back to where
you were," Rick growls through the glare. "When I call your name
again, I want you to come up here with a bit more enthusiasm."
Stunned, Jordan returns to his fence post. Rick allows thirty seconds
to pass, then calls out, "Jordan Douglas?" as if for the first time. This
go-around, Jordan walks properly to the window.

. . .

"I'm just gonna do some pervin' with the Bushnell."

And with that, the twenty-four-year-old caddie takes his golfer's
rangefinder from his bag and stands on the eighteenth tee, both
hands cupped around the device as if it were a pirate's telescope. He
does actually look like a sketchy pirate as he scans his rangefinder

down Links Road, on the hunt for passing women. His white sunglasses (Dolce & Gabbana knockoffs) are pushed high onto his head, over his caddie cap. His back is to our entire group. For the moment, the scouting is unsuccessful. Until . . .

"Oh shit! I forgot about the Himalayas!" he exclaims, and swings his Bushnell wide and left, over toward the putting green.

"Oh mannnn . . . there it *is*!" he yells, honing in on an unsuspecting voluptuous blonde. "I'm beamin' her ass at a hundred and eighteen yards," the caddie reports breathlessly.

I'm on my first round back at the Old Course. Joining me are two young trainees (from nearby Cupar, home to the pub chant "Ya think you're tough, ya think you're super, but you ain't nothing till you've walked through Cupar"), plus Bushnell Kid. And on every hole, I'm welcomed back by the other caddies. Dawn Hinds lifts her club in the air. Gary Easson gives me a thumbs-up. Colin Gerard— out by himself with four Vietnamese golfers in matching green shirts—waves to me, then signs the letters "SOS" in the air.

As we stand on the eighteenth tee now, Nathan Gardner approaches us on his way to the first green. He's carrying a little pink golf bag ahead of his Japanese lady, a huge sarcastic grin splashed on his face. His shades are on, and his knit caddie hat is fully unfolded so that it stretches above his head like a chimney pot. "This is classic switch-off stuff," Nathan says through his grin, and walks away, holding the pink bag with just a few fingers, as if it were a trash bag with a dead rat inside.

As Gardner leaves, Bushnell Kid turns to me. "This your second year caddying?"

"No, fourth," I reply.

The guy whistles. "Woo! Big number." He seems impressed.

"Yeah, I guess." I'm playing it cool. But I'm a little surprised by the number too. It seems huge. Still, I feel proud of it, because I'm starting to realize that it *means* something. I'm starting to see how returning to a place year after year can pay you back. As my years at the shack keep growing, they're becoming a firmer part of my identity, a larger part of my life. Now, at the beginning of year number four, I'm glad to be back. Well, sort of . . .

. . .

"When can you come visit in Paris?"

Sylvie's French accent, when she speaks English, is almost too cute to handle. Especially this evening, when I spent all afternoon in Dundee. Outside Sylvie's window, I can overhear the high-pitched peeps of Vespa horns and Paris traffic. Outside my window, that R & A guy is hitting bunker shots from his garden.

"Hopefully in a few weeks. I just have to save a little more money for the trip."

"I want to see you soon! I miss you! My friend and I were speaking about you today. Everyone wants to see you!"

"I miss you too, so much!"

And I do. When I speak to Sylvie on the phone, I wonder what I'm really doing here, in Scotland. Sure, I'm not exactly, like, living in a Dumpster, but the five months I just spent in Paris were so amazingly different—as if my life had actually begun. And I met a girl, who is now my French girlfriend, and who is begging me to come back and see her in Paris. So, like, isn't this what you're supposed to do when you're twenty-one? Aren't these exactly the things you're not supposed to let slip away? I miss Sylvie, and I miss being with her in Paris. And right now, when I think of her from my room, St. Andrews feels tiny, totally isolated. Of course I'm happy to be back. But suddenly I'm realizing that St. Andrews isn't the only place I want to be. Maybe I've changed—maybe I'm growing up, or my horizons are expanding, or maybe I've just got this girl on my mind. It's clear to me that there are two kinds of love: the love you feel for your eighty-six-year-old great-uncle, and the love you feel for your French girlfriend. Two very different types of haggis.

"I'll start looking at flights—I think I can get over in two weeks," I say to Sylvie, as I hear another bunker shot being struck in the

R & A practice bunker and a marbles-in-the-mouth R & A voice scream, "Oh, jolly good shot!" I wonder if I can head to the airport right now.

. . .

It's the next day. I'm on the New Course, caddying for an American guy. On the first tee, he tells me loudly, "Oliver, we're going to have a *lot* of fun today!" which, I've come to understand, is a sure sign that we will *not* be having a lot of fun today. Sure enough, the man begins by pulling his approach shot into a green-side bunker, flubbing the bunker shot, then throwing his club violently into the bag and screaming, "FUUUCKKKK!" at the top of his lungs. This transitions into what I would term a "storm cloud of immense anger." He begins scolding me for infractions as serious as 1) not telling him a putt was downhill, 2) not adequately drying his golf ball after wiping it with my towel, 3) giving him "too much club" when our approach shot from 156 yards ends up 10 feet past the pin, for birdie. By hole 3, he has thrown three different clubs. By hole 5, I hate him. On the ninth hole, as we walk toward the green, the man turns to me and asks casually, "So, do you ever have to caddie for any real *assholes* out here?"

FORTY-SEVEN

I've booked a flight to Paris!

It's all set. I'm flying on Ryanair—the dirt-cheap UK airline that offers 99 p fares around Europe, minuscule seats, and flights that land in distant, inconvenient airports around Europe. Ryanair is so low on frills, they're actually debating whether to charge for onboard toilet use. None of it matters. In less than two weeks, I'll be heading from Glasgow Prestwick (a smallish airport outside Glasgow) to Paris Beauvais (a smallish airport *wayyy* outside Paris). For one delicious weekend, I'll be in Paris, spending every minute with Sylvie. I'll be trading the Eden Estuary for the Seine, haggis for crêpes, Paul Lawrie for Jean van de Velde. I've even got my excuse for missing weekend work lined up for Rick—stomach flu, a bad one, potentially flaring up exactly two weeks from now.

I gave Sylvie the good news last night, and she's already arranged a whole weekend's worth of parties, dinners, and barhopping. I'm mesmerized by this girl. I miss her like crazy. I can't wait for that weekend to get here.

It's now Thursday afternoon, and I'm on the Old, caddying for a banker from Philadelphia who plays slowly and unsteadily. He's here with three buddies from college, all from Philly as well. The other caddies in my group are Alistair Taylor, Colin Gerard, and Neil Gibson—an actorly-looking sixty-year-old St. Andrean with a thick head of cotton-white hair, who's banned from almost every single pub in St. Andrews . . . as well as from Tesco supermarket. Neil's a top-thirty list guy. And he can be a tough caddie. He's reputed to have walked off the course on the fifth hole when his golfer hit into one of the Seven Sisters bunkers, then couldn't get out in four swings. "Fook me, I thought you said you could fookin' play!" Neil said.

"I can!" the guy replied, three feet below from the sand.

"Well, get the fook outta the bunker then!" Neil snapped, and walked off the course.

Today, though, everyone is getting on splendidly, and Neil's guy loves him. We're on the sixth hole, and after a short wait (Dougie Saunderson has come walking across our path, carrying, for some reason, an entire pull-cart over his shoulder like a mining pickaxe), one of our golfers pulls his tee shot left into the thirteenth fairway. "Abraham Lincoln," Colin announces.

"Huh?" the guy asks.

Colin explains. "Dead Yank."

This round is my initiation into the on-course caddie one-liners. I've been hearing them occasionally over the summers, but out in this group today, my three caddie-mates are on fire. "That's a South America," Neil announces when his golfer's putt stops one inch in front of the cup. "One more revolution needed." On the next green, Alistair Taylor can't figure out the break on their tricky putt. "Fook me, we've got a Salman Rushdie," he says, referencing the rather impenetrable writer.

"What's that?" his golfer asks.

"Impossible read," Alistair replies.

On the seventh hole, Colin's golfer crushes a drive down the middle, setting up an easy approach shot. "Titty licker, sir," Colin says with a grin.

His golfer turns to him, still smiling brightly after his drive, and says confusedly, "Huh?"

"Opens up the hole."

The golfer, grossed out, doesn't comment.

I'm noticing that these jokes are said more for the benefit of the other caddies than for their golfers. Colin and Alistair and Neil aren't trying to make their golfers laugh—they're just trying to crack each other up. And even though I find most "golf jokes" bone-jarringly corny, the ones from these cool Scottish caddies are somehow different. They're better. Funnier. Less PG-13.

On the back nine, there are more.

As a badly struck shot bounces up the fairway: "That's a sister-in-law."

"What do you mean?"

"You're up the middle, but you know you shouldn't be."

And others.

As a tee shot on a par-3 is duffed fifty yards: "That's a Bon Jovi."

"Huh?"

"Halfway there."

There are sports ones . . .

Upon reading a putt: "Okay, we've got a Lance Armstrong."

"A Lance Armstrong?"

"One ball left."

Movie ones . . .

After a badly read putt: "Fookin' hell, that was a Rock Hudson. Thought it was straight, but then it wasn't."

Political ones . . .

After a putt lips out: "Ach, fookin' Monica Lewinsky! All lip and no hole."

And subjective ones . . .

"That's a Kate Winslet."

"What's that?"

"A little fat."

A lot of Old Course caddies out here could moonlight as stand-up comedians. I remember once being out with Nathan Gardner on the twelfth hole—a tricky par-4 with five hidden bunkers in the middle of the fairway. On the tee box, Nathan described these hidden bunkers to his golfer, who doubtfully replied, "Really? Are you *sure*?" To which Nathan responded, without missing a beat, "Well they were there this morning . . ."

As the round continues, I grow happier and happier. I love being out here with these guys. They're so funny. So cool. And they're treating me like an equal. On the sixteenth hole, another caddie one-liner is delivered when Alistair's golfer hits a low, skulled drive that runs forever.

"Mmmm . . . that's a Sally Gunnell," Alistair announces, referencing a female British Olympic track star, famous in Scotland for being, well, not their greatest beauty.

"What's a Sally Gunnell?" Alistair's golfer asks earnestly, eating it up like it's sticky toffee pudding.

"She's ugly, but she's running," Alistair replies.

I smile. This is my favorite caddie one-liner, for a very specific reason. There's a rumor that several summers ago, a man on the Old Course was playing the fifteenth hole when he hit a similar skulled drive. "Sally Gunnell!" the guy's yellow-toothed caddie proudly proclaimed. "She's ugly, but she's runnin'!"

"That's great," the man replied. "I'm her husband."

The caddie's tip at the end of this particular round was—shockingly—not high.

. . .

"I think I'm getting in at six o'clock!"

"Oh wow! That is so great!" Sylvie is excited. I am too.

"Yeah, I'll just jump on the metro when I get there and meet you at your apartment."

My Paris trip is a week away, and I'm having trouble thinking about anything else but Sylvie. I think I've rechecked my flight details about 150 times.

"I'll call you later, Sylvie, before I go to bed. Okay?"

"*D'accord! Bon après-midi!*"

I hang up with Sylvie, but I'm still thinking about her as I walk from number 12 to number 4 Howard Place, with my computer. It's five o'clock in the afternoon, and I've got another big appointment. One that I've been waiting a long time to schedule.

"Blimey! Do ya have the whole picture on this?"

Henry is sitting with Uncle Ken on the couch. My laptop is on his lap. And Henry is in a state of amazement.

"Yep, the film's all on this computer," I say.

"By golly, well I'm blowed," Henry murmurs, shaking his head.

I've assembled the gents here this afternoon for an official viewing of the caddie documentary. I've already been giving out DVDs at the shack, and the caddies so far have been loving it (I think Rick liked it too, although he still pulled me into his office to yell at me for various moments he was "unenthusiastic" about). Today, though, it's the big 4 Howard Place screening, and I wanted to be here in person when Uncle Ken and Henry finally saw the film . . . and themselves.

"All ready?" I ask.

"Yes yes . . . ," Uncle Ken replies a little impatiently (*Antiques Roadshow* is on in twenty minutes, after all). I check the volume, make sure it's all the way up, then press play. The film fades up from black.

"Well, look at that! There's the caddie shack. And all the caddies . . ."

Henry is narrating from the sofa.

"And there's the eighteenth green of the Old Course . . ."

Henry is still narrating, pointing each location out to us, as if this were a slide show. "And there's Hope Street . . ." From my perch behind the gents, I wait eagerly—because I know what's coming next . . .

"And there's . . . *By golly* . . ."

For the first time, maybe ever, Henry goes quiet. Because right now, Henry and Uncle Ken are watching, well, Henry and Uncle Ken.

"Aye, this is what I like . . . ," video Henry says. He and Uncle Ken are wearing exactly the same outfits that they now wear on this sofa.

"Now, careful, Henry, this'll be very hot," video Uncle Ken says.

"Hee hee hee," real-life Uncle Ken giggles.

"All right," video Henry replies.

"Well I'm blowed," real-life Henry exclaims. He turns to Uncle Ken. "He's got us on sound and everything!"

"I know!" Uncle Ken giggles again. And now Henry begins laughing, and laughing loudly. The smile on his face is bigger than I've ever seen. He looks back at me for a second like I've invented electricity. And as I stand behind the sofa, watching my uncle and his best friend watching themselves, I know that all the hours I logged on this film in Sever House were worth something. Because now I'm here, in this living room, making Uncle Ken giggle his giggle, and Henry laugh his laugh, and whatever this all means, whatever it is that's making my heart race—it feels cool. It feels right. It feels like maybe, just maybe, I've discovered what I want to do with my life. Still another kind of love.

FORTY-EIGHT

It's Tuesday morning—only a few days left before Paris!

I'm sending Sylvie e-mails. I'm calling her nonstop. I'm search-ing around shops for gifts to bring her from St. Andrews. I am so excited for this trip.

I'm still thinking about Sylvie as I walk into my flat after a late double round. Both my flatmates are home.

"Jizzie Pants was at the party."

Will Skjott is nursing a White Russian from the green couch. Hilly is sitting beside him.

"Oh yeah, he came with the Shire Horse. God, he got absolutely *hooned*," Hilly says. "Sock was there too."

"Why was he called 'Sock' again?"

"Someone caught him wanking into a sock."

"Oh yeah, right."

Will sees me and, without asking, pours me a White Russian—then continues his reminiscing.

"Raisin Weekend was brilliant in the flat that year, Ollie. We had a three-story-high plastic pipe, and all our academic children had to drink from it at street level. Mate, they got *involved*."

Hilly nods. "Big style. Then our academic brother started pouring vodka down the pipe while they were drinking."

"Also I think someone peed in the pipe too . . . ," Will adds reasonably.

If the University of St. Andrews had a Mafia family, Will Skjott and Chris Hill would be the godfathers. The lads met freshman year as dormmates in John Burnet Hall—located ten seconds from the Old Course's seventeenth green. After terrorizing John Burnet together (friends of mine living in John Burnet years after Will and Hilly would still hear stories of their antics), the pair became flatmates at 12 Howard Street. Five years later, they're both still here, marching semidecidedly toward master's degrees in modern history.

As far as best mates go, they're an unlikely pairing.

Will was born in Denmark but from the age of twelve went to a fancy English boarding school called Abingdon. It's the kind of school that rivals Eton, the kind filled with sons of lords, the kind that ensures you will spend your early adolescence wearing tuxedos.

Chris Hill, by contrast, is a Northern boy. He's from Yorkshire, where he went to state school. Hilly is a seriously talented football player—he plays on several semiprofessional teams around Fife. Hilly's reputation in football at the University of St. Andrews was eclipsed only by his reputation with the female student population at the University of St. Andrews. Chris, to put it mildly, got "stuck in" while at university.

The friendship of a UK "public school" boy and a state-school boy wouldn't be a big deal in America, but in Britain it definitely is. Hilly and Will spent the first few days of St. Andrews sizing each other up, not really knowing what to make of each other. What drew the two together though, ultimately, seems to be their shared love of adventure—and of "banter."

The two boys speak in code—using nicknames for everyone they know. Pinkie. Beastie. The Spaniel. Gonetta. Beaver. Sleazie. Rambo. Horsie. Teflon. Gonno Green (GG for short). Poison Dwarf. Meningitis. Jizzie Pants One. Jizzie Pants Two. Shrew Face. Chopper. Redders. The Chatten Wenches. Trotsky. Shovel. Trow. Dump Truck. Wee Beastie. The Atholl Ax. Singaporno (from Singapore; acts like a male porn star). And so on. For Hilly and Will, each character exists within a rich framework of pranks, Scottish university high jinks, and (extremely intertwined) romantic liaisons. Almost everyone I've ever met at the University of St. Andrews is known to Will and Hilly. Remembered. Cataloged. It's an anthropological study of British university lore, but with more lager.

"The Grad Ball's coming up, Ollie," Will says. "We'll have to get you a ticket."

"Cool," I say. Frankly, I'm in awe of Hilly and Will. They're so much cooler than any American college students that I've met.

"Is the Paris trip all sorted?" Hilly asks.

"Yup! I can't wait. It's gonna be awesome!" I reply.

"What day do you leave?" Will asks, sipping his White Russian.

"Friday morning."

"Fucking loving it!" Hilly says.

I am too.

FORTY-NINE

The final few days pass by in a blur of grass and flags. Until, at last, it's the morning of my Ryanair flight out of Scotland and back to Paris. In six short hours, I can kiss Sylvie again, and smell her perfume, and try to make her laugh with my laughable French. I'm proud of this coming weekend. I set this trip up myself. I made this happen. The American kid is on his way back to France.

The preflight journey is not exactly easy. On the bus ride to Glasgow Prestwick Airport, feeling extremely fragile after a caddie night out, I ask the bus driver if we can pull over for a second, for some fresh air. The heavily tattooed bus driver (doing a bouncy eighty) stares at me in his rearview mirror.

"No fookin' way."

I gulp really hard, make an admission.

"I think I'm about to throw up."

This gets his attention. Bus driver slams on his breaks, swerves us into the breakdown lane beside a field, and, wild-eyed, wrenches open the doors. "Go go go!" he shouts. I tumble off the bus into a beautiful field of poppies. And here, as forty Scottish passengers look out through the windows, I drop to my knees; take several deep, shaky breaths; and . . . nothing. Actually, I feel slightly better. I reboard the bus, having not thrown up, and nod weakly to the driver. This is not the result he was looking for. The rest of the ride in, he eyes me anxiously in the mirror, as if I'm Mount Saint Helens.

It is six P.M., Paris time, when our plane skids into Paris Beauvais Tille Airport. This should really just be called "Beauvais Tille Airport," since we're still fifty-five miles outside Paris. Muttering this to myself, I gather my backpack and switch to yet another bus for the hour-and-a-half ride into Paris proper. Before long though, the Truffaut skyline of elegant apartment buildings magically appears, with the Eiffel Tower spearing the sky above. We're passing cafés and tree-lined streets, and people wearing motorcycle helmets and Hermès scarves. People who hold unlit cigarettes in their hands before they even step outside. People who have never tasted haggis. I watch skinny, well-coiffed Parisians commuting from their offices on 1950s Vespa scooters. It seems inconceivable that Paris and St. Andrews could share the same planet.

We pull into Porte Maillot. I hop off the bus as my cell phone buzzes. It's an earlier missed call—from the caddie shack. I don't check the voice mail. I did eight spins this week. Rick Mackenzie can wait till after the weekend. I hop on the metro, ride the four stops to Sylvie's apartment. It's a warm summer evening in the city. I buy a *Pariscope* (speaking in French). I buy a crêpe (speaking in French). I accidentally stumble into an old woman, who screams at me (speaking in, I think, Turkish). It's nice being back in Paris. It's more than nice, actually. It feels like the center of the world. It feels *right*. I call Sylvie, arrange to meet her outside her apartment. There's a party at her friend's house we're going to tonight. Then everyone's heading to some restaurant in the Marais. I race the final few blocks to Sylvie's apartment. It's going to be a perfect weekend.

Tomorrow, we'll revisit my old neighborhood again, and walk in the Jardin du Luxembourg, where the kids ride the merry-go-round, and we'll visit the Picasso Museum, and *holy shit*, I am so unbelievably happy.

. . .

Tonight, my first night in Paris, Sylvie breaks up with me.

"Wait, what?" I'm pacing back and forth outside the restaurant.

"Something is missing," Sylvie says. She's sitting on the curb of the side street, clutching her knees. And killing me.

"I don't . . . You've got to be kidding."

"Can't you see that this is hard for me?"

"Oh yeah, brutal. Couldn't you have told me this, like, on the phone, *before* I flew over here?" I'm trying to keep it together. All of Sylvie's friends are inside, except for two girls who are waiting across the street, watching. This is playing out like a corny French film. Except it was never supposed to be funny.

"I'm really sorry," Sylvie says. "I really wanted this to work—"

"Yeah, me too! That's kind of why I came over here!" Everything I've felt good about this summer, everything I looked forward to, it's all crumbling in front of my eyes. I'm trying not to cry. "Sylvie, I could stay here . . . I could move here this summer. Isn't there some way we could—"

"No. Oliver. Please. I'm sorry. I'm—"

I've heard enough. I start walking away. And then I start running. And then I start really running. This couldn't be less brave, but I don't know how to deal with what I'm feeling, and I don't care. I feel like I've just been punched in the stomach. I feel like this city has just ripped my guts out. I feel like the biggest loser in the world. Suddenly I'm alone and far from home, and all I want to do is be back in St. Andrews.

. . .

The rest of the weekend plays out much in the way that it might if your girlfriend dumped you . . . and then you still had to stay at her apartment for two more nights. Which is to say, unbelievably uncomfortably.

"Do you have a, uh, extra pillow?"

I'm at Sylvie's apartment now. I've been put in the spare room.

"Yes. There ees one behind the dohr." Sylvie is calling from the other room.

"Uh-huh, right . . . behind this far door?"

"No, the other dohr."

"Wait, what?"

"The other one."

"There's another door?"

"*Oui!*"

I pause for a few deep breaths.

"I'm sorry, I *really* don't see another door."

More sounds of motorcycles and Vespas outside. All I want to do is turn the light out—to end this day. The last thing I want to do is have another conversation. An accordion starts playing from somewhere. It's an Edith Piaf song. Are you fucking kidding me?

"What are you doing tomorrow?" Sylvie asks.

"What am *I* doing? I dunno . . . I guess I'll just go for a walk or something."

"Maybe you could go to a museum."

"Yeah, maybe."

I'm in the world's most romantic city. And the girl who just dumped me is suggesting trip itineraries.

. . .

After a lot of lengthy silences, Sunday arrives, and I have to make the turn for home. Sylvie gives me a hug at the door.

"I'm sorry, Oliver. Really. I'm really sorry."

"Yeah."

"Thank you for coming to Paris."

"Yeah, it was really special . . ."

On ScotRail's train service back from Edinburgh to St. Andrews, with the Paris Vespas and the cafés a fading memory, I hide myself in an Ernest Hemingway book (*The Sun Also Rises*) and miss my train stop. I have to catch a bus from Dundee at midnight. The girl in front of me throws up on the bus. Two guys behind me start having a fistfight. Overall, this is not the weekend I had dreamed it would be.

FIFTY

Back in St. Andrews, I can't get Sylvie off my mind. The weekend in Paris is still on auto-loop in my head. Could I have done something differently? Could I have acted more mature? Was my final parting line as the door shut ("By the way, thanks a *lot*") a little much?

I'm still wondering what I did wrong as I sign in at the shack this morning. Rick's kindly assistant, Ken, is at the window. He's got some interesting news.

"There's a job for qualifying in the Women's British Open if you want it, Ollie."

This snaps me back to reality. "Really?"

"Yep. She's a Welsh girl. Lydia Hall. Playing a practice round on Sunday, then qualifying Monday. Do you want the bag?"

This is crazy. The Women's British Open is coming to town— and it's being held on the Old Course for the first time in history. Swooping in will be Annika Sörenstam, Karrie Webb, Michelle

Wie, Paula Creamer, Natalie Gulbis. Now, if this girl makes it through the qualifier, I'll be caddying in a major championship.

I nod back as casually as possible. "Sure, that sounds good." When I'm out of sight of the window, I do a huge leap in the air. I've got a bag. And who knows, Lydia could be the love of my life.

The Women's British Open final qualifier is being held in six days. It's an eighteen-hole event. One hundred twenty ladies gunning for twenty-one spots. These odds are, as golf qualifiers go, remarkably good ones. Sure, the one hundred twenty will include ninety pros among the amateurs, most of them regulars on the Ladies European Tour, but one hundred twenty for twenty-one spots is still in a different cosmos from the Monday qualifiers on the PGA Tour I've read about, where two hundred people will play for one or two spots, max. This Sunday, it's eighteen good holes, and you're in. Eighteen holes, and it's Michelle Wie, Annika Sörenstam, and Paula Creamer. Even cooler, the qualifier is being held on the New Course—a track I've played close to a thousand times.

I take stock of the situation. I've got the rest of this week before Lydia gets into town. If I caddie nonstop for the week, I'll try to get myself into "tournament caddie shape" for the qualifier—whatever the hell that means. I'll ask the shack to put me on the New Course as much as possible. I'll prepare as best I can. It'll be the perfect distraction from Sylvie. I walk back into the shack to grab a coffee, feeling better already. I've got new women in my life now. The Women's British Open is coming to town. I want in.

FIFTY-ONE

Uncle Ken has a helper this year. Her name's Rina, a sixty-year-old St. Andrean with an overcast face who comes to check in on him every day at five o'clock. This service was set up through Ninewells Hospital, after Uncle Ken's fall in November. Rina helps Uncle Ken with the shopping, makes sure he's got everything he needs. I think Uncle Ken kind of likes this, being told what to do. It's a throwback to his old military days.

"Rina said that I *must* do these exercises, you see!"

I'm over at Uncle Ken's now. As usual, my uncle wanted to see me but invented a more practical reason for me to come over ("You know, I could really use a little help with the marigolds . . ."). We're in his kitchen now, and he's just begun doing some funny little exercise moves.

"The doctor gave me a list in November, you see, and Rina is *very strict* about my *doing* them!"

My tiny eighty-six-year-old uncle now has both hands on hips and is doing some funny hula-hoop-style twirls, like a cheerleader.

"Hold it! Hold it! One more set!"

I didn't do anything to warrant the "hold it," but I don't ask questions. My uncle puts one hand on his sink counter and now does some mini leg swings—counting out the reps to himself very seriously. "Six . . . seven . . . eight . . . two more!" Uncle Ken is in the zone.

After the exercises wrap up, we troop out together into the garden. In the late-afternoon sunshine, I dig holes by the back wall for the green beans. I plant a set of marigolds in the center display. I dig up weeds around the flower beds. I deadhead roses. I water the pansies. It's rather grueling work, and I muddy up all my clothes, but it all seems to really please Uncle Ken. As I work, he potters around, occasionally remarking, "Oh, this is excellent, Oliver!" After a while, I decide to share my news.

"You know, Uncle Ken, I've got a bag for the women's Open qualifier."

"You do? Oh, that's super! Oh, I'm very pleased about that, you know!"

"Yeah, it's this Sunday. Eighteen holes on the New Course."

"Oh, excellent!"

Uncle Ken is obviously excited. I return to my work—packing white daisies into wet soil. I'm working harder than usual, I notice. A little more earnestly. I think it's my way of dealing with what's around me. As if by doing that one extra deadhead, I can slow down time. Because seeing Uncle Ken with his cane, seeing the extra fall-prevention precautions around the house, seeing the way in which my uncle walks and talks just that little bit slower, is scaring me. It's as if our body clock is always waiting to play catch-up. That if you defy it, and take care of yourself, and keep yourself young, it's *always* lurking, looking to reel you in. One fall can do it. One fall *has* done it. Because I hate to admit it, but with his fall last year, my uncle seems to have just added fifteen years onto his age.

"Are you sorted for dinner tonight, Oliver?"

I turn to my uncle. "Aren't we having dinner together at the Grill House?"

"Well, I'd *like* to, you know, but I'm feeling a little bit under the weather . . ."

"Oh yeah, don't worry about me—I've got pasta and cheese at home," I say as brightly as possible.

"Oh good!"

Uncle Ken seems relieved. But I'm not. Uncle Ken and I have had dinner together at the Grill House virtually every week I've ever spent in St. Andrews. When my uncle passes on dinner at the Grill House, I know something has changed.

FIFTY-TWO

Lydia Hall. Nineteen years old. From Pencoed, Wales.

I'm Googling Lydia. And, wow, she seems good.

I scroll down the page of a Welsh amateur Web site, scanning a selection of her tournament results.

Top qualifier—British Girls' championship.

Silver medal—European Under-21 championship.

Winner—Glamorgan Ladies' championship.

I let out a little caddie shout.

"*Foaaahhhh!*"

. . .

It's 4:40 P.M., and I've just finished another qualifier-prepping round on the New Course. There are only three more days left, and I'm feeling ready. I'm also feeling ready for bed, as I head into the shack, to collect my bag. Rick is there, waiting. He has alternative plans.

"Mmmm . . . Ollie, I'm going to need you to go again," Rick says, pointing outside as if ordering a misbehaving dog to a kennel. "You're on the tee right now."

I wince, tell Rick, "Okay" (how can I say no?), and stagger back outside, where I find Randall Morrison putting on his bib.

"Rick said it's a very VIP job," Randall announces.

"Great."

My pulse doesn't exactly quicken. Rick promises this kind of round frequently, and it usually just means "I need you to fill this job, so you're going again."

Today, though, Rick isn't kidding. We go to meet the golfers. In our group is the son of Tony Lema—the mega-tall American golfer who was immortalized by winning the 1964 British Open, in his first-ever St. Andrews appearance. Tragically, "Champagne Tony" (so nicknamed because he used to buy bottles of champagne for all the media) was killed in a plane crash, just two years later, at the age of thirty-two, leaving behind his only son . . . who is now forty-five, making practice swings next to me on the first tee.

David Lema is a spitting image of his father. He's tall as a tower and stern as a stone. "I come here every five years to play the Old," he tells me and Randall. David's here with two friends from Las Vegas. All are 2-handicaps. All are serious golfers. And, I note, being the son of a former Open champion has its benefits. Members of the R & A come out to shake his hand before we tee off. The starter in the hut gives him a warm hello. Lema's friend, for whom I'm caddying, tells me midway down the first fairway, "Having David's father be who he was, it's opened a lot of doors for us."

Randall and I have to work hard on this round. The men are demanding. They're used to the best. But I don't mind. I like being tested out here. And right now, I like being alongside David Lema.

David was four years old when his father was killed—just two years old when his father won here. The legend of his father and that epic win at St. Andrews—these are the shadows in which David lives his life. As we play, the tall American doesn't say much. But he's observant, thoughtful. It's as if, by playing the Old, treading on the same grass that Tony Lema trod forty-three years ago, David is trying to discover the dad he never knew.

Darkness is descending on St. Andrews as we walk up 18. My guy's hit an approach shot to the back of the green, and David's hit his wedge to twenty feet. As we walk, I can see David staring up the edges of the fairway. I wonder if he's imagining what it was like for his dad on this final walk up the eighteenth. Crowds cheering. Tip Anderson beside him. Roars echoing from behind the green—roars that I always dreamed of hearing for myself, roars that I'm sure David has dreamed of too.

It's pitch-dark when David Lema stands over his putt, on the same green on which his father won. I'm not sure what it is, but this green always makes you think of the past. The way it sits at the edge of town—the history behind it. Something about this green always makes it seem, I dunno, like a platform from which you can touch the past. David takes a deep breath and strokes the putt. The ball skids up the left, takes the break, slides right. It slams in. Birdie. A birdie on 18 at St. Andrews. Everyone in our group breaks into cheers. And then, without warning, Champagne Tony Lema's son looks up, and screams out into the darkness, at the top of his lungs, *"I LOVE YOU, DAD!"*

The shout rings out into the night, booms up into the sky, catches us totally off guard.

There are chills down my spine.

FIFTY-THREE

Ricoh, the office supplies manufacturer, is this year's sponsor of the Women's British Open. And the fact that the Old Course suddenly looks like a stationery store means that championship week is approaching. It's Saturday, two days before the Monday qualifier, and already, most of the grandstands, TV towers, and bright red Ricoh scoreboards are in place (one of the scoreboards has its letters set out already, which someone has used to write the message CADDIE TIPS START AT 70). Out on the course, the greens are being rolled, the tee boxes watered, pitch marks repaired. Everything's getting ready.

I'm on the third hole of the New Course, scouting pins and calculating run-outs from the tournament tees, when Lydia calls.

Actually, it's Rob from the shack who phones me. "I've got a job back at the Links Clubhouse for you," he says.

I'm stunned. I can't believe Rob's sending me out with a potential 27-handicapper. "I can't do it, Rob, I have to pace out all the yardages for Monday!" I say.

"Well, can't you do both at the same time?" Rob sounds confused. He's obviously not hearing me.

"Sorry, Rob, I'm too busy," I say firmly.

There's a lengthy pause on the other end before Rob says, "Okay, I'll just tell Lydia you can't do it."

It's Lydia Hall. My golfer. Shit. "Oh! No, wait! Wait! No, I'm coming!" I yell, then sprint back the wrong way down the course, to the Links Clubhouse. It's swarming with female golfers, coaches, caddies, and tense-looking family members. Amid the swarm, I spot Greaves and McGinley. Both have bags for final qualifying. Both look excited. I hurry over to the front desk, where I'm shown to a young-looking girl in a black rain suit.

"Are you Ollie?" she asks.

Lydia is tiny. She would be five-foot-two-ish in high heels, *maybe*. Short blond hair pokes out from under her white Welsh Golf cap. Although her bio says she's nineteen years old, she immediately seems serious beyond her years. Serious, yet at the same time casual—a combination that somehow strikes me as very "pro."

"Yeah, hi, nice to meet you!" I say, still flustered from the run but trying to exude tournament-caddie confidence. I grab Lydia's clubs, and we set off for the first tee. En route, Lydia hands me a small notebook, in which she's written (rather exact) carry yardages for her entire bag: 228 for a driver . . . 98 for a pitching wedge . . . 92 for a pitching wedge mid-grip . . . I'm reminded of Bernhard Langer, whose caddie once supposedly told him, "Okay, we've got one sixteen from that sprinkler head," to which Langer replied, "Is that from the middle of the sprinkler head or the back of it?"

On the first tee, Lydia does some funny little warm-up exercises—short plyometrics squats and jumps—as I intro the hole. "Okay, so we only want two twenty or two twenty-five off this box," I say, trying to lean against our golf bag like Burt Lancaster would a wall. "Any more than that, we'll get into that light rough up there. Ideal line's on that green bush."

"Got it," Lydia says simply. She's in the zone already. As I look on, Lydia pulls her rescue club, makes two practice half swings, then absolutely bombs one up the middle.

"That work?" she asks. Would that ever *not* work?

"Yup," I grunt in as world-weary a tone as I can muster. I've got a player.

Our opening practice round is, to put it in technical caddie terms, sexy and thrilling. Despite Lydia's size, she bombs it 260 off every tee box. Her swing is short, compact, grooved. And deadly accurate. Everywhere I tell Lydia to hit, she hits it there. She chips in three times—once for eagle. I'm at the controls of a powerful machine. Throughout the round, I show Lydia ideal lines off every tee. I give her my best guesses for where the tournament pins will be cut. We hit multiple balls to different spots on the fourth green, hit practice putts from tricky areas of the seventh. We discuss run-outs from the eighth tee and where the trouble spots are on the par-3 ninth. This is a different type of caddying—tournament caddying—and I'm loving it. It suddenly feels like its own sport. It feels competitive, athletic. Important.

"That where you want it?"

Lydia is holding her finish, watching as our Pro V1 rockets toward the par-5 twelfth green in two.

"Yeah, good strike," I say understatedly as our ball skips up onto the green, to ten feet. I'm trying to act like all the other tournament caddies I've seen—feigning just a touch of disinterest, mixed with unwavering self-confidence. In reality, I'm just trying not to trip over our golf bag.

It's a quiet summer evening. The wind has dropped, and the light is beginning to fade, the sun settling into purple clouds overhead. Across the estuary, past Tentsmuir Forest, the clouds are darker. It seems to be raining over by Carnoustie. We start heading up to the green. As we walk, I notice Lydia continually glancing over at the empty grandstands on the Old Course. It's hard not to. The

Old Course now looks like a fully rigged movie set, waiting for the crew to arrive. In four days, this place is going to be mobbed. The show is coming. But seeing it empty like it is now, I'm reminded just how close we are to getting in. Lydia must be thinking the same thing.

"Which hole is that over there?"

Lydia is pointing over past the eighth fairway of the New, toward the Old.

"Oh, that. That's nine green on the Old. It's an easy par-four."

"Cool," Lydia says. She's quiet a moment before she says simply, "Eighteen holes."

"Yeah," I say back. Because, really, what else can you say? It couldn't be more clear-cut. Eighteen solid holes, and we're there.

Lydia started playing golf at age twelve. Her family, all obsessed with rugby, didn't play golf (and still doesn't). But they quickly saw that their daughter was serious. Lydia began taking lessons with her local pro at age thirteen. Six years later, he's still her coach.

"I'll check in with him from time to time, to make sure my swing's still sharp."

Lydia is sitting across from me at Marmaris, a Turkish food joint at the quiet end of Market Street. We're finished with our practice round, and since Lydia doesn't really know anyone in St. Andrews, I suggested that we grab dinner. Already, I feel kind of like a big brother to her.

"So your family didn't make the trip over?" I ask, sipping my Sprite.

"No, they have to run the store back in Wales. Plus, you know, the trip's kind of expensive. I'm trying to get some sponsors, but, yeah, we have to be careful with costs."

"Yeah."

It must be lonely, being here by herself. Especially before the biggest tournament of her career. Lydia starts tucking into her chicken kebab.

"So what are your plans for this fall?" I ask. "Got any other tournaments coming up?"

"Well, I'm actually going to try for Tour School this November. For the Ladies European Tour. It's in Spain."

"Oh wow. Nice!"

"Yeah, so I'll hopefully be playing some other comps before then. A lot of people, like, don't think I'm ready. But, you know, why not, right?"

As I watch Lydia sitting here, eating her dinner, I think of how, I dunno, *real* this all is. She's nineteen, and she's finished with school; she's not going to college. This is her moment now. She's going after her dream. I'm pumped to be in her corner.

The owner of Marmaris comes over to our table.

"Lee-dia, is everything good, my friend?"

He's found out that Lydia's playing in final qualifying. And he's loving it.

"Oh yeah, it's delicious. Thank you!" Lydia says, looking up from under her golf cap. She looks like she's twelve. The owner beams.

"If you win on Monday, I throw you beeg partee here at shop. Everything free!" He motions at me. "For your caddie too."

"Thanks," Lydia says.

"Thanks," I say. I imagine him running down to meet us on the eighteenth green Monday afternoon, with a giant chunk of lamb doner.

.   .   .

The night before a big tournament, it's standard practice to have a quiet night, go to bed early, and get plenty of sleep.

The night before final qualifying, a huge bumblebee flies into my bedroom.

Groggily, I grab a *Golf in Scotland* brochure and fling it at the bee. It's a good fling, and Colin Montgomery's face strikes the bee. The bee does not die. If anything, the bee becomes more alive with rage. As it begins making aerial moves in my direction that resemble those of a Star Wars TIE fighter, I retreat to the living room couch, slamming the door closed behind me. For hours, I lie beside the fish tank (and the kelp jungle) in the dark, staring up at the dead leopard on Will's wall.

It's 5:10 A.M. when my cell phone alarm goes off. It's 5:10 A.M. and ten seconds when my bedside-clock alarm, digital-watch alarm, and laptop alarm all also go off. I wasn't taking any chances with oversleeping. The bumblebee is now gone (or asleep) when I wander back into my room. I make some quick deliberations about what caddie outfit will look most professional and calming for Lydia during her round. I try on an outfit in total Tiger Sunday red, then discard it . . . too dorky. An old gray sweater and black golf cap . . . too bummy. I'm deliberating where to hang my caddie towel from (my belt? My jacket zipper? Do people even *hang* it?) when I realize it's now 5:35 A.M. I'm late.

"You heading off?"

Will has wandered out into the living room, where I'm doing final pocket checks for yardage books. Will's been eagerly listening to my qualifier updates the last few days and wanted to see me off this morning.

"Yeah, we've got the seven o'clock tee time," I reply hurriedly.

"Ace. Best of luck, mate! I've got something for you, by the way."

Will removes an enormous hunting rifle from behind the couch (directly under where I slept last night). It looks loaded. Excitedly, Will flicks some levers and removes the sight.

"Here, you can use this for today, to grab distances."

Will is now holding out the Danish sight toward me proudly. It looks as if I'm about to sniper-kill a moose.

"Uh, Will, I don't really think—"

"It has a twenty-seven-hundred-yard range."

I look at my caddie groupie. "Um, I'm pretty sure this is illegal for tournaments . . ."

Will considers this for a second, his feelings hurt.

"Okay, whatever. I'm going back to fucking bed."

Lydia and I are first off.

In our group is a twenty-three-year-old Spanish amateur with a ponytail and braces and a beautiful, chain-smoking, too-cool-for-school Italian pro from Rome. The Italian pro is about thirty-five and has just flown in this morning, hasn't yet seen the course. Her tour caddie is apparently back in Italy, so she's taken a randomly as-signed caddie this morning—whom I soon see walking up with the bag. It's Matt Fouchek, my caddie friend. He got the call-up from Rick twenty minutes ago. He looks unbelievably nervous.

"You're in the seven o'clock game too?" he asks.

"Yeah."

"Oh, thank you, *God*."

We do a brief, private fist-pound behind our golfers. It's nice to have a shackmate in the group.

The mood is weirdly quiet down by the first tee. Most of the 120 golfers are still on the range, or at the chipping green, or doing whatever intimidating preround rituals they do. A stern female La-dies' Golf Union starter calls up our three-ball, to hand out golf tees and pin sheets and to begin explaining the rules. "Welcome to the seven o'clock starting time . . . ," she says. I suddenly have to pee. Really bad. On a scale of one to ten, like maybe a seven.

Italian Pro is up first. She crushes one down the middle. Spanish Braces Girl is up second, does the same thing. (Now I have to pee at, like, an eleven.) Next it's Lydia's turn. At this moment, I can barely breathe. Lydia does a little waggle, looks at the hole. She suddenly seems so small up there, so young. I think about the weeks of buildup to get here—the finishing eleventh out of 150 players in local qualifying just to make this event; the trip to St. Andrews without any of her family; the pressure of competing against ninety professionals. Everything about this moment makes her seem vulnerable.

Lydia takes a deep breath, starts her short backswing . . . and absolutely *bombs* it right down the middle. Perfect drive.

I have a new hero.

Bags and clubs clang as our group strides off the box. I want to sound as sturdy and understated as possible and rack my brains for what a veteran pro caddie might say to his golfer after the opening tee shot. "Good move through the ball," I settle on.

Lydia smiles. "Thanks, Ollie."

I take out my pin sheet that I've scribbled notes on, as well as my yardage book, and begin preparations for our approach shot into the first green. There's fiery determination in my eyes. Eighteen holes and we're in the Women's British Open. Let's get it on.

There are a few observations that I make over this front nine.

First of all, Spanish Braces Girl is really annoying. She lets out shrieks of delight whenever she holes putts (which is often, like on the first hole from thirty feet, for birdie), and she screams and slaps her thigh even more loudly if she is disappointed. She also takes *forever*. Her green reading involves a bizarre three-pronged move in which she stands, then crouches, then kicks into a Camilo Villegas sniper position. Her caddie, a young Scottish kid from Kingsbarns, seems inspired by this and begins doing the same sniper kick for green reading. Soon our group is holding up the entire tournament behind us. As a side observation, I also think that Spanish Braces Girl is sleeping with her caddie—she gives him extended, vaguely fondling hugs whenever he makes good clubbing suggestions.

Italian Pro, our other playing partner, could not be any cooler. Maybe it's her casual smile, or her skinny frame that still busts 270-yard drives, or her Italian cigarettes, but she brings to mind a glamorous international spy, working undercover on a golf course. Nothing can shake her. Between cool drags on cigarettes, she makes effortless par after effortless par. Matt Fouchek, by contrast, looks like he's about to faint.

Over in the Lydia-Oliver corner, however, things are more shaky.

Tee to green, Lydia is exceptional today. Her drives are huge. Her irons are dialed in. And I'm becoming less alarmingly nauseous with fear. That's all going fine. Our problem is on the greens. The New Course greens are different this morning. They've been double cut and double rolled. They're like lightning. And maybe that's the reason, or maybe it's just nerves, but today, Lydia's pace is off. We three-putt the first hole from twenty-five feet. We three-putt the sixth hole from twenty feet. On 8, Lydia leaves an eighteen-foot downhill putt halfway there and falls to her knees. Somehow she holes the remaining ten-footer for par. Behind her, at the side of the green, I close my eyes. This is as relaxing as a quadruple bypass. By the time we make the turn, we're 3 over. Spanish Braces Girl and Italian Pro are both even.

It's frustrating. We're still really close to the cut number; we're just not scoring. In my head, I think that even or 1 over par should definitely get in. Whenever I pass other St. Andrews caddies, we're subtly trading our golfers' scores from adjoining fairways—with a quick flick of the fingers and then a thumbs-up or -down for over or under par. Most are way over. I see Greaves going up the fourth hole, chain-smoking away and caddying for a Japanese lady (4 over). I see McGinley (4 over), Joe McParland (3 over), Big Malcky (5 over), and Alistair Taylor (who smiles brightly at his golfer, then turns and secretly flashes me the universal hand-on-throat choking sign). It's an inner community of Old Course caddies in the midst of this tournament, and we all want one another to get in. I think I might have the best chance.

The twelfth hole is a par-5, but a short one. Lydia slams a drive down the middle, then hits a 3-wood to the edge of the green in two. We've now got thirty-five feet, right to left. I show Lydia the line (three cups out right). "Give it a chance," I say. She strokes the ball. Her putt crests the hill, takes the break, slams into the pin . . . and drops. Eagle. Lydia leaps into the air. Suddenly, we're back to 1 over.

"See what happens when you get the right speed?" I say, trying to keep everything calm, but my pulse is privately lunar-launching. We're now leading our group and definitely inside the cut line for the tournament. For the first time all day, something's gone really right. Cool Italian Pro pars the hole and grins at Matt. Sweating a little, Matt gives her a strained thumbs-up, then whispers to me, deadly seriously, that he's thinking of asking her for his first-ever cigarette.

Lydia and I par the tricky par-3 thirteenth. Then Lydia hits a perfect 3-wood down the par-4 fourteenth and an 8-iron to just short of the green. This is looking good. Like, really good. A par here, and maybe just one more birdie, and we should definitely qualify for the Women's British Open. As I watch, Lydia chips to ten feet . . . then makes a perfect stroke on her par putt. The putt lips out. Shit. Unfazed, Lydia walks around the other side and taps the remaining three-footer. Which misses too. Double bogie. My mouth drops open. I'm in shock. I think Lydia is too.

Shaken, we bogie 15. And then 16.

And then, just like that, it's over.

. . .

Lydia's 77 is the first score slotted onto the enormous green "Ricoh Women's British Open FQ 2007" scoreboard outside the Links Clubhouse. Seventy-seven. Five over. Four fucking over for the last five holes. For a while, the wind begins to freshen, and it looks like maybe, just maybe, 5 over could sneak through. But then reality arrives, in the form of a half-dozen 72s and 73s, and the new cut line drops from 5 over to 4 over. It's official. The first-ever Women's

British Open to be held on the Old Course is not going to include Lydia Hall.

We both turn away from the scoreboard, and the large crowd milling in front, and just stand beside each other. Lydia's already phoned her coach with the bad news, texted her parents with the bad news, shared this bad news with the fifteen different tour pro friends who have asked. It's time to say good-bye. I should give Lydia some encouragement.

"Well . . . ," I start to say.

And then it hits me: the full wave of emotion. The relentless pounding disappointment. *Shit*. And then. *Fucking hell*. And then . . . *Why? We were there! The Women's goddamn Open Championship!* I can't even complete my pep talk for Lydia because I'm so overcome by my own frustration. Beside me, I expect Lydia to be a puddle of tears.

Instead, Lydia looks up at me, shrugs, does a little smile, and says:

"Tough day at the office."

There's a pause. I don't know what to say back.

I look down at this five-foot-one, nineteen-year-old girl, whom I expected to be crushed—and I know that she's the real deal. That she's already absorbed this defeat. That she's *not* letting her dream be shattered.

I'm proud to have been her caddie.

· · ·

It's the next evening.

Lydia has gone home. We exchanged e-mail addresses and phone numbers, and I wished her the best in Tour School this fall. It's the end of a great partnership—it's just ending six days too soon. Now everyone who qualified is preparing for Thursday's first round, playing practice rounds on the Old. The TV crews are in town. The crowds have started to arrive.

I'm out playing on the Jubilee Course, by myself.

I can't stop replaying yesterday's round in my head, blaming myself in a million different ways. *If I'd just given Lydia a 7-iron on 14 instead of an 8-iron, then her chunk would've made the green! If I'd just anticipated that she'd pull her putt on 10!*

These thoughts aren't helping. Playing golf by myself isn't helping. Nothing's helping.

On the par-3 fifth hole, I hit an ugly hook with my 7-iron. The ball screams left and disappears over the embankment, onto the adjoining New Course. Without thinking, I head over the hill to find my ball. When I arrive there, it's as if the golf gods have played a cruel trick on me.

I'm in the middle of the New Course's fourteenth fairway, precisely where Lydia and I crumbled yesterday.

And suddenly I begin to cry.

Through the tears, I'm shocked by own reaction. *Why the hell am I being so affected by all this?* And then, I know why. I see myself at age sixteen, the four-time junior club champion at Rockport Golf Club and the three-time junior club champion at Bass Rocks Golf Club, absolutely convinced that I would someday be a professional golfer. I see myself in the big tournaments where I imploded, the tryouts where I failed, the gradual unraveling, thread by thread, of my particular golf dream. Was it ever a sure thing? Of course not. But I was good. And I was promising. And it was *my* dream. It mattered to *me.* Now I realize that yesterday's failure feels like my *own* failure. That there's been a kind of transference.

I think again of Lydia.

Lydia. This young girl I just met from the middle of nowhere in Wales, with a kind of absolute ability to not be defeated by loss, to be able to just say, "Tough day at the office." And in her, I see a strong woman. From her, I take courage.

I head back over the hill with my ball, to the Jubilee Course. Now I'm thinking about another shattered dream from this summer. Maybe Sylvie, too, was just a "tough day at the office."

· · ·

"You heading to the Dunny?"

Patrick McGinley and I are standing on North Street, by the New Picture House movie theater.

"Uh, maybe. I want to get some pizza first. Why?"

"I think Lorena's family's having their party there."

It's Sunday evening. The first-ever Women's British Open held on the Old Course has concluded. Lorena Ochoa has won. It's her first-ever major. Back in Mexico, people are celebrating in the streets. Here in St. Andrews, Ochoa has flown in about twenty family members. Celebrations should be going deep tonight.

"Just get pizza after!" McGinley whines.

"Nah, I'm hungry now, I'll catch up with you there," I say. As we stand here talking, I see Greavesy on the other side of the street. He crosses over to us, panting a little.

"Paula Creamer's heading to the Dunny. It's her twenty-first birthday tonight."

Earlier this evening, after finishing tied for seventh, Creamer was seen on BBC coverage drinking birthday champagne on her Old Course Hotel balcony. Greaves and McGinley both look at me.

"Well, maybe I'll just get pizza later," I say.

When we enter the Dunvegan, we're in a scene out of a movie.

The pub is packed with golfers, tour caddies, Old Course caddies, and Women's European Tour organizers. On the left-hand side of the room, Lorena, her caddie, and twenty of her family members are standing on the cushioned seats by the windows. An eighty-year-old man with a saxophone, standing next to Lorena ("That's her caddie's dad," McGinley whispers to me), plays "Tequila." Everyone is going crazy.

We head over to Matt Fouchek, who's here with a bunch of other caddies.

"How great is this?" Matt shouts, laughing.

Now Lorena is dancing in the center of the room with her dad, and everyone is clapping. "Lorena! Lorena!" they shout. Soon a bag-piper comes inside, and from the entrance begins playing "The Blue Bells of Scotland." The music cuts into the room. It strikes me that for the moment, here in this room, I'm at the epicenter of golf.

And then she comes in.

Paula Creamer. Looking unbelievably cute. She's here with two friends, here to celebrate her turning twenty-one—the same age as me. They take a seat by the windows.

"She's nice!" Fouchek says.

"Seriously nice," Greaves adds.

"Yeah," I say.

And then inspiration strikes. I run for the bar.

"Where are you going?" Greaves shouts.

I order two shots of tequila and grab two limes, plus two salt-shakers. The bartender puts everything on a tray for me. And then I head directly for the window. There's a kind of lull in the music as I walk up.

"Excuse me, Paula?" I say.

The Pink Panther looks up at me. "Yeah?" Paula says.

"I got you a birthday present," I say, and hold up the tray. Adults all around us see this and burst into a chorus of "Way-hayyyyyyy!"

Paula starts laughing. "Uh, thanks. You'll have to show me how to do this!" she says. Then she reaches for her lime.

"No, it's salt, tequila, *then* lime," I say.

A year at St. Andrews has educated me well on the tequila front.

With the entire room now watching, we clink our glasses and down our tequila shots. Everyone cheers. Pictures are taken. I no-tice, at the other table, that Paula's dad and caddie are glaring mur-derously at me, but I don't care. Happily, I plop myself down on a chair next to Paula.

"I thought you did really well this week, Paula . . . ," I say, and for the next fifteen minutes, I proceed to unabashedly (and com-pletely unsuccessfully) hit on her. Behind me, the Ochoa family has started dancing again. Caddies and golfers are joining in. I look around me. I think of Lydia. And her dream. And being able to say, "Tough day at the office." She'll get here one day. I know she will. The music crescendos. It's been a good week, among these new women on the Old.

FIFTY-FOUR

It's August.

Senior year is looming. My summer is winding down.

I'm out on the Old.

My golfer is a mega-rich businessman from Thailand. Caddying for this guy is an experience. And not a good one. Despite speaking perfect English, the man addresses me only as "caddie." He also makes me pick his ball out of every cup. He also has a head cover on every iron. I have yet to meet a golfer I like who uses a head cover on every iron.

The round is going nowhere speedily when on the fifteenth tee, a text buzzes in from Matt Fouchek. Casually, I flip open the message.

"larry david just teed off on 1"

This gets my attention.

"WHAT!! WHEN???" I text back.

"5 mins ago"

"HOW MANY CADDIES IN GROUP??"

"1. For 4 guys. No one else around."

A plan forms in my head. I will push my group onward, as fast as inhumanly possible. Then, when we reach Larry David, I will ask to join his group.

"Okay. Good to go! Good to go!" I shout, and begin gunning my guys along, as if piranhas are tailing us. On 17, I spot them coming up the second fairway: three guys and a tall, loping Larry David. "I'll be right back," I yell to my Thai golfer, but already I'm dashing away. Steering clear of Larry David (that'll be too obvious), I walk up to another golfer instead. "Hey, guys," I say as casually as possible. "I see you've only got one caddie . . . just so you know, I'm happy to catch you guys up, after I finish my round." As the guy considers this, I suddenly recognize who I'm talking to: Peter Farrelly, one half of the film-directing Farrelly brothers.

Peter Farrelly looks me up and down. "You a good caddie?"

"*Yeah*, I'm a good caddie!" I reply.

Larry David walks up. "You fun?"

I look back at Larry. "Eh, I'm okay . . ."

Twelve minutes and thirty-seven seconds later, I'm fizzing my bike along the shell-covered path, back out onto the Old. I catch everyone in the middle of the third fairway, and with nowhere to lock my bike, I simply hurl it into the middle of a large gorse bush. "Hey, everybody," I pant as I jog up.

"Jeez, you got here quick," Larry says.

"Yeah, well . . . I . . . hi," I reply. Peter Farrelly puts me on his bag. This round has begun.

"So this is your fourth season over here?" Larry asks.

It's the seventh hole, and the creator of *Seinfeld* and I are walking up the fairway together.

"Yep," I reply.

"Cool! I bet it's fun."

"Oh yeah." We walk for a second. And then I blurt out . . .

"Hey, Larry, I know like every single line from *Curb*."

This information could have perhaps been delivered in a smoother way.

Larry laughs. "Really? That's awesome! Thank you!"

"Yeah. 'The Ski Lift' is probably my favorite episode ever. 'The Carpool Lane' too."

Larry smiles. "Thanks! Yeah, those were fun." We keep walking side by side—just me and Larry David. Larry seems pleased. I am too. Larry turns to me.

"So you got a girlfriend over here, Oliver?"

The sun is setting as we walk off the eighteenth tee. It's time for the Swilcan Bridge picture—possibly the best-known tradition on the Old Course. Peter Farrelly hands me his camera as the group starts walking toward Swilcan Bridge. Peter . . . the other two guys . . . everyone, except Larry. I look left and see Larry David walking away from them, toward the wooden maintenance bridge.

"Hey, Larry!" I call out. "You're going over the wrong bridge."

Larry turns to me, then looks over at Swilcan Bridge and replies, "Eh . . ."

"Larry," I yell, "come on, everyone's taking their picture on the bridge. It's a tradition."

Larry considers what I've said, then shrugs. "Nah, I'm good."

"Larry! Come on, just do the picture!"

Larry seems to weigh this in his head for a second. Then he speaks.

"Eh . . . it's just a fucking bridge!" he says in classic *Curb Your Enthusiasm* form . . . and walks over the maintenance bridge.

Tequila shots with Paula Creamer. Caddying with Larry David. It hasn't been a bad summer. Peter Farrelly turns to me.

"You got a girlfriend over here, Oliver?"

FIFTY-FIVE

"Oliver Horovitz and Mike Brown."

I shuffle over to the shack window ahead of Mike, a young trainee caddie from Cupar. It's my final day in St. Andrews. My flight home is all booked for tomorrow. Senior year is looming. I wonder if I should have eaten all six of the jelly donuts Big Malcky brought down to the shack this morning.

"Ten forty on the Old," Rick says to us, taking our fivers and handing us pin sheets. I take mine.

"This is my last round of the season, Rick."

Rick looks back at me. "I never thought this day would come."

As we leave the window, Mike the Trainee looks at me excitedly. "Should we go up now and meet our golfers?"

I recognize his eagerness a little too easily. "No, give it a minute, they haven't gotten to the tee yet," I say, and gulp down the last of my 30 p shack coffee. I hope this kid's not going to be annoying out there today.

It's funny how the caddie shack moves in cycles. You arrive for your first season, knowing nothing, and by the end of the summer, you've started to figure out the script. The next summer, there are other newcomers to take your place. You see the new trainees making the same mistakes you made—correcting veteran caddies on the course, grabbing too few pins, giving too much information—but instead of helping them, you kind of just let it happen. Like it's the natural order of events.

Our golfers today are two husband-and-wife couples from Long Beach, California. I'm caddying for a nice guy named John. Mike the Trainee has John's friend: Randy. Picking Randy's bag, it soon is revealed, was a mistake of uncharted proportions.

Randy is hellish. On the greens, he's apparently decided that Mike will be held to a standard of putt-reading more precise than pommel horse judging. "Okay, Mike, I'm trusting you here!" Randy will announce over putts, then if they miss, add accusingly, "Well, that was on your mark . . ." Each putt read is a murder trial. A trial for which the verdict will be delivered into poor Mike's ear for sometimes three minutes afterward.

"I feel like I'm being abused," little Mike whispers to me, quietly, on the tenth tee box.

It's tough to watch. Mike's just a trainee. He doesn't know these greens that well. If Randy wants this so bad, he should do what the pros do and read his own putts. He should give Mike a fucking break. But he's not. In fact, Randy is becoming angrier, more demanding.

At last we get to 18. Randy (who's announced that he is 3 over, which I know is untrue) hits his approach shot to thirty feet. Then he turns to our group and makes another announcement. "Okay! I

277

wanna get a birdie here! Birdie on eighteen . . . come on, Mike, we *have* to get this."

I can see Mike swallowing hard. This is exactly what you do *not* want to hear from your golfer. Especially someone like Randy. As Mike surveys the putt from up top, he looks terrified . . . and completely unsure of how it's breaking. "How great would birdie be here?" Randy is saying to his wife. That's it. I need to step in. I walk behind Mike, who's crouched down behind the ball, and whisper, "Hey, man, what are you seeing?"

Mike looks up at me nervously. "Oh, way out left . . . four feet left," he says.

I look at the putt, then back at Mike. "I think it's only a foot," I whisper, then walk away.

"Okay, what's the story here, Mike?" Randy says loudly, oblivious to our conversation.

"One foot out left," Mike replies.

"You sure?"

Mike winces slightly. "Yep."

"Okay . . . ," Randy says, before adding, "I'm trusting you."

Randy hits the putt, starting it exactly one foot out left. The ball trundles downward, picking up speed. I watch from the other side of the cup, privately praying that I didn't just screw up Mike's read. The ball moves faster and faster now. Five feet from the cup, it begins to break. Slowly at first, then harder. And now Randy is backing up. His putter is in the air. And the ball is still turning. *Come on! Stay up. Stay* up! The ball does one last dive, holds its line, and slams into the center of the cup. It drops in. *Birdie!* A crowd of twenty-five people behind the green break into roars. Randy is in orbit.

"Oh my God! Birdie! On eighteen at St. Andrews!" he shouts. Then he does a you-da-man point at Mike. "Great read, Mikey!"

Mike's eyes light up. He looks directly at me, as if I'm his big brother who just knocked out the school bully with one punch. "Thank you!" he mouths silently from across the green. I just wink back at Mike. *No prob.* Then I turn away, and let my caddie mate enjoy the moment. And as the rest of the group now swarms Randy and Mike, laughing and congratulating them, I lean against our flagstick, and quietly watch.

If there's such a thing as a caddie torch, I think it just got passed.

FIFTY-SIX

"Would you look at those wee pansies . . . by golly!"

Henry is loving the flowers. So is Uncle Ken.

"The Taits always do well here," my uncle says as he putters around the large plant bed, inspecting. We're at the Hidden Gardens tour, an annual occurrence in St. Andrews known mainly to the Gardeners' Club members, or to those people over eighty years old. During the Hidden Gardens, roughly a dozen families in St. Andrews with particularly impressive private gardens will open them to the public, with the proceeds going to various charities. The entry fee for this tour is not exactly steep—the garden we're currently visiting, which sits on the cliffs overlooking the North Sea, cost 30 p to enter.

"Aye, will you look at that shrubbery pruning!" Henry is impressed.

I've taken a few hours off from packing to accompany my two ancient mates on this tour. Both Henry and Uncle Ken use walking sticks; both wear tweed coats, tweed caps, dress shirts, sweaters, and ties. Henry has brought along a little camera for the tour, which is dangling from around his neck.

"What time is your flight leaving, lad?"

"Noon, tomorrow. From Edinburgh."

"Oh aye. I hope you don't get caught up in these twisters they've been showin' on the news."

"Well, those are in Kans—yeah, I'll try not to, Henry."

"That reminds me, Oliver," Uncle Ken adds, "you'll have to bring your bike round later, so I can store it over the winter!"

"Yeah, definitely. I'll bring it over after this evening, before the Grill House."

And then I have a thought.

"Hey, guys, can I get a picture of all of us together? I want to send it to Mom and Dad."

I give my camera to a Hidden Gardens volunteer, and have them snap a photo of me standing between Uncle Ken and Henry. They both smile brightly, their canes in their right hands.

"Thanks, guys," I say, putting the camera back in my pocket. I just fibbed. That picture wasn't for Mom and Dad. It was for me. I'm going to miss my mates this winter. More than I'd ever tell them. Because as we do one final stroll around the garden—Henry marveling at the pansies, Uncle Ken giggling—I think about how these ancients are getting ever more ancient. I think about how the new caddies down at the shack seem younger and younger every summer, while the veteran caddies get older and older. And I wonder how this all fits into my particular life. Where will I be at age eighty-six? Or even in ten years' time? What will my life be like? Where is this all heading?

PART
FIVE

FIFTY-SEVEN

I'm in Harvard Yard.

It's June. Graduation weekend. Nine months later. All 1,656 members of our class of 2008 have just been shepherded into Memorial Church. Outside, our parents are going crazy—both emotionally and photographically. Tomorrow we're graduating. In thirty minutes, we're having our official class picture taken, on the steps of Widener Library. But first, Drew Faust, Harvard's new president (and first female president—she replaced Larry Summers, who was removed last year after his helpful "suggestion" that women might be innately worse at science than men), is about to give us a private speech here in Memorial Church. No one's allowed in besides us. No parents. No professors. No other adults. Just President Faust and us.

It's hot inside the church. We're all crammed into every available pew, sweltering in the heat, waiting. As required, everyone's in their caps and gowns, although for today, you can wear whatever you want under your gown. In the row behind me, a friend of mine named Ben is wearing a black and yellow MILF HUNTER T-shirt (referencing a porn website) underneath his gown. Ben has always kept it classy.

Drew Faust arrives at the podium. The chatter from our pews dies down, replaced by a quiet(ish) rustle of significantly divided attention. Everyone's politely thinking the same thing: *Not another fucking speech.* I sit next to my roommates Jake and Jordan, awaiting, along with everyone else, the obligatory "go out into the world" sermon. We've been hearing them all week, and they're all slowly blending into one long inspirational corn-fest. Drew Faust looks out at us and begins speaking. Her opening is unexpected.

"I'm worried that so many of you are going into I-banking and consulting."

The rustling stops. Our class goes quiet. Suddenly, 1,656 people are listening. Really listening. As if, at the exact same moment, everyone's had the same microsecond flicker that an adult is actually *talking* to us. Everyone seems shocked. I watch from the balcony, staring down at Harvard's president. I've sort of been thinking the same thing.

All of my friends are going into consulting. Senior year at Harvard has been a never-ending stream of unfamiliar names. Bain. McKinsey. BCG. Oliver Wyman. Deloitte. Names I've never heard of. Names that are suddenly tossed around the dining hall with reverence, as if the firms are a new feather in your identity cap. "Bain's like the *party* consulting group," I overhear a girl in the Eliot dining hall telling her friends.

They're calling it the magic option. The industry for which everyone's qualified. You could study English. Religion. Ancient Greek. Ancient Greek religion. The firms still want you. On paper, it seems sensible. A two-or-three-year stopgap in which you can make $60,000 your first year (plus $5,000 in moving expenses) and figure out what you want to do later. They'll train you. They'll send you places. Shit, they'll even pay for you to go to business school afterward! Like the British Open into St. Andrews, the firms have all swooped into Harvard's campus, throwing splashy evening events at Harvard Square hotels, opening their warm welcoming arms to the entire Harvard class of 2008. Friend after friend of mine comes back to Eliot House bearing gifts of the newly converted—new Bain foam-ball globes, shiny McKinsey pens (the kind Viagra used to give out), bright red Deloitte brochures. Everyone, it seems, has drunk the consulting Kool-Aid. No one, it seems, will tell me what you actually *do* in consulting.

The kids who aren't going into consulting are heading to Wall Street. Lehman Brothers. Goldman. Morgan Stanley. Here, the starting salaries are higher; $140,000 for an "all-in comp" (including bonuses) is fairly typical. I know maybe thirty kids from my class heading to Goldman Sachs in New York. My freshman intramural basketball team roster reads like a who's who in rookie-year investment banking.

Flying even higher than the investment bankers are the hedge fund kids. People know even less about the hedge funders, except that these seniors tend to be the bookish econ majors, the quieter ones, who have now been head-hunted by small boutique hedge funds in downtown Manhattan or Westport, Connecticut. Cerberus. D. E. Shaw. Sankaty. This world is even more mysterious, even more removed, except for the salaries, rumors of which are throttling through our classrooms and libraries and Harvard gyms. The English major who will be making $400,000 next year. The kid who's being flown to Dubai for final interviews. Together, the hedge funders and the I-bankers are full of heady enthusiasm. It's mid-2008. It's still a good time to be on Wall Street. The hedge fund faucet is flowing. Signing bonuses could buy you a car. Life, as they say, is good.

And in the middle of all this, I am instantly a lost cause.

I know I'm not a fit for Wall Street—I have no interest in finance, the only econ class I took was in sophomore year of high school, and the last time I tried to calculate splits on a restaurant bill, I overcharged my friends for sushi by $35. Instead, throughout much of senior year, I've thrown myself into my thesis film, as if by burying myself in that, I'd be able to put off the question of my own future. While prepping my film, I also prepped an application for a Fulbright scholarship. I'd go back to Paris, apprentice to a French filmmaker, then shoot my own film in the second half of the year. It all sounded good, and I wrote a fistful of Fulbright essays, had my Fulbright interview in September, found out in December that I'd advanced to the final stage, and then, two weeks ago, discovered that I hadn't been picked.

Through it all, I can't stop thinking about St. Andrews. I've been speaking to Uncle Ken once a week by telephone, and I also check in with Greaves, who's bagged a job as a junior assistant producer with European Tour Productions (the UK equivalent of the Golf Channel). And from my Harvard dorm room, back in November, I followed Lydia's progress in Ladies European Tour Qualifying School. As I tracked her live hole-by-hole results on my laptop, the nineteen-year-old girl who everyone told not to go to Q-school shot *8 under* in her first round, 6 under through the next four rounds, and out of 150 players, finished second. Lydia's on the tour.

Now I don't know what to do next. It's great to hear from my St. Andrews mates. But back in Cambridge, all I'm hearing about is consulting firms. As if it's, like, *expected* that you'll follow the crowd. And maybe this *is* the smart track to follow. I just don't see where I fit into all of this. I feel stupid for passing judgment on my friends. What right do I have to criticize their choices? What am *I* doing that's so revolutionary? I don't have an answer. But I do know that this whole undertone of senior year has just felt . . . wrong. Like a mass sell-out. Like all of us have shifted our priorities from learning, from figuring out our world, to how much our signing bonus is going to be compared to those of our roommates.

"Please consider what I've said. Thank you."

Drew Faust has finished speaking. The message is over. The moment has passed. Students are filing out the doors now, back into the morning sun, to Widener Library, their families, and their lives. As I exit Memorial Church, my smile goes back up. I'm playing out my role as the happy graduate—for my family, for my friends, and for myself. But it's a fraud. I have no job lined up. I don't know what I want to do with my life. I feel lost.

. . .

Graduation comes and goes. Mainly goes. I take a job as a teaching assistant in Harvard's film department. I'm a TA in VES 50: Fundamentals of Filmmaking—the ten-person class I took as a sophomore, in which you shoot docs on 16 mm film, edit on Steenbecks, cut using splicers. It's the same classroom in which I spent sophomore year, the same basement in which I spent my college career. All my friends move to New York, to $2,500-a-month apartments in Manhattan. They're in the real world. And I'm teaching sophomores. I really shouldn't complain. It's a good job. It's more than a good job. I love the professors that I'm TA-ing for—Ross McElwee, Robb Moss, Alfred Guzzetti. They were my favorite guys in the department. I get to hang out with Pete and John too, my old buddies in the equipment room, and now we have time to really shoot the shit after work. I'll grab them coffees from down the street, before classes, and we'll talk films, or music, or how exactly John can unstick lenses using Scotch tape. And I like teaching. It's cool. The students are really nice. But something's missing. Deep down in my mind, I know that I was supposed to move away from here when I graduated. But I'm still here. It's safe, it's secure. But I can't really say that it excites me like caddying used to, like being in St. Andrews used to. Which is to say, truthfully, that I still miss St. Andrews.

New England fall turns to New England winter. New England winter turns to much-more-miserable New England winter, then stays that way until every Massachusetts resident has seriously contemplated a move to Phoenix. Then it gets even colder. I spend the winter calling back to Uncle Ken frequently, in St. Andrews. For the most part, he sounds good—but I know he's had more falls. He's gone down twice in the past month, once not too badly, once *much* too badly. The second fall, on the front steps outside his door, ended in a broken pelvis and a stay in the hospital. As always though, Uncle Ken's upbeat on the phone. But he sounds like he misses me. And although he won't admit it, he sounds disappointed that I won't be back this summer to caddie.

. . .

I teach at Harvard the next year too. Another twelve months pass. Now students who crewed on my thesis film as freshmen and sophomores are roaming the halls as upperclassmen. I share an apartment in East Cambridge with a couple of MIT grad students in physics. I watch a lot of movies and wonder what I'm going to do next. Time is speeding up just as I want to slow it down. During winter break, I spend a huge chunk of my savings and go with three friends to climb Mount Kilimanjaro, in Tanzania. It's exactly what I need—it's an adventure, it's different, it's thrilling. But then I'm back in Cambridge, Massachusetts, in midwinter. By the spring, as my second year wraps up, I know what I need to do. Not what others think I should do or what's logical for me to do. What I *want* to do. I call the caddie shack and tell them I'm coming back. I book flights with the rest of my savings. I call Uncle Ken. My roommates are surprised. My friends are surprised. My parents are surprised. I'm just excited. I'm heading back to St. Andrews.

FIFTY-EIGHT

"One second, one second! Hee-hee-hee."

The high-pitched giggle has never sounded so sweet as footsteps draw nearer to the door. As I wait outside with my suitcase, I think about how strange it feels to be back. And how awesome it is.

The door is unlocked. And opened. And then I'm hugging my eighty-nine-year-old uncle. And I can't believe I've been gone for so long. It's as if I've just woken up from a long, deep sleep.

"I've pumped up all the tires on your bike!" Uncle Ken says proudly, beckoning me in.

"That's brilliant. Thanks!" I say.

"Oh, pleasure!" Uncle Ken replies Englishly. "Did you have a good trip over?"

"Sure, yeah, it was fine."

I walk down the hallway. Everything's the same. I run my hand along the wallpaper, hear the grandfather clocks ticking. I'm back with my best friend.

. . .

There are some differences down at the shack.

The ballot has gone "digital." Instead of a paper copy of the ballot hanging outside the shack, there's now a computer monitor, enclosed behind glass, displaying an electronic version. Caddie badges are now electronic ID cards—swiped before each round when you get your pin sheet and entered into a computer database. There's also a new system for allocating caddie jobs. Caddies are now assigned to one of four (creatively named) lists: List 1, List 2, List 3, and List 4. Now, during the week, there is no first come, first served policy. Instead, everyone calls into a special caddie voice mail each night and finds out what time their list should be down in the morning, or who the first fifteen names on each list are for the following day. List 1 is the new top-thirty group. They have to double every weekday, but they'll be off the course first each afternoon. Next out on the course is List 2. List 2 is for people who still want doubles most days but want a little more flexibility in their schedules. List 3 is for guys who mainly want singles. List 4 is the seniors list. The most obvious effect of this list system is that things are calmer. During the week, no one has to get down at four A.M. anymore to get a good number. The caddie day has a more officelike structure. Saturday is still a free-for-all, however, with some caddies getting down at two A.M. to be first for sign-up.

There are other changes too. The shack now has two bathrooms instead of one (the other used to be Rick's personal toilet). There's a flat-screen HD TV now mounted on the wall (the remote is still missing). There are new cubbyholes for bags. There are new caddie caps (in baby blue, which I'm not crazy about). There are new caddie waterproofs (now Gore-Tex, and now actually waterproof). And there are new caddies. Lifers from Gleneagles and Kingsbarns who have made the switch to St. Andrews. Characters who seem to have arrived via Pluto. There's Naci Karsli, a Super Mario–looking Turkish guy, who's lived in Scotland for years (he used to own his own

Turkish food joint called the Hungry Horse) and who makes a point of always barking extra-Scottish phrases, like "Ach, this young laddie! You're a good laddie!" or "Ach, this fucker! This wee shit!" There's the "Stirling Mafia"—the raucous fifty-year-old duo of Malcolm Cowan and Rob McCormick, who race their Vauxhall Carlton and Peugeot 306 each morning at 90 miles an hour, from their shared house in Anstruther to St. Andrews (along tightrope-narrow roads), then back again at the end of the day. And there's Gordon McIntyre, an eccentric sixty-year-old Zimbabwean with a large white beard and farmer's hat, who spends each winter on an Israeli vegetarian kibbutz and greets me in the shack each Friday with "Shabbat Shalom, young man."

In matters of caddie finance (read: the matter that matters most), the caddie fee has risen. It's now forty-five pounds plus tip for full caddies. This makes sixty quid an almost guaranteed minimum and slides the Hawaii-Five-0 into new, previously unfathomable strata of offense. Caddies also now have a seventh course on which to ply their trade—the Castle Course, built in 2008, and instantly proving the most brutal course to caddie on that I've ever seen. The Castle has its own (smaller) caddie department, and on slow days, caddies from the Old will sometimes shoot over for jobs at the Castle. (The guy who designed the Castle clubhouse also designed our Old Course caddie shack.) Behind the eighteenth green, Hamilton Hall has now been sold. Sadly, it's no longer a University of St. Andrews dorm, and Herb Kohler, the new owner, is turning it into luxury apartments called the Hamilton Grand. Apparently the price tag is around three million dollars per apartment (a slight change in ambiance from when I was a student, walking along one of the Hamilton hallways at night, when a room door was suddenly flung open and a student projectile-vomited into the hallway).

There are changes inside the shack office too. Ken has retired as assistant caddie master and now works part-time up at Kingsbarns as an on-course ranger (I see him up there one day, with his binoculars proudly around his neck, clearly loving it). Helping to run things now are the new assistant caddie masters, both former caddies: Dave Hutchison (Loppy) and Paul Ellison (Switchy). Both have hung up their bibs and stepped into "the office," a change I'm sure they find just as weird as their friends find it.

But of all the changes in the shack, one is the most dramatic, by *far.*

Rick Mackenzie is no longer the caddie master.

Yep. Rick is gone. There was some kind of incident—something happened, and although nothing's been proven, Rick has been removed from the job. I am absolutely shocked by this news. In his place is Rob, Rick's former assistant. An even-keeled thirty-year-old from St. Andrews, Rob worked for the Links Clubhouse before moving into the shack. Of greater importance, Rob caddied on the Old as a sixteen-year-old. Rob's hardworking, intelligent. He has a desert-dry sense of humor. He's also levelheaded, the Mikhail Gorbachev to Rick's Stalin. While Rick ruled by fear and terror, Rob has instantly created a calmer, more predictable work space. The daily threat of firing is gone. There's a sense that things are more, well, fair. I can't help feeling glad for the change. And yet, I also can't help remembering Rick's shockingly honest speech to me years ago, about how the shack was his life. I realize now that that life has been taken away from him. And I can't forget how, amid everything else, Rick always took me back, year after year . . . always had a bib ready for me . . . even prompted my first razor blade shave. Bizarrely, I can now only feel terribly sorry for this man who used to strike terror into my heart. I didn't think I would ever feel this way, but my heart goes out to him.

Other than that, most of the guys are still here. Gordon Smith. Andy Black. Big Malcky. John Rimmer. Big Eck. Dougie. Jimmy Reid. Coynie. Neil Gibson. Bruce Sorley. There are new trainees of course (there always are . . .), and I find that in the shack, to my amazement, these new kids are now looking to me as a veteran caddie. A fifth-year guy who was caddying "back when Mackenzie was here!" It's weird. And I can't say I hate it.

* * *

I'm in the shack today, my second day back, when Gardner walks in.

"What the fook . . . *Horovitz!?*"

Gardner is wearing his knit caddie hat fully unfolded, so that it now extends at least a foot above his head. In the space for his caddie card, there's a picture of a brown Labrador and the name "Gardner's Revenge." Nathan bends down to his gym bag, from which he inexplicably pulls out a teakettle and toaster, then plugs both into the wall. Above him, tacked to the notice board, I observe two fresh newspaper articles that have been tacked up, side by side. One headline reads: SUPREME SCRAP. The other reads: I WORK WITH NUTTERS.

"Hi, Nathan."

Gardner looks pleased. "Couldn't fookin' stay away, huh?"

I nod, with a hesitant smile you might give to your older brother's lunatic friend, who is about to either joke around with you, or beat you up. "Actually, yeah, pretty much."

Gardner digests this reply, and grins. I think he approves. Outside the open shack door, up on the first tee, some Americans are driving off. The first guy hits a low burner and screams, "Run like an open sore!" Everyone else in the group winces.

Gardner looks over at me. It hits me that over the years, these guys have come to know me as I've grown up. From an eager-eyed eighteen-year-old to the twenty-four-year-old standing before them now. Each summer that I come back, I've still got a place here.

"Welcome back, ya spanker!"

I'm not sure what "spanker" means, but I have a guess.

FIFTY-NINE

In June, the Old Course closes, for preparations for the 2010 British Open. Just like the last time the Open was here, in 2005, the month serves as a kind of forced vacation for the caddies. This time, I'm popping back over to the States for the wedding of two friends of mine from Harvard, Damien and Jasmine. The wedding's in Martha's Vineyard, which is kind of hard to pass up. I'll stay in the States until British Open week, then fly back to St. Andrews in time for the tournament.

As I leave, Uncle Ken is set for an operation that he's been wanting to have for years, a heart-valve replacement. It's being done at the Royal Infirmary of Edinburgh. Mom and Dad are flying over to Scotland as I leave, so they'll be there to help him recover.

Damien and Jasmine's wedding is unbelievably fun. It's the first wedding of friends my own age, and it's like a bar mitzvah with alcohol. I head back to New York after the wedding—suntanned, well fed, and Martha's Vineyard happy—to see family. It's there that I first hear that Uncle Ken isn't doing that great.

The operation seems to be a success. Uncle Ken comes out of it well. For the first few days, he improves steadily and is set to stay in the hospital for a week afterward. But then suddenly things take a turn. He picks up a hospital-dwelling infection that settles in his lungs. He remains weak. Suddenly Mom and Dad are out at the hospital every day, by his side. I get updates from them, check in constantly by phone from New York. It's not great. Soon it's really not great. Aunty Jacqui, my mom's sister, comes up by train to Edinburgh, then postpones her return. I'm getting worried. But it's Uncle Ken. I know he'll get better. He's survived much tougher things. Wars, and falls, and landings in lightning storms. This too will pass.

* * *

I'm in East Hampton with my sister Rachael and her family when I get the voice mail.

"Please call, Ollie," my dad is saying, his voice beginning to crack. "It's . . . it's not good news."

I dial Scotland, already knowing what will happen when the call connects. The call connects. Dad picks up.

"It's over, honey," he says.

That next second seems to last a century. The first thing that pops into my head, and the first thing that I say back is "It doesn't feel real . . ."

And then, on this street corner, in front of dozens of happy passing tourists and beachgoers, three thousand miles from Uncle Ken's kitchen, I begin to cry. I don't want to hang up the phone with Dad, because he's in the hospital room next to Uncle Ken, and while I'm on the line, it's the only physical connection I have left to my uncle.

I push up my flight to St. Andrews. I pack a dress shirt and black tie for the funeral. And before I go to bed, not knowing what else to do,

I upload a picture of Uncle Ken to Facebook, with his funny smile, dressed in classic tie, sweater, and tweed coat, along with the caption "Uncle Ken, May 14th, 1921–July 8th, 2010. Will be greatly missed."

When I get up the next morning, what I see makes me cry again. All the caddies have left comments on the photo. "Rest in Peace Uncle Ken." "Uncle Ken was a legend." "Thinking of you, Ollie." Most of the guys knew Uncle Ken personally. Some lived on his street. Some grew up visiting his house for doctor's appointments, where his wife, Dr. Isobel Cochran, ran her practice. It's beyond touching. And it helps.

. . .

It's weird being back. The clocks in Uncle Ken's house still chime. His pictures are still up. He never expected, when he packed a bag for the week and left for Edinburgh, that he'd never be back. That fourteen days from that afternoon, we'd be arranging his funeral. So it's hard. And as the British Open rages on outside, I find myself still winding all the clocks for Uncle Ken, watering his plants, deadheading his roses, walking the rooms, looking at all the photographs. And I find other photographs in the house, hidden in cupboards and boxes. Uncle Ken as a twenty-five-year-old Royal Air Force pilot, with a mustache and short shorts, looking exactly like Alec Guinness in *The Bridge on the River Kwai*. Uncle Ken meeting the queen. Uncle Ken driving around royal dignitaries. But it's the photo of Uncle Ken as a twenty-five-year-old that sticks with me. He's so strong, so confident. So powerful. As if he'd never be an eighty-nine-year-old, obsessed with his garden and worrying endlessly about his great-nephew's supper plans.

The funeral is held in tiny All Saints' Church, just off the end of the Scores. It was Uncle Ken's church, and he went every Sunday. The 2010 British Open ended yesterday, and the crowds have largely gone home. But there's a big crowd at the funeral—gardening-club members, locals, retired RAF servicemen, former town councilors. And several rather high-up members of the Scottish parliament, here to acknowledge Uncle Ken's years of service. There are family, friends. Dave, my flatmate from that first summer on Market Street, comes with his mother, Anne. A few of us share some thoughts on Uncle Ken. I wrote a speech last night, downstairs in the basement of Uncle Ken's house, and I recite it today in front of the congregation. I talk about Uncle Ken's giggle. I talk about Bonnie, his old dog. I talk about the Grill House dinners, and the garden chores, and the puttering about the house humming. I tell it all. And as I say the lines I wrote, I feel close to my dear friend again.

.   .   .

Everyone stops me on the street to offer their condolences. A funny fifty-year-old caddie named Scott Kennedy, who often loops while wearing an ascot, tells me that he's lived at 7 Hope Street, across from Uncle Ken, since 1970. "I always used to call your uncle *Squadron Leader*!" Scott tells me. At a garden party for the residents of Hope Street and Howard Place, the organizers make an opening address to the whole crowd, saying, "We lost a great man recently. Ken Hayward."

And I'm checking e-mail in Beanscene, the coffee shop on Bell Street, when I run into the manager of the Grill House. He's a tall skinny guy in his early thirties. Immediately, he looks like he might cry. "I was so upset to see the news in the paper," he says. "I'd just seen Ken walking in the street a few weeks ago!" This is a standard occurrence for me. People are shocked to hear that he passed away— they didn't know about the operation, they can't believe how quickly it happened.

I tell the man how much Uncle Ken loved the Grill House; I tell him how many "loyalty cards" we went through, with Uncle Ken always losing them just before the sixth punch and the free meal. The guy tells me how much the staff in the Grill House loved Ken—

how he seemed so at home in the restaurant, with his walker and tweed coat and hat, and his giggle. I thank him, tell him I'll come into the Grill House soon. And then I leave.

That night, I have dinner with Uncle Ken's old neighbors Jake and Edith at their house on the Scores. It is hilarious—they force wine on me, whiskey, gin and tonics; they easily outdrink me as eighty-year-olds. Edith says to me, "Ken would *always* worry about you. He'd say to me, 'Oliver is so *forgetful* all the time! I worry where he's putting his caddie money! He's making so much of it, you know.' " Edith smiles at me. "He was always thinking about you, Ollie. He loved hearing about your studies, your caddying, your golf exploits. He loved you so much, Ollie. You were the son he never had."

SIXTY

"Thanks for coming down here, Oliver."

Henry is sitting in his easy chair, surrounded by his plants.

"Oh, it's great to see you, Henry!" I reply.

I've come down to the end of Tom Morris Drive, to visit Henry at his house. It's very hard for Henry to get outside these days. Because he's not doing so well. Mentally, Henry's the same as ever, but physically, his tree-trunk-tall body is starting to betray him. His legs have somehow lost circulation, and they're very swollen. Bandages cover the lower parts of both legs. Louise, Henry's daughter, has to change the dressings twice a day. It seems as if Henry is in a lot of pain. Even so, he is dressed, as usual, in tweed jacket, tweed cap, dress shirt, and tie. Gentle, English, and old-school. And he looks eager to see me. My dapper mate points over to his dresser with importance.

"That's the program from Ken's funeral. Louise brought it back for me. She said it was a *lovely* service."

Henry wasn't allowed by the doctor to come to Uncle Ken's funeral. He shakes his head sadly.

"Do you know, I'll never forgive myself for not being there," he says.

"You were there in spirit, Henry," I say, trying to cheer him up. Henry nods, like a boy who's just been told *why* he can't have a second ice-cream cone.

"Aye. I was. But still, I wish I had been there . . . to give him a good send-off."

I think about what it must be like to lose your best mate of sixty years. And how hard it must be for Henry, a man *made* for the outdoors, to be now forced inside by his own insides. But if he's to be trapped anywhere, this is as good as it gets. Because Henry's house, which he shares with his wife, Grace, and their daughter, Louise, is a fitting place for a lifelong gardener. Everywhere I look, there are flowers.

"Those are tulips over there, Oliver." Henry, perhaps to lighten the mood, has transitioned into a flower tour of the house. "And over there, those are primulas, and African violets past them." It's amazing. In this living room alone, there are orchids and azaleas, great green umbrella plants and red-leaved poinsettias. There are peach-colored geraniums on the tables and yellow begonias along the carpets. Outside in the back garden, I see even brighter explosions of color—purple hydrangeas and sunny yellow forsythias. Deep pink cyclamen and dainty white fuchsias. Daisies and pansies. Pink viburnums and purple climbing clematis, evergreen hebes, creamy violas, and a sea of geraniums, crocuses, and snowdrops, all dancing in the wind outside the window. Flowers that Uncle Ken and Henry have pointed out to me year after year. An ocean of flowers.

"These are lovely, Henry!" I say.

"Aye, they've done well this year," Henry says, peering around contentedly at his brood. He looks proud. His flowers. His plot. A comfort for an old gardener who's just lost his oldest friend.

• • •

The call arrives a few weeks later. It's from Louise, Henry's daughter, and it's in the middle of the night.

"Oliver, this is Louise here. I'm sorry to bother you, but I thought you should know. Henry had a fall tonight and hit his head on the staircase. He hit his head very hard. They rushed him to the hospital, but . . ." There's a long pause. "But he passed away there."

I'm silent. I'm in shock. Two best friends, in the space of a month, going down together. It's just too much.

"Oh, Louise, I'm . . . I'm so sorry," I say.

"We're all very upset," she says. "But, you know, he's with Ken now."

I instantly think of Henry, waiting at the bus stop on Market Street, all those afternoons before he'd visit Uncle Ken. I used to think that Henry was just stopping for a chat, but eventually I realized the truth. Henry just didn't want to arrive before his one P.M. arranged time. He would purposefully kill time so that he'd arrive precisely on the hour. "I'm sure he is, Louise," I say. And I think of Henry and Uncle Ken now having tea together in heaven, sharing their heavenly gen.

. . .

I'm staying in Uncle Ken's house. August has come and gone, but I'm still here. There's nothing particularly important back in America that I have to return for. And just staying here, for now, feels good. Feels right. It's just me now in Uncle Ken's house, winding his clocks and watering his plants and thinking about him all the time.

September marches on, and the air grows colder. The nights are drawing in. High season on the Old Course has gone. A quietness settles over St. Andrews during these times in September. The R & A has taken over the Old Course for its two-week autumn meeting, reclaiming the land for its members—a sea of tweed caps and heavy accents. The members assemble from all over the world, descending back on the town to compete, eat sumptuous meals, and wear their red trousers. At the tail end of the autumn meeting is the R & A Captain's Drive, a centuries-old tradition, in which the incoming captain of the Royal and Ancient strikes a tee shot down the first fairway—literally driving himself into office—and all the caddies scramble to get the ball (the caddie who succeeds in catching the ball returns it to the captain, who presents him with a gold sovereign, worth roughly three hundred pounds). For these weeks, the American tourists disappear. The students aren't yet back. The Dunhill Links Championship is still two weeks away. For now the town is local, peaceful. People walk around North Street at a slower pace. Easing into the fall.

Ring ring ringgggg . . .

I force open my eyes and lock in on my bedside clock. I groan. It's 6:55 in the morning. And the house phone is on its twentieth ring.

Upstairs, at the top of Uncle Ken's house, I pull a second pillow over my ears. Whoever's calling, they're going to have to wait. The rings finally stop, but I can't fall back to sleep. Finally, I give up. I groan again (dramatically, for the benefit of absolutely no one, since I'm alone in the house) and make my way downstairs, for the phone receiver. I check the voice mail.

"Hellooo . . . this is Hamish Matheson calling . . ."

I know Hamish. Hamish is an eighty-five-year-old Scottish über-stalwart member of the Gardeners' Club. He's been a member for years with Uncle Ken and Henry. And Hamish's priorities, it's safe to say, are 100 percent Gardeners' Club. If a large asteroid were heading for earth, Hamish's first thought would likely involve where to hide the petunias.

I have a feeling I know why Hamish is calling, and I think it's because he stored some pots and bowls in Uncle Ken's cellar at the beginning of the summer, two months before Uncle Ken passed away, for the fall St. Andrews flower show. In this message, however, it's as if Hamish is sending out SOS distress calls during World War II.

"This is Hamish. Urgent call. Repeat. Urgent. I need to pick up the cups and bowls at Ken's house . . ."

I roll my eyes. The flower show is still two weeks away. This is like a sitcom.

". . . please would you ring me back at . . ." Long pause. "Oh dear, I've forgotten my number. Apologies. I will ring back later. Urgent."

I just want to go back up to bed, but poor Hamish sounded so worried. And I like the fact that he signed off his voice mail with one final use of the word "urgent." This is classic Gardeners' Club behavior. *All* of the members (all in their mid-eighties) plan their lives around the Gardeners' Club shows. The Gardeners' Club is their world. Nothing else really matters. Even with the deaths of my uncle and Henry, two presidents who have fallen, the show must still go on. I guess I should do my bit.

I find Hamish's number in Uncle Ken's red leather-bound address book and dial him back.

"Hellooo?"

"Hi, Hamish, this is Oliver, Ken Hayward's nephew."

There's a sharp intake of breath on the other line. "Thank *God* I got you on the phone," Hamish says in his slow, old-world Scottish accent. "You're going away soon. We've *got* to get the pots back. D-Day is approaching!"

I digest this information as I stand in the upstairs living room in my flannel boxers.

"Umm . . . I could do it this evening at six, when I've finished caddying . . ."

This is the answer that Hamish hoped to hear. He sounds enthusiastic. "Yes! That would be excellent. Do you have a mobile? I'll give you mine. Mine is . . ." Another long pause. "*Damn* . . . I've forgotten that as well . . ."

. . .

Eventually I finalize plans to meet Hamish at six o'clock—plus some other Gardeners' Club members who will be "aiding" with "transport"—and then head back upstairs for another sleep attempt. I caddie later in the morning and finish my round at three thirty P.M. I'm about to head home for Hamish when Rob calls me back to the window. There are VIP jobs—four CEOs of French businesses playing the Jubilee at 3:40—and Rob needs me to go with them. My cell phone is out of battery, and I realize that I have no way to alert Hamish to this change. I go out on my second round, distressed about stranding poor Hamish. I ask my golfer to borrow his phone, but he tells me, "*Desolée*, I never bring mine on the golf course." I finish the round, fairly certain that this mess-up will not be taken completely in stride.

Sure enough, when I return home at eight thirty P.M., I find a small note taped to the door.

> *Hamish Matheson Called in at 6:01 p.m.*
> *Departed at 7:58 p.m.*
> *Young Oliver Nowhere to be found.*
> *Emergency.*
>
> > *Hamish.*

SIXTY-ONE

Uncle Ken's house is being packed up.

It's being left to the Scottish National Trust, as dictated in Uncle Ken's will. It's what he and his wife Isobel wanted. My aunty Jacqui and aunty Christine have been up from England to start sorting through the house's contents—deciding what's to be kept and what's to be sold. It's hard to see the house bundled into boxes. As if I'm witnessing the dismantlement of my connection to St. Andrews.

Down at the course, at least, I have a distraction.

The Alfred Dunhill Links Championship has arrived. It's a European Tour event, held on three different courses—Kingsbarns, Carnoustie, and the Old Course (the "Compilation Course" is set up for visiting tourists during Dunhill Week, consisting of the New and Jubilee Courses). The Dunhill is part individual tournament, part pro-am, with celebrities playing alongside pros—the European equivalent of the AT&T Pebble Beach pro-am. Samuel L. Jackson plays in the Dunhill. So does Hugh Grant. And Michael Douglas. And Bill Murray . . .

I'm at the shack window now, waiting for a bag.

Jobs are assigned during Dunhill Week through a rota system. Caddies sign up for either the Pro List or the Amateur List, then show up at the crack of dawn Monday to get a low sign-up number. Getting a bag isn't easy. Some caddies just take the week off. Others refer to the tournament as "the Dunghill." But like most things in the caddie shack, Dunhill Week is usually about luck. You can get a great bag in the tournament. Or you can be like Jerry Van Zyl, the nice South African caddie who showed up at four o'clock this morning to get a low tournament number, and instead got sent to the Compilation Course with a visiting 27-handicapper (the only Compilation request of the day). It's a caddie crapshoot.

"Oliver Horovitz."

My name is called from the window. I head over to Rob.

"What's up?"

"You're in the next game out, with either of the gentlemen on the putting green."

The other caddies by the window hear this and turn around. Willie Stewart sees it first.

"Fook! That's Huey Lewis over there!"

. . .

Huey Lewis, the lead singer of Huey Lewis and the News, is stroking two Pro V1s toward tee pegs when I arrive (1.3 seconds later) at his bag.

"Hi, I'm your caddie," I say. Huey Lewis looks up at me, sticks out his hand, and grins.

"Huey!" he announces in a deep voice that seems to say, *I played quarterback in high school.*

"Ollie," I reply in a voice that says, *I did not.*

Huey squints his eyes slightly. "You American?"

"Yeah."

Huey thinks about this for a second, then nods. "Cool." He strokes another putt. "We're gonna play well this week, Oliver." He strokes another putt. "We got this." He strokes another, looks back up at me, and grins. "I'm not here for a good time."

And just like that, I've got Huey Lewis in the Dunhill championship.

. . . .

My first practice round with Huey Lewis is, in one word, awesome. In nine words, I can't get Huey's tunes out of my head.

"What do we have in, Ollie?" Huey asks from the middle of the third fairway.

"We've got one forty-two front"—(*It's hip to be squaaaaarrree!*)—"and, uh . . . one fifty-seven to the"—(*That's the powwwwer of lovvve!*)—"to the . . . uh . . . flag . . ."

This is Huey's fifth year playing in the Dunhill championship—he also plays each year in the AT&T Pebble Beach pro-am—and he's clearly one of the fan favorites. Everywhere we walk, people recognize Huey and yell out to him. Whenever we wait for groups in front, Huey is either signing autographs, or talking to fans, or imitating people's Scottish accents.

"What ya doin' Wednesday, pal?" Huey asks me (in a fake Glaswegian accent) as we walk up the sixteenth fairway.

"Nothing special."

"Ga-reat! Ah fookin' luv it!" Huey now switches back to American. "I'm playing here again Wednesday morning. Final practice round. You're coming too."

. . .

It's Wednesday, and I'm standing on the putting green beside the first tee—with Huey Lewis hitting practice putts toward my feet.

"Straight back—straight through," Huey says.

"Stroke looks good," I say, casually flicking each ball back to Huey the second it comes to rest (as I think I've seen pro caddies do in the past).

There's a loud commotion behind the first tee. A crowd has formed. I crane my neck to see who's arrived and spot Michael Douglas. He's playing in the Dunhill for the first time since 2006 and is now warming up on the first tee. I'm psyched to see him here. Even being fifty feet away from him is kind of cool.

"Okay, Ollie, let's go."

Huey Lewis is looking at me.

"Huh?" I say back.

"Let's go, we're on the tee," Huey replies. I look at the tee box and recognize the other golfers who are standing there. *Holy shit.*

Our group today is Huey Lewis, Tico Torres, Andy Garcia, and Michael Douglas.

Dazedly, I move our bag onto the first tee. The others see me.

"Hi," says Andy Garcia.

"Hey," says Michael Douglas.

"Yo," says Tico Torres.

"This is my caddie, Ollie. He's from New York," Huey says.

This is a bizarre Wednesday morning I'm having.

. . .

Our pro for the Dunhill is Simon Dyson—a cool blond-haired Northern English guy who actually won this tournament in 2009. Right out of the gate on Thursday, Dyson is a machine. He shoots a 69 at Kingsbarnes, then a 71 on Friday at Carnoustie. On Saturday at the Old—when we're paired with Martin Kaymer and his dad—

Dyson goes *9 under* through his first fourteen holes, letting out a schoolboy whoop each time he makes a birdie. Huey's loving it. Dyson's loving it. I'm *really* loving it. When the dust settles, Dyson has carded a 63 and moved himself into a tie for second place.

It's now Saturday evening, and I'm furiously checking the European Tour Web site to try to figure out our pairings for tomorrow. I hit refresh for the thirty-ninth time, aware that because of Dyson, we're going to be in one of the last groups, with either Padraig Harrington, Graeme McDowell, Rory McIlroy, Louis Oosthuizen, or Michael Hoey. The screen refreshes. Still no news. I switch off my computer, head out into town. Midway down Howard Place, I get a text from Greaves. "Holy shit! Ollie and Rory tomorrow! Fooooahhh!"

We're in the second-to-last group tomorrow, for Sunday's final round.

With Rory McIlroy.

I do not fall asleep easily that night.

. . .

"Hi, I'm Rory."

Rory McIlroy is stretching out his hand to me with a big smile. He's tiny. I tower over him. "Hey, I'm Ollie," I reply, and shake the hand of the defending U.S. Open champion. It's a good start to my Sunday afternoon.

My suspicions are first aroused that today is going to be interesting when Rory holes out his second shot from 134 yards in the middle of the third fairway, for eagle. It's clear Rory is just outrageously good. He has no fear. He goes at the hardest pins on the course—4, tucked back-left; 11, right up top. His dad, Gerry McIlroy (Rory's amateur partner), looks on the whole time—proudly, but matter-of-factly. Just another day at the office.

"Yeah, cheers, Simon, I'll putt."

We're now on the tiny seventeenth green. I'm holding the flag (and a golf towel that Gerry has given me) as Simon Dyson waits and Rory putts. All the cameras are trained on our group. A huge crowd watches from the grandstand. Huey Lewis stands beside me. It's surreal. Tomorrow this place will be empty, but at this instant, it's electric. At this instant, we're at the center of the golf world.

I look around at all the crowds, at McIlroy and his dad, at Dyson, at Huey Lewis. I think about how this job can get you inside the ropes, rocket you to the extreme front lines of professional golf, connect you to movie stars and rock stars, Japanese business titans, Rory McIlroy . . . and plumbers who have saved up for years to book their trip. Everyone's here for the same basic reason; everyone's made the pilgrimage for the same basic goal—to be at the source.

I get it.

. . .

The Dunhill finishes. St. Andrews empties out once more. The town is returned to the people. Any local can pitch up now to the first tee of the Old and get right out. It's the town of Uncle Ken and Henry again. And I'm still here. The days are closing in. The nights are getting colder. The wind is chillier. The sky seems to hang lower. You can taste winter.

Up in the dorms, in the classrooms, the University of St. Andrews students are back in full force. But for the first time, I'm not in their world anymore. I'm a caddie. And I hang out with the caddies. We're in the final weeks of the season, and I notice a sense of contentment hanging over everyone. When you make it this far into the season, you feel like you've accomplished something. It's a long season, and it's not easy, but it's a cool feeling to have "finished it out."

I spend my days when I'm not caddying walking around the town, revisiting my old haunts, soaking everything in. I'm here later now than I've been since I was a student, and with the tourists gone, I feel a million miles away from New York. I can't do this forever. I can't stay here forever. I have to take the next step in my life. But it hits me that I've learned so much from this job of carrying people's golf bags while shepherding their wildest dreams. And it's possible I've stayed at it just long enough to realize what's really important in this life.

Suddenly I feel as if Uncle Ken and Henry are standing nearby.

SIXTY-TWO

I'm walking up 18.

It's my final day in St. Andrews, before I head back to New York City. I've decided to play one last round on the Old Course. Aunty Jacqui is in the house—we've been packing up the last of Uncle Ken's things, and this morning, I discovered his old putter. It's an ancient putter, paper-thin, with a hickory shaft and the name "Vanessa" on it for some reason. Without thinking, I put the putter in my golf bag, to bring it around the Old Course for one more round.

I'm playing with two Irish guys from Dublin, cabdrivers who have been hit hard by the recession in Ireland (one of them had to stop being a chef) and are here on a package deal with the Old Course, saving money by playing in the winter. They're incredibly nice and are in total wow mode. Throughout the round, I've been helping them out, and I find myself telling them all my best caddie stories. In fact, the guys have been calling me their "St. Andrews hero." On 12, one of the Irish guys notices the old putter in my bag and asks me about it. I tell them about Uncle Ken. On 14, we see Eck Spence, a cool older ranger, dressed in head-to-toe foul-weather gear. "That's good that you're with Ollie, he'll take care of you," Eck says to the Irish guys. I also see Neil Gibson and Colin Donaldson, out together on a caddie round, who know I'm headed home tomorrow. "All the best, Ollie, have a great winter!" they yell.

The light is beautiful as we walk up 18—a low winter light that is soft and muted and gentle, and looks like it's ten P.M. even though it's only two P.M. I've absolutely bombed my drive, and since we're way downwind, the ball's ended up just short of the green, in the Valley of Sin. Walking up the fairway, I realize that I've only got a putt for my second shot. And for the first time all day, I decide to pull out Uncle Ken's putter for this last attempt. *Come on, hit it close, give him a birdie!* I think to myself.

I stroke my eagle putt from where Costantino Rocca holed his Daly-tying putt in 1995. But my putt comes up way short. Fifteen feet short. Now I've got a tough birdie putt. I give it a read and do some practice strokes. The putt is inside-right, uphill. The light is fading, and everyone in my group is watching. Just like I've done a million times here, I look out over the different shops and Hamilton Hall and all the buildings, and soak everything in. Uncle Ken's putter is so ridiculously thin, it's beyond difficult to putt with. I don't have high expectations for this putt. I just want to give it a chance. I stroke the putt. Midway to the hole, it definitely has a chance. I hold my breath, not daring to get my hopes up. The ball charges onward, straight for the hole. Everyone shouts. The putt hits—drops in, dead center. Birdie. Uncle Ken has made one last birdie on the Old. Everyone goes nuts. One after the other, the golfers come up to hug me. My arms are in the air, and I have never felt this good. All at once I'm thinking of when I broke par here for the first time, of all my years in St. Andrews, but mainly I'm thinking of Uncle Ken. I remember Tony Lema's son playing here and making his own birdie, and suddenly, without hesitation, I yell loudly into the evening sky.

"I LOVE YOU, UNCLE KEEEEEEN!"

My voice echoes back at me, bouncing off the R & A, and Hamilton Hall, and the shop where Tom Morris handmade gutta-percha balls and hickory-shafted mashie niblicks. And I'm overwhelmed by a feeling of contentment, and pride.

Golf. There's absolutely nothing like it.

Epilogue

It's 7:55 A.M., Thursday, September 22, 2011.

There's a crowd of over three hundred R & A members, plus townspeople, standing there. Above the first tee. They fan out around the steps. Down both sides of the first and eighteenth fairways. The men wear coats and ties. The women wear petticoats. Everyone's in their Sunday best. Even though it's Thursday. They stand there, the R & A members, alongside their wives and children, just as their fathers and their fathers' fathers have done for hundreds of years.

They're all watching us.

I'm among thirty heavily caffeinated caddies, all trekking out down the first fairway. In five minutes, Alistair Low, this year's incoming R & A captain, will be swatting his drive down the first. I'm back for another year.

"Ach, he cannae hit it far, it's intah the wind!" Rob McCormick, a lifelong caddie nicknamed "Big Raab," yells (as much to himself as to anyone else). We all take up positions facing back on the first hole from the opposite direction that we normally do, each one of us privately deliberating where the hell this tee shot is going to go. It's a chilly morning. The Scottish sun, this late in September, has barely risen, and it's now peeking over the top of the R & A Clubhouse, directly into our faces. It's blinding.

I'm at a spot twenty yards past Granny Clarke's Wynd—about 150 out, which I think is a decent guess for where the ball should bounce (the wind is into us . . . and Alistair Low is in his midsixties). I'm also standing way to the right—almost in line with the eighteenth green. I think he's going to pull it.

"This is it, boys!" Scott Bechelli yells. A small roar goes up from the R & A section. Alistair Low has arrived at the first tee. He wears green pants, a dark blue sweater. He shakes hands with three other R & A members. The crowd has swelled in the last few minutes. Looking out, I feel like we could easily be in the year 1870. I know Uncle Ken would be among the crowd as well if he could, watching.

Around me, caddies stretch, do quick jogs in place now, shield their eyes from the sun. It all looks so distant from our caddie location out in the fairway. And now, after all the waiting, things are suddenly speeding forward. Every caddie locks in—goes quiet, concentrates intensely in his own small world. Because now, in the distance, Alistair Low is doing a single practice swing. And now he's over the ball, and he's taking back the club, and making his downswing, and . . .

BAMMMMM.

The cannon fires. The ball is away.

A roar goes up from the crowd, way up ahead, but out here in our fairway, it's eerily silent. Because every caddie is sidestepping rapidly, frantically trying to spot the ball. And then, as people have described the milliseconds before a car crash, everything slams to slow motion.

I am running left. My first instinct, before the ball disappeared into the sky, was that Mr. Low blocked it right. If that's the case, then the ball is going to land thirty yards left of where I am. I charge, searing the sky with my eyes as I move, searching desperately for anything resembling a ball. The seconds are passing in slow motion. And I'm running, running, running . . .

And then, as if out of nowhere, the ball reappears in the sky.

There it is. I see it!

It's still climbing in the sky, thirty yards to my left, and moving, tracing perfectly against the clouds, as if in slow motion, as if it's been placed there for me and only me. And now I'm running flat out, sprinting, and the ball is starting to come down, and I'm running, speeding, charging, and now my left hand is up, and I'm getting closer, and now I'm leaping . . . I'm in the air . . . and the ball is falling . . . and . . .

HOLY SHIT, I'VE GOT IT!

The ball slams into my outstretched left hand, its momentum halted, and drops down beside me. Dazedly, I bend down, scoop it up, and hold the ball, staring at it, dumbstruck. Silence. My world is this three-foot radius. And now, everything around me is getting louder, and people are cheering from everywhere, and the caddies start shouting, "Run it up there!" "Run it in, Ollie!" "Run it in!" I look back at them as the shouts continue. "Run it in!" "You got it!" "Run it in there!"

So I run.

I run toward the first tee, clutching a golf ball as tightly as I ever have, running quicker and quicker, into the arena of cheering St. Andreans. The applause builds, and everything gets louder as I approach, as if I'm bringing the torch into the Olympic arena. And I'm smiling stupidly. Ridiculously. I can't stop smiling. I can't wipe this stupid smile from my face. Because ever since I arrived in St. Andrews for my first year, every time I walked up the eighteenth fairway, I secretly imagined a crowd gathering around the fairway, like this, behind the green, cheering my British Open victory. I secretly dreamed this, secretly expected it, and was secretly crushed when that dream faded. But in this split second, as I'm running this ball in now, I realize that *this* is my British Open, *this* is my story, this is my moment. Behind me, caddies are shouting, "Well done, Ollie!" I run faster and faster now. I know that somewhere up there, Uncle Ken is watching, giggling, and telling Henry.

I reach the tee. I present the ball to Alistair Low. He shakes my hand. "Well struck, sir," I say, out of breath. "Uh . . . well caught," Mr. Low replies, sounding a little surprised. I don't think he was expecting my American accent. Cameras are snapping all around us. A TV crew is rolling. The Royal and Ancient captain for the year 2011–2012 hands me the gold sovereign. We pose for the photos together. Then I stumble back toward the shack, R & A members running up to congratulate me. "Well caught, young man!" "Jolly good catch!" And now I arrive at the shack. And caddies are coming up to me and shaking my hand. Congratulating me. Everyone wants to check out the sovereign. They inspect it like it's a Game 7 ball in the World Series. My phone is already buzzing with text messages from other caddies who have heard the news. Andrew Rennie, who caught the ball last year, writes, "Well done, champ!" Craig Scott writes, "Immortality." And now I realize something. The caddies are happy for me. Happy that one of their own made the catch.

"Oliver Horovitz."

My name is being called on the caddie shack intercom. I walk to the window. Rob's standing there, just as Rick used to. "Ollie, I need you on the New Course."

"Sure thing."

I put on my bib, grab my jacket, tuck the sovereign carefully inside. And then I step back out of the shack into the cool morning sunlight, for my next caddie round.

By the door, I see Jimmy Bowman, about to head inside for his coffee. He nods at me, gives me a pat on the shoulder. "Good catch, Horovitz." I nod back to Jimmy, thank him, offer up my sunniest smile.

And then I get going.

ACKNOWLEDGMENTS

Thank you to Sibeal Pounder for your endless support and confidence and to Cara Spitalewitz for always-useful advice.

Tom Greaves, my caddie mate through so many summers, was an invaluable sounding-board, and Alyssa Wolff and Mark Eglinton provided pitch-perfect pointers whenever I asked. Chris Hill, Will Skjott, and Iain Webster were steadfast supporters of my writing, as was David Field, who helped me keep it real. Thanks as well to Jake Foley, Jordan Weitzen, Ben Kultgen, Sean Harris, Michael Kramer, Joe Kavolus, Tom Nash, Damien and Jasmine Chazelle, Justin Hurwitz, Heidi Dallin, Sol Frieder, Graeme Lennie, Betsy Andrews, Mike Harvey, Claire Pascolini-Campbell, Aunty Jacqui, Aunty Shirley, David Joy, David Coyne, Daniel Ross-Rieder, John Cella, Ryan Murphy, Lissi Erwin, and Tiana Matthews, for encouragement on both sides of the pond.

Jerry DeGroot gave me working space and Thanksgiving turkey, and Sharon Roe listened to all my caddie stories with a smile. The Williams family—David, John, Anne, and Colin—provided accommodation and friendship over many summers. Jake and Edith Davidson, and Louise Anquitel, made home seem much less far away. Mike Woodcock, with the St. Andrews Links Trust, was funny, friendly, and always helpful. Shout-outs to Peter Hood, Steve Clayton, Bass Rocks Golf Club, and Rockport Golf Club for getting me hooked on golf in the first place. At Harvard, thanks to Robb Moss, Ross McElwee, Alfred Guzzetti, Pete Grana, and John Rybicki for teaching me about film and life, and to Thomas Batchelder, for steering me through it all.

New York University's Bobst Library provided the perfect writing environment while I was in New York City. In St. Andrews, Taste Coffee was my go-to spot for caffeine and free Internet. To the University of St. Andrews Library—sorry for sneaking in coffee that spilled in my backpack, then returning borrowed library books, pretending they were already coffee stained.

My parents, Israel and Gillian Horovitz, are a giant part of this book coming to life. Thank you, for everything. A special shout-out to my dad, who spent countless hours working with me, passing on wisdom and wicked good advice.

Thanks also to my wonderful sisters and brothers: Hannah, Rachael, Matthew, and Adam, and to my uncle Richard Price, who read an early draft and gave crucial golf-nut feedback.

My brilliant agent and friend, Ryan D. Harbage, guided me from start to finish with the greatest of skill and wisdom. Thanks as well to Bill Shinker at Gotham, and to my editor, Jessica Sindler, whose comments and ideas were superb throughout.

I am indebted to Robert Thorpe, my Old Course caddie master, for his unflinching support and understanding, even as my double-rounds began to, um, slacken. . . . Thanks as well to Ken Henderson, Peter Rees, Paul Ellison, and David Hutchison in the caddie shack office, as well as John Grant with the St. Andrews Links Trust. And thank you, Rick Mackenzie, for taking on that eighteen-year-old (talkative) American kid back in 2004 and somehow letting him return each year.

Lastly, I'd like to thank my fellow St. Andrews caddies, past and present. Words cannot adequately express how important you've become in my life. To all of you . . . FOOOOAHHHH!!!!!!!!!!

ABOUT THE AUTHOR

Oliver Horovitz is a writer, filmmaker, and caddie on the Old Course in St. Andrews, Scotland. He has written for *Sports Illustrated*, *Golf World*, and *Golf Digest*. A native of New York City, he was the founder and captain of Stuyvesant High School's championship golf team and is the former New York City Heisman PSAL Wingate Trophy winner for golf. An active filmmaker whose work has screened around the country, Horovitz received the 2008 Edward H. Potter Prize at Harvard College and directed a 2007 documentary about caddying entitled *The Caddies of St. Andrews*.